The image of Hitler as a demagogic 'pied piper' leading astray the 'little people' of Austria is as misleading as it is powerful. *Nazism and the working class in Austria* is a case study of the ambiguous relationship between state and society under the Nazis. It places the experience of Austrian industrial workers in the Third Reich in a broader historical context, from the origins of the earliest 'national socialist' movements in the backwaters of the Habsburg empire to the end of the Second World War. Workers did not seriously attempt or even expect to overthrow the Nazi regime in the face of unprecedented surveillance and terror; but neither were they won over, and their oppositional strategies and disgruntled political opinions reveal a truculent workforce, rather than one which was contented and converted.

Nazism and the working class in Austria

Nazism and the working class in Austria

Industrial unrest and political dissent in the 'national community'

Tim Kirk

University of Northumbria, Newcastle

CAMBRIDGE
UNIVERSITY PRESS

CAMBRIDGE
UNIVERSITY PRESS

University Printing House, Cambridge CB2 8BS, United Kingdom

Cambridge University Press is part of the University of Cambridge.

It furthers the University's mission by disseminating knowledge in the pursuit of education, learning and research at the highest international levels of excellence.

www.cambridge.org
Information on this title: www.cambridge.org/9780521475013

© Cambridge University Press 1996

First published 1996
First paperback edition 2002

A catalogue record for this publication is available from the British Library

Library of Congress Cataloguing in Publication data
Kirk, Tim, 1958–
Nazism and the working class in Austria: industrial unrest and political dissent in the 'national community'/ Tim Kirk.
    p.   cm.
Includes bibliographical references and index.
ISBN 0 521 47501 5 (hardback)
1. Working class – Austria – History – 20th century.　2. National socialism – Austria.　3. Austria – Economic conditions – 1918–1945.　4. Austria – History – 20th century.　I. Title.
HD8410.K57　57　1996
305.5'62'0943609043–dc20　95-48269　CIP

ISBN 978-0-521-47501-3 Hardback
ISBN 978-0-521-52269-4 Paperback

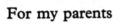

For my parents

Contents

Tables

Acknowledgements

I should like to thank the staff of archives and libraries in Austria, Germany and Britain for their assistance and encouragement. Particular thanks are due to Dr Siegwald Ganglmair of the *Dokumentationsarchiv des österreichischen Widerstands* in Vienna, Herr Hofrat Dr Lorenz Mikoletzky of the Austrian State Archives, Dr Werner of the German Federal Archives in Koblenz, and the staff of the German Federal Military Archives in Freiburg im Breisgau and of the Upper Austrian *Landesarchiv*. I should also like to thank librarians at the Austrian National Library, the Austrian Institute, the German Historical Institute and at the University of Northumbria, especially David Cheetham, Kath Holmes, Margaret Howey and the staff of the inter-library loans section, and above all Jane Shaw, for whom nothing was ever too much trouble.

For their help, advice and encouragement at the beginning and over the years I should like to thank Jill Lewis, Ernst Hanisch, Francis Carsten and above all Gerhard Botz. I am grateful to Peter Kammerstätter and Karl Flanner for their time and advice many years ago. Thanks are also due to Liz Harvey, Stephen Salter and Ian Kershaw, who read and commented on the typescript at various stages. Their constructive criticisms were invaluable, and the remaining flaws are my own. I should also like to thank Roger Newbrook for his help in preparing the manuscript for publication.

I was able to carry out the research for this book over the years thanks to financial support from Manchester University, the German Historical Institute in London and a small research grant from the University of Northumbria.

Above all, I should like to thank Drs Kurt and Irmgard Mustafa, and their sons Georg and Stefan for their friendly and generous hospitality in Austria over many years.

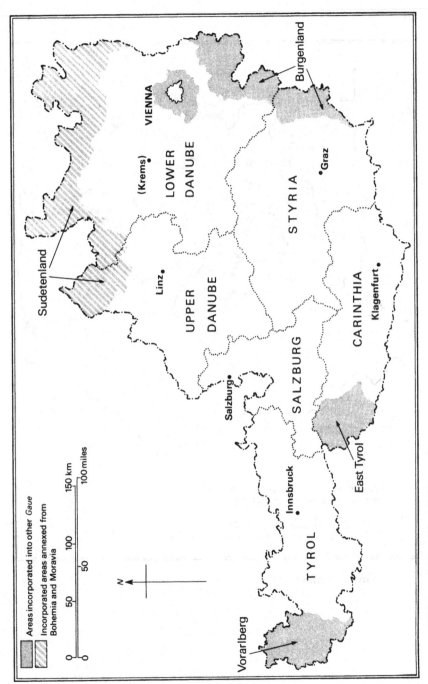

Areas incorporated into other *Gaue*

Incorporated areas annexed from Bohemia and Moravia

Sudetenland

(Krems)

LOWER DANUBE

VIENNA

Burgenland

Graz

STYRIA

Linz

UPPER DANUBE

CARINTHIA

Klagenfurt

SALZBURG

Salzburg

East Tyrol

Innsbruck

TYROL

Vorarlberg

N

0   50   100   150 km

0   50   100 miles

'Alpine and Danubian *Reichsgaue*', 1939

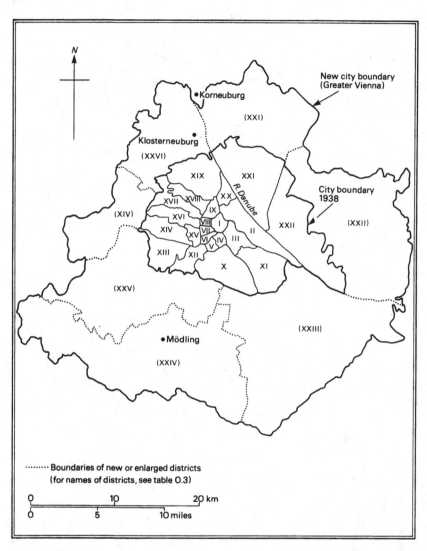

N

●Korneuburg

New city boundary
(Greater Vienna)

(XXI)

Klosterneuburg ●

(XXVI)

XIX

XXI

R. Danube

City boundary
1938

XVIII
XVII   XX
XVI   IX
XIV   VIII I
(XIV)   XV VII
         VI IV III
XIII XII V   II
                X   XI

XXII

(XXII)

(XXV)

●Mödling

(XXIII)

(XXIV)

.... Boundaries of new or enlarged districts
(for names of districts, see table 0.3)

0   10   20 km
0   5   10 miles

Greater Vienna, 1939

Introduction

A study of Nazism and the working class in Austria is compelled to engage with a number of historical debates at once, all of them rendered more or less controversial by the politics of the present.[1] Discussion of Austria's recent history has proved problematic for Austrians and foreigners alike, not least in the wake of the Waldheim affair and in the context of the continuing electoral success of the far right Austrian Freedom Party (*Freiheitliche Partei Österreichs*, FPÖ). Discussion of the historical relationship between fascism and the working class is similarly bound up with controversy: the focus of the discussion has shifted from the 'discovery' of widespread working-class resistance and opposition after two decades dominated by cold war historiography back to assertions of the central importance of workers – the 'little people', '*das einfache Volk*' – in bringing the Nazis to power and sustaining the regime.[2] A national study of working-class opposition to fascism in one country raises both general historical questions about relationships between societies and their rulers, and historiographical questions about post-war hierarchies of 'national' culpability and their validity. The more general relationship between Nazism as a political movement and Austrian society in particular is an especially vexed one, which raises further questions about 'national' resistance and, indeed, national identity.

The following discussion will outline some of the historiographical issues, and conclude with an examination of society and economy in the First Austrian Republic, before setting out the aims of the book, and the methods and sources on which it is based.

Peculiarities of Austrian historiography

Austria has been ruled for much of the last fifty years by a grand coalition of Social Democrats (the *Sozialistische Partei Österreichs*, SPÖ) and clerical Conservatives (the *Österreichische Volkspartei*, ÖVP) whose proclaimed purpose has been (among other things) to avoid the political conflicts of the First Republic. The principle of proportionality (*Proporz*) which has underpinned the coalition politics of the post-war era extends to society at large, and not least to public opinion and intellectual life. One effect of this consensual corporatism has been a relative reluctance, even on the Left, to address the issue of Austria's indigenous fascist dictatorship because the ÖVP is the political heir of the Christian Social Party whose leaders imposed it.

The single most paralysing influence on the Austrian historiography of this period, however, came originally from outside. Although Austria had been incorporated into the Reich in 1938 and remained a part of Germany throughout the war, its position was rendered ambiguous during and after the war by the Allies themselves. In 1945 Austria was divided by the Allies into four zones of occupation, and Vienna, like Berlin, into four sectors. Austrians were tried for war crimes, denazification procedures were established, a process of 'political re-education' was initiated and claims were made for reparations. The conditionality of Austria's eventual independence was formalised in a constitutional guarantee of neutrality demanded by the Soviet Union which remained valid for decades. In many ways Austria's post-war experience was closer to the more punitive treatment of Germany than to that of a 'victim' of Nazi aggression. The British government, for its part, continued to regard Austria as enemy territory; the two states remained technically at war until 1948. A peace treaty was drafted for Austria by the Allies at the same time as those for other enemy states such as Italy (which was otherwise treated with less severity than Austria), Finland, Hungary and Germany's other Balkan satellites.[3]

Yet at the Moscow Conference of 1943 the Allies had identified Austria as Hitler's first victim, and declared the Anschluss null and void (although both Britain and the United States had barely protested at the time, limiting themselves to disapproval of the use of force).[4] At Moscow the Allies committed themselves to the restoration of a 'free and independent Austria' after the defeat of Germany. However, the Moscow declaration was qualified by a reference to Austria's shared responsibility for the war, which would have to be redeemed by the Austrians' contribution to their own liberation.

The importance of the Moscow declaration to the Second Republic's first generation of political leaders need hardly be emphasised. It was seized upon not only as a legal guarantee of Austrian independence, but as a confirmation of Austria's status as victim rather than accomplice.[5] It seems unlikely, to say the least, that this was the intention. The origins of the Moscow declaration have been traced to the British Political Warfare Executive, which expressed the opinion that there was increasing resistance to Nazi rule in Austria, and that it ought to be encouraged by an Allied commitment to restore Austrian independence after the war. This was not the general consensus at the time, and it was certainly not an opinion shared by the Foreign Office, which was sceptical and referred to 'passive grumbling rather than resistance'. Talk of Austria as a 'victim' of the Nazis contradicted the fact of British recognition of the Anschluss, and the Foreign Office watered down the proposed declaration on Austria;[6] and if the declaration's value as propaganda was in doubt, it certainly never seems to have been intended as more than that.[7]

The real importance of the Moscow declaration lies in the diplomatic use to which it was put after the war by the Austrian authorities. International lawyers took up differing positions regarding Austria's legal status in 1945, but their arguments and expert opinions were ultimately less important than the *Realpolitik* of the cold war. In the context of continuing Allied occupation, the Austrian government mounted a determined political offensive, particularly in the United States. The US government was happy, for its own reasons, to support Austria's interpretation of the Moscow declaration, and did so most emphatically and decisively on the occasion of a visit by Austria's foreign minister, Karl Gruber, in 1946.[8]

The internal effect of the Austrian government's determination to exploit the Moscow declaration was the development of a 'victim' mythology which came to dominate Austrian contemporary history. Characterised as 'self-infantilisation' by one Austrian historian,[9] the notion of Austria's helplessness in 1938 has nevertheless been officially promoted since the appearance of the *Rot-Weiß-Rot-Buch* in 1946.[10] Dissent from the consensus has been difficult for most of the post-war period, and it is only in recent years that more critical approaches to Austria's recent past have emerged.

In this respect the Waldheim affair was something of a watershed. The most obvious immediate effect of Kurt Waldheim's candidature for the Austrian presidency in 1986 was, of course, the damage it caused to Austria's international reputation. The country was transformed, in the words of one commentator, from the 'isle of the Blessed' into a 'pariah nation'.[11] Certainly, public and popular opinion outside Austria rapidly became very sceptical, not only about Waldheim's equivocations, but about the role and attitudes of Austrians generally during the war. If western public opinion had once been inclined to accept a

'Sound of Music' image of Austria under the Nazis, it suddenly saw only a nation of 'little Waldheims'.[12]

The reaction of many Austrians was to close ranks around the beleaguered presidential candidate. His conservative sponsors for the presidency in the ÖVP concluded their campaign with the slogan 'Waldheim, now more than ever', ostensibly a gesture in defiance of attempted foreign interference in Austrian internal politics.[13] The response of others was to restate long-standing agreed positions on Austria and National Socialism, collaboration and resistance.[14]

In this context critiques of Austria's attempts at *Vergangenheitsbewältigung* ('mastering the past') prompted hostility in some quarters. The most notable example was the extraordinary response to an article by the British historian Robert Knight in the *Times Literary Supplement*.[15] Copies of the offending article were circulated to academic historians in Austrian universities by the then foreign minister Peter Jankowitsch, who effectively summoned them to the defence of the Republic. Knight's arguments were also severely criticised in the Austrian press, most notably in the conservative daily newspaper *Die Presse*.[16]

To say that the Waldheim affair ruptured the post-war consensus on fascism is not to discount forerunners – principally younger historians on the Left – who had already raised some of the thornier issues associated with the politics of the First Republic and the war. Gerhard Botz, for example, had addressed the controversial issue of defections from the Left to the Nazis in 1934;[17] and more recent volumes of Austria's official documentary history of the resistance had broken away from the established approach of associating opposition with institutions or ideological camps (*Lager*) and complemented the 'official' resistance history with material on 'individual' and informal opposition.[18] Similarly, historians have adopted an increasingly critical approach to the history of 'Austrofascism'.[19] Finally, much more sensitive issues have begun to be addressed, such as the Nazi persecution of 'unrespectable' victims, and the question of compensation for victims.[20] In this respect Austrian historians, like their counterparts in other parts of Europe, have moved closer to a demythologised history of fascism.

Fascism and the working class

Contemporary observers among the leaders of the European labour movements of Mussolini's rise to power, and not least 'Austromarxists' such as Otto Bauer, were in no doubt about the nature of fascism. It was a movement of the political Right; it was part of a broader international development; and it was hostile not only to Bolshevism, but also to the liberal ('bourgeois democratic') institutions which had been established after World War I, and which allowed the Left a measure of political space.[21] Liberals and Conservatives, on the other hand, while they rejected his 'demagogic' politics, were nevertheless willing to concede that Mussolini had contained the threat of revolution just as Nazi Germany was later seen as a bulwark against Soviet Russia. If the Second World War and the holocaust modified western liberal opinion, bringing more liberal sections of the Right behind a broadly anti-fascist consensus for the next thirty or forty years, they also served to restore the initial conservative impression: all 'mass' politics was bound to come to no good, to end in 'totalitarianism'.[22]

The notion that the rise of fascism had been a matter of the 'little people' being led astray by rabble-rousing demagogues was a comfortable one for the compromised ruling classes of post-war Europe and one which dominated the historiography of the cold war era in the West. That it was challenged in the 1960s and 1970s was not so much a consequence of the use of hitherto undiscovered sources (although new sources, and more importantly new types of sources were used), but a result of new approaches made possible by the changed intellectual and political climate. It was increasingly possible for historians to discuss the history of the Left and of the working class.

The historiography of the relationship between fascism and labour reflected these new approaches, and included a desire to reclaim and celebrate a hitherto hidden history not deemed 'respectable' by the academy. The relationship was thus presented as an oppositional one, and histories of socialist and communist resistance, emphasising the importance even *in absentia* of the parties, dominated the early historiography of labour under fascism.[23] The new work nevertheless insisted on uncomfortable facts: that in sheer numerical terms the resistance of the underground labour movement, and (most uncomfortably of all) that of communist parties especially, had dwarfed that of other groups. A resistance was revealed which was never truly 'national' in any sense, but remained largely factionalised.

Nevertheless, the communist resistance was not the working class, and the majority of workers remained outside it. Workers resisted the rise of fascism in the polling booths and on the streets, but did not flock to join the resistance against it once it was established in power. If class consciousness and class conflict persisted, it was channelled into more informal and traditional forms of industrial protest, recalling practices which pre-dated the establishment of open and legal trade unions and socialist parties.

This discussion has developed in a number of different ways over the last two decades. Tim Mason's work re-set the agenda for the discussion of industrial relations under Nazism, by showing how a class conscious but politically disabled working class developed new strategies for developing individual and collective interests.[24] Since the publication of Mason's early work, however, there have been a number of detailed studies of the history of the industrial working class under Nazism.[25] Many of these have found Mason's theses wanting; and indeed, Mason himself refined his original position.[26] On the whole, however, the revisionism of recent years, like that of the 1960s, owes as much to altered political perspectives as to new sources or approaches, and not only to those of an assertive intellectual 'new Right', but also to a broader and more nuanced view of working class experience on the Left.[27] To this extent, historical writing on fascism has reflected more general political developments. Discussion of class has been rendered unfashionable, and a new generation of conservative historians has dismissed 'history from below' as '*passé*'. In fact, the new revisionism has forced all kinds of social history into something of a general retreat. The editor of a series of essay collections whose agenda is explicitly revisionist (in the broadest sense) has written that the crisis of Marxism, particularly since 1989, has given rise to doubts not only about Marxist history, but 'the entire field of social history', and that 'the whole basis of social history has been questioned. Disillusionment with social history simultaneously opened the door to cultural and linguistic approaches largely developed in anthropology and literature.'[28] The first impact of such approaches was felt elsewhere, particularly in historical writing on the French Revolution where, it has been argued, '[r]itual, drama, rhetoric and symbolism have become causal forces in their own right'.[29] The same observer concluded that 'although it is undoubtedly a question of time, Leni Riefenstahl and Albert Speer still await their Mona Ozouf' and explained the reticence of revisionists to enter this field in terms of the historical immediacy of fascism and the continuing controversy surrounding it. In short, 'it would be a travesty to give an account in terms of competing discourses and the like'.[30] Since then, Alf Lüdtke has suggested that 'the Nazi language of labor expressed meanings attached by ordinary workers to work that the Marxist language of class did not'.[31] More generally, historians of Nazism have, indeed, become more concerned with issues of race and gender than with class. Class-based interpretations of Nazism and the Third Reich have occupied the attention of historians less and less, in relative terms.[32]

Cultural interpretations of working-class acquiescence under the Nazis are still few, however, and the main thrust of revisionist argument remains one which assumes the existence of a working class pursuing its legitimate interests, but either doing so unsuccessfully, or ceasing to do so because – at least from the late 1930s until the last year or so of the war – those interests were largely met by the rearmament boom in any case. Social and economic developments during the Nazi period contributed to a cumulative weakening of class identities. As David Schoenbaum argued in the 1960s, this was 'marginal protest . . . economic, not political, a matter of wages and hours, and not, it seems of fundamental opposition.'[33] Before the war workers were simply relieved to be in employment again; in the victorious years they were won over by military success, and in the face of imminent defeat they were distracted by the everyday realities of war.[34]

Discussion of the relationship between fascism and the working class has been dogged by a number of problems, not least that of defining class in general and working class in particular. The terminology itself has varied. Some approaches have been vaguely descriptive, such as 'industrial workers' (the Nazis themselves, and other contemporary and present-day observers, tended to use a similar term: *Arbeiterschaft*).[35] Others have aspired to an objectivity based on income level, occupational status and other 'neutral' indicators. The construction of such notionally empirical categories is an exercise which is itself by no means free of values, and the failure to recognise this is a fundamental flaw which undermines their pretended 'objectivity'.

The discussion below is based on the assumption that class cannot simply be equated with social stratification, but implies a conscious awareness of a collective identity. This may coincide with a political commitment to organisations claiming to defend the interests of the class as a whole, as it did with the majority of Viennese workers during the First Austrian Republic, but the labour movement and its subculture was not the working class *per se*, and a discussion of the labour movement and its institutions cannot stand in for the political history of the working class.

This is particularly true in a historical context marked by rapid political change and the re-negotiation of class relationships, where class was important as a historical relationship rooted in lived experience.[36] It will be implicit in the argument of this book that the experience of class as a relationship is particularly important after the establishment of fascist regimes, when the 'formal' class politics of liberal states was absent in the wake of the destruction of trade unions and political parties,[37] but class relationships, as will be shown below, quite clearly survived under fascist rule.

The consciousness of class was fundamental to the politics and the mentalities of early twentieth-century Europe and the language of class dominated the political debate of the period, in a way that is now scarcely recognisable. Fascism in Italy and Germany was stimulated in its early years by counter-revolutionary impulses, and was eventually brought to power in part, if not primarily, by interests which sought to reverse the 'revolutionary' settlements of the early 1920s, both domestically and internationally (aims which were not without sympathy and support in the West). Neither the Italian Fascist Party nor the Nazi Party *seized* power (in the sense of their own revolutionary mythologies), whether by *coup d'état* or in the course of a 'national revolution', and neither was elected into office, although electoral support and (later) plebiscitary acclamation were important to the fortunes of both.

The emergence of the clerical fascist regime which preceded the Anschluss in Austria was rather more complicated. It grew out of a government which had been elected, but had little hope of retaining office without the series of unconstitutional measures it took between 1930 and 1934. In that sense, perhaps, there was a seizure of power, but one from above: a *Staatsstreich*. The simultaneous radicalisation of the Christian Social Party from within was motivated by the same pressures for a reversal of the post-war political settlement as were present in Italy and Germany. Fascism came to power in all three countries as part of a more general resolution of class antagonisms in favour of the ruling classes and employers.

This reordering of class relations was also the most important preoccupation of fascist regimes during the consolidation of their power: from 1922 in Italy, and from the early 1930s in Germany and Austria, the industrial and political organisations of the labour movement were first undermined, and then suppressed, their leaders arrested and imprisoned. This onslaught was the first priority of all three regimes, and once the aim of destroying the labour movement was achieved any attempt to revive it was prevented by varying degrees of surveillance and terror. In its place the new regimes established various corporatist organisations, which claimed to represent both workers' and employers' interests. Yet the 'national community' where conflicts of sectional interest were subordinated to the greater national good never became a reality. Workers in particular (but increasingly, other groups as well) were prevented from pursuing their interests openly and collectively, and resorted to a variety of other methods to achieve their aims or even simply to express opposition. The authorities themselves were aware that the containment of open political and social conflict (whether by repression or political mobilisation) did not amount to consent, and this is evident from the internal reports of the regime, and the activities they recorded.

This is not to argue that class conflict was the central concern of fascist regimes. Clearly, fascism – and Nazism in particular – was more than a reactionary, counter-revolutionary project; but it was essential to address the problem of class conflict in industrial societies before other more far-reaching objectives could be pursued. The German Right especially, preoccupied as it was with the 'stab-in-the-back' myth, felt that war could not be waged if there was a possibility of revolutionary unrest at home.[38]

Nor does it mean that class relations remained unaltered or class consciousness uneroded. Despite the efforts of exiles, the underground press and foreign broadcasters, the party, the state controlled media and the 'co-ordinated' education system were the most important influences on popular opinion. In addition an older generation of workers organised by the Social Democratic and Communist Parties was gradually replaced by a new generation with a limited experience of trade unions, or of industrial relations practices which involved them. Finally, of course the nature of industrial work itself changed, and with it the character of working-class communities. Sub-cultures built up since the nineteenth century were eroded and workers' activities thereby considerably 'depoliticised', producing, it has been argued, the atomised working class of the post-war period.[39] Such changes *accompanied* fascist rule, rather than followed directly from it: the part played by fascist regimes in 'modernising' European economies and societies is still very much open to argument.

Resistance and society

For individuals, institutions and entire nations, a demonstrably anti-fascist past has fulfilled an important legitimating function in the politics of post-fascist Europe (although one whose significance has diminished dramatically in recent years). Individuals (politicians, for example, or industrialists), particularly in those countries ruled or occupied by fascist regimes, have sought to distance themselves from any hint of collaboration. Similarly, institutions and organisations (for example the churches or the Communist Party) have asserted claims to a history of persecution and resistance for themselves and to some extent, on behalf of groups they represent (for example Roman Catholics, industrial workers). In order to do so the institutions themselves have needed to be relatively powerful, and the groups they represent sufficiently large or deserving of sympathy. The distinction between such victims and those deemed less deserving of sympathy (gypsies, homosexuals, tramps, criminals and marginal Christian sects can all be said to fall into the latter category in one way or another) is an important one, establishing as it does a continuity of principle, if not of degree, between fascist societies and the liberal democracies or 'socialist' states that succeeded them.

This has meant that the history of resistance has been dominated by the churches, political parties, armed forces and articulate individuals from the upper or upper middle classes.[40] The ambiguous attitudes of eminent individual resisters, and the rather belated and limited anti-Nazism of some of the 1944 conspirators is now well documented.[41] Similarly, histories of society in the Third Reich have revealed more complex attitudes to Nazism than histories of resistance with an institutional or organisational focus.[42] Popular opinion and political attitudes, unlike party programmes and statements of ideology are temporary and shifting. For the majority, opposition to the Nazis was mixed with approval, however limited or grudging and even with acclamation. If it was possible, as it was for the Bishop of Münster, for the same individual to denounce euthanasia and yet to welcome the invasion of the Soviet Union, then it was much more possible for social groups or communities to hold approving and disapproving opinions of the regime simultaneously.

The balance and focus of approval and disapproval, acclamation and opposition depended on existing ideological prejudices, and those social groups who already had a coherent set of beliefs or political schooling were more resistant (*resistent*) to Nazi ideological penetration than those whose ideological *Heimat* was less secure. Martin Broszat has identified Roman Catholics and industrial workers as the two most important such groups displaying what he has called '*Resistenz*' to the Nazis.[43] The agenda of the 'Bavaria project' (whose results Broszat was discussing when he introduced the term) was explicitly dominated by the notion of rulers and society in conflict, however much that conflict was latent and suppressed; and the term *Resistenz* has made it easier to discuss the structural opposition of such groups in the absence of any articulated intention of political opposition. Such 'functional' opposition was often directed at specific measures or policies in particular contexts, and often succeeded in achieving limited aims. Whether an accumulation of such instances of functional resistance had a more general impact on the regime and its policies is a different question, however, and we should beware of designating resistance behaviour that was neither political in intent nor seriously disruptive in effect.

Ian Kershaw has developed a related approach to informal expressions of opposition in his work on popular opinion and political 'dissent', a term used to 'cover the voicing of attitudes, frequently spontaneous and often unrelated to any intended action, which in any way

whatsoever ran counter to, or were critical of Nazism . . . reactive, spontaneous, ill-defined expressions of discontent – often "political" only
because the regime defined them as political.'[44]

Alongside active political resistance to Nazism there existed, then, a
whole range of informal oppositional behaviour and dissenting opinion.
This should not be conflated with resistance proper, which remained a
minority affair. We now know that the relationship between state and
society in a dictatorship is not necessarily one founded exclusively, or
even primarily, on popular opposition to repressive rule.[45] Resistance to
modern dictatorships from within has generally been a minority affair.
'The majority complies', as Karl Stadler argued in the introduction to
an early account of such behaviour in Austria. Most people, he went
on, tried to remain respectable: 'They want to survive, almost at any
price . . . On the other hand our documents show that there were forms
of . . . resistance which were perhaps not so serious, occurred spon-
taneously and sporadically, and yet could carry the severest consequences for those involved.'[46]

Most people, perhaps, complied sufficiently to ensure that even if
there was no stable consensus, there was never a serious internal threat
to the regime either. We should beware of overestimating dissent, and
producing a distorted, or even apologetic picture by ignoring the regime's popularity; and we should bear in mind that the behaviour of the
majority was complex. Acquiescence was not approval, and compliance
was not consent; responses to the regime were not uniform, but varied
from one social group to another and were complicated by a whole range
of variables. Similarly, there were many kinds of deviant behaviour, not
all of which constituted political dissent. Deviant behaviour might be
individual or collective, spontaneous or organised, overt or covert; it
might or might not carry the conscious intention of political opposition
or protest.[47]

Some of this deviant behaviour was only illegal in Nazi Germany or
other authoritarian states. Sometimes it has been illegal in less authoritarian societies in special circumstances (black market slaughter during
the war, for example) or its legal status has fluctuated with the political
climate (abortion and homosexuality). Finally, of course, despite the
formal criminalisation of behaviour, the law would or could not always
be enforced. Conversely, other types of behaviour, while not technically
illegal might be inadvisable. It is one of the principal objectives of the
discussion which follows to identify various types of 'dissenting' behaviour among the industrial working class in Austria and to assess its
extent and importance.

The First Austrian Republic: society and economy

In 1914 Austria-Hungary was the third largest state in Europe and had a population of some fifty million. After the Treaty of St Germain, which confirmed the loss of all Austria's non-German provinces, along with considerable numbers of German speakers in the South Tyrol and the Sudetenland, it was about the size of Scotland or Bavaria, and had a population of around six and a half million.[48]

The loss of Austria's imperial provinces was a blow to what had been a diverse and complementary economy, and one which had undergone a degree of economic integration in the period before the First World War.[49] The economic performance of its western, industrialised provinces had been comparable with that of the industrialised regions of western Europe, while the eastern, agrarian provinces were more backward. In the face of the economic difficulties which the new 'rump' Austria seemed to face, most of its citizens despaired of the First Republic ever becoming economically viable and pinned their hopes on union with Germany.

The new republic of 'rump' Austria was characterised by a particularly uneven distribution of population and economic resources, both of which were disproportionately concentrated in the capital. In 1934 more than a quarter (1.87 million) of Austria's population lived in Vienna and it was here too that industry, trade and administration were overwhelmingly based (table 0.1). There were no other cities of comparable size; only two had a population of over 100,000: Graz, an old university town and Austria's 'second city' (153,000), and Linz, which with less than 109,000 inhabitants, had a smaller population than some districts of Vienna. No other Austrian town had as many as 100,000 inhabitants.

Vienna enjoyed an ambivalent reputation and fluctuating fortunes between the wars. Its economy went into rapid and apparently irreversible decline once much of its economic hinterland was lost, and the city lost a quarter of its population between 1914 and 1939. Nevertheless, its continuing importance as a European city far outstripped the significance of the new Austrian state as a European power; and its political position was further bolstered by its constitutional autonomy as a free-standing federal state. The progressive social policies of 'Red Vienna' won admiration abroad, but provoked the hostility of the city's own resentful middle classes, and deepened the national political antagonisms of the First Republic.[50] As a consequence the erosion of the city's political autonomy and economic independence came to be central to the strategy of creeping authoritarianism which characterised the Dollfuss administration.

Table 0.1. *Distribution of resident population in each economic sector*

	A Austria	B Vienna	C B as % of A
1 Agriculture/forestry	1,849,518	16,679	0.9
2 Industry/commerce	2,125,060	726,848	34.2
3 Trade/transport	984,685	458,530	46.6
4 Finance	64,749	41,758	64.5
5 Public service	224,677	84,047	37.4
6 Free professions	249,468	118,151	47.4
7 Domestic service[a]	88,659	50,650	57.1
8 Unemployed[b]	1,009,682	336,557	33.3
9 No profession given[c]	163,735	40,910	25.0

a Non-resident domestic servants. Resident domestic servants are allocated to the economic sector of their employer.
b Without profession.
c Includes employed people for whom no further information is available
Source: Statistisches Jahrbuch für den Bundestaat Österreich. Die Ergebnisse der österreichischen Volkszählung vom 22. März 1934 (Vienna, 1935), pp. 2–5.

The antipathy of many Austrian conservatives to their capital city reflected not just the vested economic interests of farmers, landowners and metropolitan bourgeoisie, but deeper-rooted anxieties about modern city life which were shared with the Nazis. Indeed, the triumph of Nazism has been called an 'uprising of the provinces against the metropolis', and Adolf Hitler a 'product of the socialisation process of the Austrian provinces'.[51] Yet, despite Hitler's own professed aversion to Vienna (and grandiose plans for Linz),[52] it was the Nazi administration which sought to reverse the city's decline and create a Greater Vienna which would be the Reich's second city and the gateway to the Balkans. The size of the city was quadrupled with the incorporation of neighbouring rural districts and the population increased by 213,000. The Nazi authorities commissioned a detailed analysis of the city's economy which was pessimistic about the present decline of trade and industry (tables 0.2 and 0.3), but more upbeat in its expectations of the future – if the right policies were applied, and opportunities seized.[53]

Outside Vienna the new Austria was overwhelmingly a country of rural and small town communities (table 0.4). Agriculture was the most important activity, of course, but there were significant industrial centres in the Vienna basin, notably St. Pölten, Wiener Neustadt and elsewhere. Steyr, in Upper Austria, was an industrial town important in motor vehicle and armaments production. The greatest concentration of heavy industry outside Vienna was in Upper Styria. It was here, in

Table 0.2. *The Viennese population according to economic sector, 1910–1939.*

	1910	1923	1934	1939
Agriculture	1.0%	0.95	1.1%	2.7%
Industry/commerce	50.2%	48.2%	47.5%	48.5%
Trade/transport	28.1%	33.0%	32.0%	27.3%
Services	11.4%	11.6%	12.8%	16.7%
Domestic service	9.3%	6.3%	6.6%	4.9%

Source: 'Wien im großdeutschen Reich', in Botz, *Wien*, p. 603.

Table 0.3. *Industrial workers in Vienna 1939 as a proportion of total population*.

I	Innere Stadt	3.6%	XII	Meidling	33.4%
II	Leopoldstadt	0.6%	XIII	Hietzing	24.1%
III	Landstraße	18.9%	XIV	Penzing	27.2%
IV	Wieden	8.8%	XV	Fünfhaus	29.4%
V	Margareten	23.2%	XVI	Ottakring	37.9%
VI	Mariahilf	14.2%	XVII	Hernals	37.9%
VII	Neubau	13.6%	XVIII	Währing	14.4%
VIII	Josefstadt	9.9%	XIX	Döbling	17.0%
IX	Alsergrund	11.1%	XX	Brigittenau	34.5%
X	Favoriten	40.8%	XXI	Floridsdorf	37.0%
XI	Simmering	37.3%	XXII	Großenzersdorf	28.9%

*After boundary changes. See map on page xiv. Districts XX and XXI include areas incorporated in 1938. Other incorporated areas (the new districts XXIII–XXV) are excluded.
Source: *Statistik des deutschen Reichs*, vols. 550/27 pp. 54ff

towns such as Leoben, Donawitz and Zeltweg, and to a lesser extent in Carinthia, that the Austrian steel industry was established in the nineteenth century.[54] Otherwise only Vorarlberg had any manufacturing on a significant scale. But although the province's industrial and commercial sector was – ostensibly – proportionately larger than that of Vienna, much of it was small scale manufacturing in the old established textile trade, and the total size of the industrial workforce was equivalent to that of one of the districts of Vienna.

Austria's provinces had nothing to equal the relentless industrial sprawl of Germany's Ruhr valley. Wiener Neustadt and Steyr were essentially small mediaeval towns despite their later importance as arms manufacturing centres during the war; and the string of industrial towns

Table 0.4. *Distribution of resident population by economic sector in the federal provinces.*

Percentage in nine economic sectors (as table 0.1)								
	1	2	3	4	5	6	7	8	9
Austria	27.3	31.4	14.5	0.9	3.3	3.5	1.3	14.9	2.4
Vienna	0.9	39.1	24.6	2.2	4.5	6.3	2.7	18.1	2.2
Lower Austria	34.4	31.6	10.4	0.5	2.5	2.7	0.7	14.5	2.6
Upper Austria	37.5	29.5	10.4	0.5	2.7	2.4	0.7	14.2	2.1
Salzburg	32.9	24.7	14.8	0.6	3.9	3.2	1.1	15.4	3.3
Styria	39.8	26.2	10.4	0.5	2.7	2.8	1.0	14.4	2.1
Carinthia	39.3	26.5	10.6	0.4	3.1	2.4	0.8	13.9	3.0
Tyrol	35.2	25.2	14.6	0.6	4.1	3.6	0.7	13.3	2.6
Vorarlberg	26.6	39.3	13.0	0.6	4.3	3.2	0.4	9.7	2.8
Burgenland	55.2	23.6	6.0	0.1	2.7	1.7	0.3	7.6	2.7

Source: Volkszählung 1934, pp. 2–5.

and conurbations set in the sub-alpine countryside of Upper Styria were tiny in comparison with Gelsenkirchen or Bottrop.

In addition much of Austria's manufacturing industry was based on small workshops employing small numbers of people, and this was also true in some parts of Vienna in a range of craft based branches, such as leather goods or printing. Equipment was often outdated and inadequate, and employment insecure. In the countryside, underemployment was widespread in agriculture, and unemployment in small provincial towns was disguised by the employment of family members in small businesses and shops. Many of those employed by large firms in Vienna (and elsewhere) were often on short time and, of course, real unemployment was high throughout Austria, in all sectors of the economy, for over a decade. Economic 'unviability' was not only the preoccupation of government ministers, but the daily concern of households throughout the country, and one against which the political developments should be read.

Aims, methods and sources

The present work is an examination of the extent and importance of informal working-class opposition to the Nazis in Austria between the Anschluss and the end of the war; it is an attempt to locate what survived of the political consciousness of the working class and its communities within a changing society and in a new relationship with authority which required compromise and consent. Its focus is the behaviour and opinion of Austrian workers at work and at home, as expressed in industrial relations on the one hand, and popular opinion in working-class districts on the other. This discussion will be placed within the broader context of recurrent political crisis and creeping authoritarianism in Austria from the last years of the First World War, and set against the background of rapid economic expansion brought to Austria by the Nazi war economy, and the social upheaval generated by the war and the war economy.

The reconstruction of mentalities, attitudes to work, pay, and conditions, to the Nazi regime and the political events of the day is inevitably less straightforward in a dictatorship at war than in a society where the expression of both industrial conflict and political opinion is open. Under the Nazis neither was possible. Fewer grievances were expressed openly, but there was an increase in the covert or indirect expression of dissent: graffiti and whispering propaganda; absenteeism and sabotage.

Censorship and state control of the mass media (press, radio or newsreel) meant not only that freedom of expression was impossible, but that the very formation of opinion was distorted. Fear of denunciation meant that it was rarely expressed, even in close-knit communities, and if it was, it was rarely recorded except in the reports of the authorities, 'compiled for particular administrative and political purposes', and above all the regime's internal reports on morale, undertaken on behalf of a variety of institutions, including the party, the police, the judicial authorities and the security service of the SS (*Sicherheitsdienst*, SD).[55]

Such sources are problematic. They are selective in what they report, and their content is frequently refracted through the ideological prism of the regime. Nevertheless there are also advantages. The regime undertook surveillance on a grand scale, and although the entire record of all that surveillance has not survived, the regime's internal reports are a very rich source.[56] In addition, the provenance of the reports is varied, reflecting the 'polycratic' nature of the political system. A range of different (sometimes self-consciously competing) authorities compiled information from different sources, in different ways and for different purposes. There is a certain degree of consistency between the various types of report, and with the content of similar reports compiled by agencies outside the regime, such as the exiled German Social Democratic Party (*Sozialdemokratische Partei Deutschlands* or 'Sopade').[57]

A dictatorship which suppressed free public opinion and replaced it with propaganda, yet needed to assess popular morale and the extent of support for its policies clearly needed a reliable internal flow of information. The circulation of such internal reports was widespread, providing the state and party bureaucracy at local and national level with a relatively reliable alternative to its own propaganda. The reports are not untainted with the ideological perspective of the reporters: no historical records are. But the more crass or dogmatic expressions of Nazi ideology are the exception. The tone and approach are rather those of an upper middle market conservative newspaper of the time, not unexpectedly given the social, educational and political background of the majority of the regime's senior civil servants and secret policemen.

Two important sources of this kind for Nazi Germany are, however less useful for Austria. For the Sopade reporters, Austria was marginal even after 1938, and although the Austrian socialists also reported on the situation, in the pages of the exile journal *Der sozialistische Kampf*, for example, such reports are much rarer than for Germany itself during the 1930s. The occupation of Austria was swiftly followed by the occupation of Prague, where exiled German and Austrian socialists alike had been based, near to the borders of the Reich. The work of the Sopade and other exiles was continued in Paris, but was increasingly difficult after the outbreak of war, and impossible after the fall of France.

The regime's own reports continued to be produced throughout the war, of course, but here there are different problems. Relatively few of the original SD reports for Austria have survived, and are mainly from Vienna and Upper Austria. Within months of the Anschluss the national SD reports, overviews compiled in Berlin from the regional and local reports, have little more to say about Austria specifically. Separate references to Austrian towns or regions are rare, references to Austria as an identifiably separate part of the Reich rarer still. The general impression gained from these sources is that Austria *qua* Austria was not a problem for the regime.

These sources are supplemented by more consistent local sources: reports on industry from the two Austrian defence districts and their sub-offices to the *Wehrwirtschaftsinspektion* (Inspectorate of the Defence Economy), and the war diaries and local reports from *Rüstungskommandos* (Armaments Commands); reports of the local police and judiciary, including case files of people appearing before *Sondergerichte* (special courts) and works disciplinary tribunals; the 'daily' reports ('*Tagesberichte*' were not always compiled every day) of local Gestapo offices; and a wide range of other types of documentary evidence from a range of sources. The challenge to the historian of Austria during this period is, of course, also an advantage: if, apart from one or two collections, the sources are uneven or even, occasionally, fragmentary, the sources will inevitably be more varied, and not overly reliant on the perspective of the SD or Sopade reporters.

In the event, the primary sources for this period are scarcely less problematic than the secondary sources. The combination of Austria's peculiar relationship with the Third Reich (and its legacy) and the politicisation of all discussion of fascism, is compounded by the continuing problem of locating effective resistance and genuine opposition in societies whose historiography has been dominated by hagiography and the apportionment of blame.

Austrian fascisms, 'Austrofascism' and the working class

Austrian politics

The history of modern Austrian politics has generally been described in terms of three broad political movements or 'camps' (*Lager*): the labour movement, the 'Catholic-conservative' camp and the 'national-liberal' camp.[1] All three movements originated to some extent in the broad spectrum of radical political opposition to Austrian liberalism in the last quarter of the nineteenth century, and their earliest leaders moved in the same political and intellectual circles in Vienna.[2] This tripartite structure has constituted the framework within which parliamentary parties have operated in Austria since the emergence of popular politics, and has proved a remarkably stable model, still recognisable in the political history of the Second Republic.

There is much to be said for the 'tripartite interpretation' of Austrian politics; it is worth distinguishing, for example, the clerical from the anti-clerical Right. Nevertheless, it is not without its problems, especially when applied to the political Right between the wars. The Christian Socialists and the German nationalists acted in accordance with the practical political imperatives that united them, rather than the ideological differences that divided them. Although the existence of three separate parties always made other types of coalition possible, the only one that was ever formed after 1920 was a 'bourgeois bloc' made up of the Christian Social Party (CSP) and the Greater German People's Party (*Großdeutsche Volkspartei*, GDVP). Coalition with the Social Democrats was unthinkable for either. Similarly, although both the rank and file of the two parties and their electoral constituencies differed, both parties represented essentially middle-class interests, and each was motivated by a determination to exclude the Social Democratic Workers' Party (*Sozialdemokratische Arbeiterpartei*, SDAP) from power.[3] In 1927, indeed, this co-operation was temporarily formalised when the two parties submitted a joint 'unity' list (*Einheitsliste*) for the parliamentary elections.

The tripartite model also provides us with a neat framework for interpreting the political radicalisation of the 1930s. Alongside the moderate party within each camp it identifies more radical groups: Communists as well as Social Democrats, the *Heimwehr* alongside the Christian Socialists, and the Nazis as well as the German nationalists. This neat categorisation misleadingly suggests an equality of political 'moderation', shared by the mainstream parties which did not exist. Not all of the First Republic's 'mainstream' politicians, or their supporters were similarly loyal to the constitution, to the parliamentary system of the First Republic, and to non-violent means of resolving conflict.

The German nationalists inherited much of their ideological baggage from the radical Pan-German Right of the empire, and had already co-operated with the old Austrian Nazis, before the wholesale Nazification of the national *Lager* in the 1930s. Similarly, the Austrofascist dictatorship of the 'Corporate State' was not established by a *Heimwehr* coup within the clerical camp, but by the Christian Social Party after years of increasingly anti-constitutional if not technically *unconstitutional* politics. Like their conservative counterparts in Weimar Germany, the leaders of the Christian Social Party sought a radical solution to the perceived political problems of the Republic, which would place their increasingly authoritarian government on a firmer, more permanent footing.

The tripartite model also obscures important realignments which took place during the critical period between 1927 and 1939, both within the broader ideological camps and between them. The labour movement fragmented under the impact of the defeat of 1934, which drove large numbers of disillusioned radical Socialists over to the Communist Party. For many people on the Right, particularly on the radical Right, political boundaries were renegotiated and ideological identities reconstructed more than once. Behind the superficial unities, the Austrian Right proved to be as fragmented, and its constituencies of support as volatile as they had been in the early days of 'mass' politics.

The radical Right before 1914

A popular politics of the Right emerged in Austria in the last quarter of the nineteenth century, not as a political party nor even as one ideological tendency, but as a welter of political groups and associations both within and outside parliament. In keeping with the tripartite model of Austrian political history, two dominant strains have traditionally been identified: German nationalism, and political Catholicism or Christian Socialism.

German nationalism, and more precisely Pan-Germanism acquired political significance in the Habsburg empire during the last quarter of the nineteenth century. Its growth was stimulated and its particular ideological complexion was influenced by a number of decisive turning points during the German wars of unification: the defeat of Austria in 1866; the *Ausgleich* (compromise), which more or less granted autonomy to Hungary in 1867; and the establishment in 1871 of a united German Empire, which excluded Austrian Germans. Pan-Germanism in Austria was a subversive phenomenon. Its ultimate aspiration, the union of all Germans in a single state, necessarily entailed the separation of the German-speaking territories in Austria and Bohemia from the other Habsburg territories, and therefore the dissolution of the empire. Necessarily disloyal to the state and the constitution, Pan-Germanism in Austria possessed an altogether more radical profile and subversive potential than its German counterpart. Pan-German Nationalists, many of whom were too young in any case to engage in formal constitutional politics, were more at home in a non-parliamentary – often explicitly anti-parliamentary – sub-culture, a network of nationalist associations which encompassed both political splinter groups and sports clubs but was dominated by the anti-semitic student corporations (*Burschenschaften*) which flourished in Austria (as in Germany) during the nineteenth century.[4]

Much Pan-German politicking was the generational revolt of young upper-class men, expressing their frustration at the 'ramshackle' old monarchy left behind by the dynamic new Germany. They were at the centre of a '*völkisch*' political movement which very explicitly defined nationality in terms of 'race'; and 'race', in turn, in terms sufficiently pseudo-scientific to invest it with the reflected authority of a spurious scholarship.[5] This was an ideology which could accommodate both the racial anti-semitism that was increasingly modish among the 'lumpen-intelligentsia' of the radical Right, and a racial sense of being German which found its ultimate cultural expression in some of the more eccentric fads and cults of the *fin-de-siècle*, ranging from an excessive linguistic purism which sought to revive a pre-classical, Teutonic nomenclature for the calendar to the worship of Woden at the solstice.

The career of Georg Ritter von Schönerer, the leading figure of the Austrian Pan-German movement, reconciled sub-culture and parliamentary politics. Although he was by no means disinclined to indulge in the more eccentric enthusiasms of the *völkisch* movement and its nostalgia for a mythical Teutonic past, he was also a member of the *Reichsrat*. The son of an ennobled *arriviste* family, he was elected for the rural constituency of Zwettl-Waidhofen in Lower Austria in 1873, and sat on the Left in parliament. Technically a supporter of the liberal government, he was also a member of the radical Progressive Club, and in practice a more vociferous critic of the government than its notional opponents on the Right.

At the beginning of his career in parliament Schönerer was a rather conventional member, largely preoccupied with mundane legislation, and prompted to speak more often than not on arcane aspects of land law. His speeches to the house quickly took on an increasingly German nationalist tone, however, and he repeatedly compared Austria unfavourably with the Reich. He denounced the *Ausgleich* as the symbol and embodiment of a wrong-headed re-orientation away from German central Europe, and objected to the government's policy in the Balkans, demanding that Austria be finally freed from 'Bosnia and company', even if it required civil disobedience. It was such rhetoric that made him a hero of the student nationalist movement, whose anti-semitism he radically assimilated into his own increasingly radical *Weltanschauung*. His proposals for ghettos and the restriction of Jewish employment have been described as forerunners of the Nuremberg Laws.[6]

The Pan-German movement failed to achieve a coherent organisational form or political identity before the First World War. Schönerer promoted his ideas energetically until his career came abruptly to an end when, after leading a violent attack on a group of journalists in 1888, he was imprisoned and lost his civil rights. He founded a number of nationalist organisations, and a journal, *Unverfälschte deutsche Worte* which, however, achieved a circulation of only a few thousand.[7] An invitation to the journal's readers in 1885 to declare in writing their support for Schönerer's parliamentary candidature solicited 3,260 replies and afforded a revealing glimpse into the geographical distribution and social background of his followers. A quarter worked on the land; a further 20 per cent were provincial officials or small office holders, such as councillors or village mayors, and some 4 per cent, members of the old free professions, such as teachers and doctors. 11 per cent were small businessmen, and well over half of these were publicans, while a smaller proportion (about 2 per cent) owned factories. Artisans and small craftsmen constituted some 15 per cent. The importance of students to the movement was demonstrated when his civil rights were restored and fourteen student corporations from Vienna sent their congratulations, along with a further seven from Graz and two from Innsbruck.[8]

Few of Schönerer's supporters seem to have come from the German crown lands, while over a third came from Bohemia and Silesia where the German-speaking population felt vulnerable in what were essentially ethnically mixed regions along the 'linguistic border' between German and Slav. It was fuelled, after the 1867 *Ausgleich*, by Czech nationalist demands for a federalised Cisleithania, with autonomy for the Czech lands similar to that enjoyed by Hungary. Although by the turn of the century Czech national leaders had more or less abandoned attempts at constitutional reform, conflicts continued at the level of local government, largely over the use of the Czech language, which German local authorities were trying to restrict.[9]

Anti-Slav prejudice and economic anxieties generated a moral panic among Germans in Bohemia which spread as far as Vienna. Czech immigration from the countryside during the rapid growth of Prague had transformed it from a German town into an essentially Czech city, and many Viennese Germans were afraid that even the capital itself might go the same way of Prague.[10]

During the revival of his career at the turn of the century, Schönerer attempted to exploit popular fears of the 'steadily growing peril . . . from Prague', which were as important an element in the manifesto of his '*Los-von-Rom*' (Break with Rome!) movement, as opposition to the church or the Jews: 'Slav insolence and Roman lust for power', he declared, had conspired in the old German *Ostmark* to 'annihilate Germandom in this empire which has been built up on German foundations'.[11]

It was anti-Slav agitation of all the ideological constituents of German nationalism in the empire that brought the first workers into the *völkisch* movement. Within the labour movement proper, the Social Democratic Party and the Free Trade Unions, Czechs and Germans were committed to internationalism, and worked together, but increasingly they were inclined to organise separately, along national lines, both in Vienna and in the Czech lands.[12]

German workers in the towns of Bohemia and Moravia, already resentful of the influx of cheap labour from the countryside into industrial towns, were particularly incensed by the Czech strike-breakers in the great strike of 1900. Their disaffection was exploited by breakaway *völkisch* unions with racist membership criteria, and by the political party they founded in 1904, the German Workers' Party (Deutsche Arbeiterpartei, DAP).[13]

The DAP has been called a 'pre-fascist party'. Its membership was distinctly proletarian, its political objectives radically democratic. It was not only opposed to 'reactionary tendencies, feudal, clerical and capitalist privileges', it also rejected the notion of uncritical obedience to leadership (at least where the autocratic ambitions of Georg Schönerer or

Karl Hermann Wolf were concerned). In the Austrian political spectrum the party was situated on the left rather than on the right.[14]

The DAP was clearly racist: hostility to the Czechs was its initial *raison d'être*. But, it was only later, under the influence of Walter Riehl, that the racism was extended to the Jews and translated into violence on the streets; and Riehl's efforts notwithstanding, anti-semitism was neither a central preoccupation of the party's members, nor the most prominent point of its ideology. Nevertheless the DAP was a clear precursor of the fascist movements that sprang up across Europe after World War I.

Support for the DAP was very limited.[15] It won 3,500 votes in 1907 and 26,670 in 1911 (of which some 22,000 were in the three northern Bohemian constituencies where its candidates were successfully elected).[16] Apart from a handful of supporters in Graz and Klagenfurt, support was largely restricted to Bohemia and Moravia, and the party was left stranded when the independent state of Czechoslovakia was established after the war. Renamed German National Socialist Workers' Party (*Deutsche Nationalsozialistische Arbeiterpartei*, DNSAP) after the war, it split into two 'branches' of unequal size. The prospects of the Austrian branch, led by Riehl, were not so bleak as they first appeared: support was reinforced by the immigration from Czechoslovakia of Germans dismissed from the state service. It won 23,000 votes in 1919, and 34,000 in 1920. Although this constituted less than 1 per cent of the vote, and the party failed to win a single seat in parliament, it was a considerable improvement on its pre-war performance on the same territory, and it did manage to win seats in the diets of Salzburg and Carinthia.[17]

German nationalist movements enjoyed no more than limited popular support during the last decades of the Habsburg monarchy, despite the emergence of a new 'mass' constituency. It was clear from the last elections before the war that the SDAP had established itself as the party of the industrial working classes on the left and the Christian Social Party as the party of the lower middle classes on the right; indeed, it has been argued that the CSP was the party of a middle class (*Bürgertum*) more united in political purpose than at any time since 1848.[18]

The Christian Social Party of late imperial Vienna was one of the most successful radical parties of the Right in Europe before the First World War. The ideology of the early Christian Social movement, expounded by Karl von Vogelsang in *Das Vaterland* echoed the new social doctrines of the church after the accession of Leo XIII. This ideology was anti-liberal and, like German nationalist ideology, recalled a mythical past characterised by social harmony, which might be restored by a 'return' to a corporate society where conflicts arising from class differences would be transcended.[19] In this point it anticipated important features of the social ideology of fascist regimes across Europe, including Italy, Portugal and Austria itself under Chancellors Dollfuss and Schuschnigg.[20]

In practice, of course, there were significant differences between Vogelsang and Karl Lueger.[21] The Christian Social movement mobilised support not so much by propagating arcane theories of society, as by addressing the grievances and manipulating the prejudices of its supporters, and above all by a straightforward appeal to anti-semitism. That this was, famously, a pragmatic strategy for winning power, rather than a reflection of real conviction on Lueger's part, and that it built on 'traditional' clerical and cultural anti-semitism, rather than promoting the more fashionable 'scientific' racism of the day, hardly diminishes its dubious contribution to Vienna's political culture: to leave the city with a tradition of public political discourse in which the expression of anti-semitism ranging from pornography to high politics was not only tolerated but rewarded with political success.

The relationship between the Christian Social movement of the 1890s and fascist movements after the First World War is problematic. There is a great deal in Vogelsang's conception of the state that anticipates the 'Ständestaat', and there is also much in Lueger's populist approach to politics that carries the resonance of a later political style; Hitler's admiration of the latter's career is well documented in *Mein Kampf*, where, ultimately, Lueger is preferred to the more ideologically appealing Schönerer, simply on account of his political skill.[22] His great achievement was to unite the greater part of both the lower middle classes (*Mittelstand*) and the educated, professional and propertied middle classes (*Bürgertum*) behind a single middle-class party against the rise of a socialist workers' movement. In doing so he created a political party that was thoroughly modern in terms of organisation, popular appeal and the breadth of its social basis. There was much here, too, that anticipated the successes of later right-wing populist movements.

The importance of the decades before 1914 for the history of fascism was not that they produced semi-formed 'proto-fascisms' waiting only for the catalyst of war to become fully-fledged fascist movements, but that they saw the emergence of a popular politics capable of mobilising mass support for the right. These radical political organisations were, perhaps, not yet fascist parties, but they drew on a proliferating corpus of radical right-wing ideas which can be described as proto-fascist, in so far as their central themes anticipated much of the fascist ideology of the inter-war years (where they did not actually create it).[23]

Austrian fascisms and the working class in the First Republic

Austria's right, fractured between clericalism and nationalism, produced two parliamentary parties after World War I. Despite its waning strength in the capital (even before 1914),[24] the Christian Social Party went on to become the party of government in the First Republic. The Greater German People's Party (*Großdeutsche Volkspartei*, GDVP), formed in 1920 from the majority of national and liberal groups, became its junior partner. If its ministerial portfolios in Vienna lent the GDVP respectability, however, the swastika emblem employed by its provincial organisations symbolised the party's closeness to a more radical *völkisch* tradition, and advertised its readiness to work with other groups who had remained outside the party, including the Nazis.[25]

The latter were organised within the DNSAP, successor to the pre-war DAP. Initially marginal to Austrian politics, the party's membership stood at 34,000 in August 1923, and it won nearly 8 per cent of the vote in municipal elections in Linz the same year.[26] Party leaders promoted co-operation with 'national socialists' in Bohemia, where the movement was stonger, and in Polish Silesia, through an Inter-state National Socialist Bureau of the German Language Territory, based in Vienna. The Bohemian Nazis were at first the strongest in this forum, but they were quickly overtaken in political importance by the newly-founded party in Munich, which also joined the Inter-State Bureau.

In the crisis years of the early 1920s the DNSAP came increasingly under the influence of the Munich party. When, in 1923, Hitler's supporters on the pro-Munich wing of the party won a majority committing the DNSAP to a putschist strategy, they plunged the Austrian Nazi movement into a lengthy internal battle, and it was during these upheavals that the emergent Austrian Nazi party became a more fully fascist organisation than its Bohemian predecessor.[27] Its social composition was transformed; older members with a background in the 'national' trade unions were increasingly marginalised, and by 1926 younger, more middle-class pro-Hitler members had gained the upper hand.[28] The Austrian NSDAP (Hitler Movement), recognised by Hitler that year, more or less replaced the Austrian party as the principal Nazi organisation in Austria. The dwindling old guard remained within the DNSAP, which was subsequently of negligible political importance.

Alongside the 'national fascism' of the DNSAP and, later, the Austrian NSDAP, there grew up a 'clerical fascism', whose organisational roots have been located in the *Heimwehren*.[29] These 'home guard' units sprang up at the end of the war for a variety of reasons to defend

Austria against incursions by foreigners at a time when the uncertain future of territories in the south and east threatened the integrity of what was already a tiny 'rump' state whose ability to survive was in question.[30] Yet, although they were armed by the government, national defence had never been the sole intention of the *Heimwehren*. Many had originally been units formed to prevent looting, and later, by extension, to defend illegal grain hoards against anticipated requisitioning. As the threat of foreign incursions onto Austrian territory subsided, their programmatic statements were increasingly directed at the 'enemy within', and they were generally supported by the local authorities and government security forces in the provinces.

They were also supported by the right-wing Bavarian paramilitary organisations which flourished after the overthrow of the Councils Republic in Munich, above all the *Organisation Escherich* (*Orgesch*) and the *Organisation Kanzler* (*Orka*). Supplied with weapons on the authority of the defence ministry in Berlin, these organisations were eager to support not only anti-socialists in Austria, but opponents of pro-Habsburg legitimism and supporters of Anschluss with Germany. Supplies of arms were exported by these groups to the alpine provinces of Austria, where staunch patriots persuaded themselves that treason supported by a foreign power against the federal government (an all-party coalition) was a noble struggle against 'the Bolshevism of Vienna'. The first clashes between *Heimwehren* and Social Democrats occurred in 1920.

The *Heimwehren* provided a focus for a range of disparate groups on the far Right, which nevertheless resisted centralisation under a national leadership. It was a movement which very much suited the particularism of provinces with assertive identities such as Styria, Carinthia and the Tyrol. Although the *Heimwehren* were important in the formation and development of clerical fascism in Austria they were also socially and ideologically eclectic. Much of their manpower was provided by the Catholic peasantry, but German nationalist students and restless ex-officers also constituted important sections of the movement, and co-operation with German groups such as *Orgesch* attracted many Pan-Germans in the early years. On the whole, however, the *Heimwehren* remained within the Catholic-conservative camp, and were absorbed into the Austrofascist regime of the mid 1930s. The exception was the Styrian *Heimatschutz*, which re-aligned itself with the Nazis in the 'national fascist' camp in the early 1930s.

It would be misleading, in fact, to over-schematise the divisions within Austrian fascism. There were differences between the ideologies and proposed policies of the two movements, in so far as the Nazis' policies were essentially those of the German NSDAP, while the aims of the *Heimwehr* movement, expressed in the Korneuburg oath of 1930, were more conservative in orientation; and naturally, then, there were differences in foreign policy. The Nazi party, was naturally not only pro-German, but persistently pro-Anschluss long after other parties had overcome their initial bout of despair of Austria's chances for survival as an independent state.[31] The *Heimwehr* fascists were more conservative in their foreign policy aims, preferring Austrian independence, and links with Italy and Hungary.

In domestic policy the two differed little. Both sought the permanent replacement of parliamentary democracy with a more authoritarian political system, and the destruction of the labour movement and its political and industrial organisations. Anti-semitism was also a common feature, although the clerical camp seemed less anti-semitic, despite the legacy of the Lueger era, as the racial anti-semitism of the national camp became increasingly virulent. They shared, too, a vision of society in which class conflict was absent, replaced by the social harmony of – variously – the *Volksgemeinschaft* or the *Ständestaat*.[32] Clerical ideology and propaganda was conservative in tone and emphasised the restitution of a supposedly traditional authority; that of the Nazis was more radical, and dwelt on the need for the rejuvenation of the nation and the regeneration of society.

Recruitment of support did not necessarily reflect the emphasis of ideology. Women joined the Austrian Nazis in their earlier radical days, but less so as the party became more explicitly fascist. On the whole, they were marginal to the membership of either type of fascism.[33] At elections they were marginally less likely than men to support parties with an extremist or violent reputation, but otherwise their voting behaviour differed little from that of their husbands or fathers, suggesting that class, age and regional loyalties were more important determinants than gender, despite the very clear difference in professed attitudes to women between the parties of the Right and those of the Left.

Younger people were attracted to the more radical parties, particularly to their paramilitary formations, and to the Nazi stormtroopers above all. But it was not young people *per se* who were attracted, so much as the war and post-war generations, and the Austrian Nazi party aged over the years.[34] Unsurprisingly, early fascist movements attract those members of the war generation most affected by the war itself, ex-combatants, and particularly ex-officers who felt betrayed by the 'stab-in-the-back' of Jewish-Bolshevik revolution against empires unbeaten on the field of battle – a composite of myths rapidly constructed and assiduously propagated (and to a large extent believed) by the right in order to explain unexpected defeat.[35] Young men who had left school for the front before work or university found re-integration into civilian society difficult: work was scarce in any case, and a university degree did not necessarily make it easier to find employment. Many students and university drop-outs joined *Heimwehren* or other right-wing paramilitary groups, and they were also massively over-represented in the Austrian Nazi party.[36] This was not necessarily only, or even primarily, a matter of their youth so much as their social class. It was not only students, but the entire university educated population that was over-represented in both types of fascist movement, and particularly among fascist leaders.[37] If there is any truth in the popular myth that high levels of unemployment stimulated the growth of fascism, then much of it was graduate unemployment among the educated middle classes.[38]

In general, much less is known about support for the *Heimwehren* than for Austrian Nazism. We know that its social base was much more rural than that of the Nazis (its leaders landowners, its members farmers), and that rural groups were under-represented in the Nazi movement, as they were in Germany. Nevertheless, civil servants, the self-employed and clerical workers in the private sector were also well represented.[39]

The Nazi party on the other hand attracted few peasants, but disproportionate numbers of clerical workers from both the private and public sectors, and self-employed artisans and craftsmen. The new *Mittelstand*, over-represented as it was in all European fascist movements, had a particularly high profile within the Austrian Nazi movement. Employees in the public sector, including transport and the postal service had not only formed the core of old DNSAP membership, but were particularly vulnerable to unemployment as cuts were made in public expenditure in order to 'stabilise' the economy; similarly private clerical workers were affected by the finance and banking crisis of the depression.[40]

Workers, and industrial workers in particular, were under-represented in the membership of all European fascist movements. This does not mean that there were no workers in the party, and fascist parties were not the first middle-class parties of the Right to recruit from the industrial working class. Nor was their impact on parties or branches negligible: the sheer size of the industrial working class in the first half of the twentieth century ensured that, under-represented as they were, workers often constituted one of the larger social groups in individual branches. Fascist parties were hierarchical: the leadership was drawn from the middle classes, while workers were disproportionately present among militant paramilitary groups, charged with inciting the street violence from which more genteel members distanced themselves.

Workers were under-represented in both Austrian fascisms. This was especially so in the *Heimwehr* movement, which was essentially rural in any case, and whose clerical affiliations impeded recruitment among a secularised working class. The *Heimwehren* were also used as auxiliary police and strikebreakers during the depression, and were associated with the conservative Christian Social Party, with traditional authority, and with long-standing tensions between town and country. For Fascists to recruit workers who did not already belong to the established constituency of working-class Conservatives, then they would have to take support from the Left, and the secular Nazi Party was better placed to do this than the clerical *Heimwehr* movement. The Austrian Nazis did manage to attract some working-class support during the mid 1930s, but workers were still massively under-represented in the party, constituting some 53 per cent of the working population in 1934, but less than a quarter of party members. During the depression and the clerical dictatorship the proportion of workers in the party rose to just under a third,[41] but it was only in Upper Styria that workers were recruited to a fascist organisation in significant numbers. Here the dominant local employer, the Alpine Montangesellschaft made membership of a *Heimwehr* union, and later of the Nazi Party, a virtual condition of employment during the depression.[42]

The working class on the defensive: economic and political crisis and the rise of fascism 1927–1933

Although the onset of the depression in 1929 marked the beginning of the terminal crisis of the First Republic, the events of 1927 are widely regarded as a watershed in the history of the First Republic. In January of that year right-wing *Frontkämpfer* shot and killed a war veteran and a young child in a violent clash between rival demonstrations at Schattendorf in the Burgenland. When those responsible were acquitted by a Vienna court in July of that year, workers in the capital responded with spontaneous strikes and demonstrations outside Parliament. The crowd became unruly and in the ensuing battle the Palace of Justice was burned down and ninety demonstrators were killed.[43]

The leaders of the Social Democratic Party were taken by surprise by events, and responded in a conciliatory manner, deploying the *Republikaner Schutzbund* (the party's paramilitary organisation) only in an attempt to contain the situation, which it failed to do. A strike declared by the Free Trade Unions the same evening lasted barely three days, and the incident served only to underline the waning strength of the labour movement as a political force. A year earlier, at the Linz party conference, there had been talk of the threat of counter-revolution; this was not yet it, but it was a clear warning, and one which seemed to allow for no illusions about the neutrality of the state or the equilibrium of class forces. The direction of government thinking was unambiguous and, in the years that followed, the labour movement faced an increasingly self-confident challenge, both on the streets and in parliament. At the same time the material position of the working class was being undermined by the depression.

The Austrian economy never achieved lasting stability between the wars. The early years of the Republic had seen high inflation and high unemployment, and even in the relatively buoyant years of the mid 1920s Austrian unemployment had never fallen below 8 per cent. Between 1925 and 1930, before the full onslaught of the depression, some 150,000 jobs were lost in Austrian industry.[44]

The effects of the world economic crisis that started in 1929 were exacerbated in Austria by the collapse of the Creditanstalt, the country's leading bank, in 1931, which in turn triggered further economic crises. Austrian governments responded to the slump with a continuation of their deflationary economic policies, punctuated by appeals to the League of Nations for assistance, and attempts to come to some sort of accommodation with Germany that would permit closer economic co-operation between the two.

The effects of the government's policies were to be seen in the continued stagnation of the Austrian economy right up to the German invasion of 1938. By 1932 industrial production had fallen to 61 per cent of its 1929 output, and unemployment had reached 21.7 per cent of the workforce. It remained at this level throughout the mid 1930s, and still stood at 20.4 per cent in 1937, when the proportion out of work had fallen to 4.5 per cent in Germany and stood at 9.4 per cent in Britain.[45]

The standard of living for those in work declined as wages fell further and faster than prices. Unemployment benefits were meagre and lasted for only one year, so that the long term unemployed – perhaps half as many again as the number of claimants had no means of support.[46] The effects of the depression on an ordinary working-class community in Austria have been described in the famous sociological study of the village of Marienthal.[47] Three quarters of the families in this community were dependent on unemployment benefits; those still in work were mainly shopkeepers and local state officials. For most families meat virtually disappeared from the diet, and such meat as was eaten was now more often rabbit, horse meat and even cats and dogs.[48]

Rising unemployment strengthened the hand of the employers in the labour market, and they attempted to dismantle what was left of the

Table 1.1. *Industrial disputes in Austria, 1927–1932.*

	1927	1928	1929	1930	1931	1932
Strikes	195	242	202	83	56	30
Strikers (000)	28.8	32.9	23.8	6.2	8.5	5.4
Factories affected	440	687	535	169	253	150
Workers (000)	37.5	44.0	37.5	10.7	11.7	6.6
Days lost (000)	476.7	563.0	286.5	40.9	100.4	79.9

Source: Statistisches Handbuch für die Republik Österreich (Vienna, 1928–1932); *Statistisches Jahrbuch für den Bundesstaat Österreich* (Vienna, 1934).

Republic's labour legislation. In 1931, for example, all 1,300 miners at a Styrian pit were made redundant and then offered re-employment on the basis of individual contracts which excluded the possibility of collective bargaining.[49] The impact of unemployment on working-class militancy is difficult to assess. There was a noticeable effect on the incidence of industrial action. The number of disputes fell from 242 in 1928 to 30 in 1932, and over the same period the total number of strikers declined from 562,992 to 79,942, reflecting the erosion of economic security (see table 1.1).[50]

The impact on political activity was more complex. Membership of the SDAP, arguably the strongest and most united Social Democratic party in Europe, peaked at 718,056 in 1929, when party membership accounted for over a tenth of the entire Austrian population. In Vienna the number of card-carrying party members in the same year was equal to a third of the city's electorate.[51] Loyalty to the party was high, even among the unemployed. By the end of 1932 there were over 123,000 unemployed party members in Vienna alone, 31 per cent of all party members in the city.[52] The party had also lost 60,000 members nationally. Some of these went over to the Communist Party (*Kommunistische Partei Österreichs*; KPÖ), but the numbers involved were modest. Communist Party membership doubled in the first half of 1931, but only to 6,813.[53] On the other hand the loss was perhaps not as great as it might have been. In Styria, where both party and unions had suffered dramatic losses in the mid 1920s, SDAP membership remained 10 per cent higher than it had been in 1925.[54]

Changes in levels of trade-union membership were more complex. Official statistics already show a decline in membership of the Free Trade Unions before 1929, reflecting the steady rise in unemployment during the late 1920s; and the decline accelerated during the slump, reflecting the sharper increase in joblessness. Right-wing unions escaped the decline in union membership. The rising membership of Christian

Table 1.2. *Trade union membership in Austria, 1927–1931.*

	Free	CS	National
1927	772,762	78,906	47,877
1928	766,168	100,087	51,247
1929	737,727	107,657	47,250
1930	655,204	111,939	48,899
1931	582,687	108,240	49,645

Source: Statistisches Handbuch (Vienna, 1928–1932).

Social unions slowed in 1928, and went into reverse in 1931; the rise in membership of the 'national' unions was patchier, but more persistent. Membership of the Free Trade Unions declined both absolutely, and relatively (see table 1.2).[55] The divergent experience of the different types of union is not easily explained. Members of clerical and German nationalist unions were generally better off than their average counterparts in other unions. The professions and regions in which right-wing unions recruited best were less severely affected by the depression. They attracted white collar workers and, to a lesser extent, transport workers, a trend that was stronger in the provinces than in Vienna.[56]

The clearest regional pattern was the divide between Vienna and the provinces. From 1930 to 1931 membership of the Free Trade Unions declined in all the federal states while membership of the right-wing unions continued to rise in some parts of the country. Although there was a decline in national membership of Christian Social unions there were marginal increases in membership in Salzburg, Carinthia and the Burgenland. German nationalist unions increased their membership in Lower Austria, Upper Austria, in Salzburg (albeit by only nine members), in Styria and in Vorarlberg. There was also a net increase in the overall membership of national unions in Austria, and they were the only ones to open new branches. (Their rivals were compelled to close down branches.) Only in Salzburg was the rise in membership of right-wing unions shared, and in Vienna and the Tyrol membership of unions of all ideological complexions declined.[57] Political pressure by employers was, of course, more easily brought to bear on workers in times of high unemployment, and the workers' choice of trade union was not always free: the pressure exerted on Styrian workers by their employers at the Alpine Montan is no doubt an extreme case, but not an isolated one.[58]

The gathering political crisis was tellingly reflected in the electoral politics of the last six years or so of the First Republic. In the general (*Nationalrat*) election of 1927 the SDAP increased its share of the vote.

Table 1.3. *Parliamentary elections in Austria, 1923–1930 (% of votes per party).*

	1923	1927	1930
SDAP	39.6	42.3	41.1
CSP	45.0		35.7
Unity List, 1927}		48.2	
GDVP	12.8		
Agrarian League		6.3	
Schober bloc			11.6
Heimatblock			6.2
Other	2.6	3.2	5.4

Source: Bukey, *Patenstadt* p. 67.

The party held its improved position well at the next general election in 1930 and, more importantly, in the Republic's last provincial (*Landtag*) and municipal (*Gemeinderat*) elections between 1930 and 1933. Such losses as there were seem to have been compensated in part by communist gains.

The electoral behaviour of conservative voters was obscured by the search for a stable anti-socialist politics by the Right, and the shifting alignments and realignments that seemed to entail (table 1.3). These shifts had already begun in 1927 when the Christian Social Party ran with the German Nationalists on a common anti-Marxist 'Unity List' (*Einheitsliste*), but failed to win many more votes than the CSP had managed alone in 1923. Many German Nationalists voted instead for the Agrarian League.[59]

If there was a radicalisation of the Austrian electorate during the depression it took place on the Right. In 1930 the CSP, now disaggregated again from the 'Unity List', won its smallest share of the vote since the establishment of the Republic (35.7 per cent). Parties on the non-clerical right, now organised in the so-called 'Schober bloc' performed creditably, and won 19 seats. But some 9 per cent of the vote was shared by Austria's two fascist movements. Most of this (6.3 per cent) went to the radicalised *Heimwehr*. Fresh from the Korneuburg rally where its leaders publicly professed allegiance to fascist values and principles,[60] the *Heimatblock* felt confident enough to campaign separately from the CSP. While its performance was something of a breakthrough for a fascist movement in Austria, however, it was nevertheless disappointing (the German Nazi Party had won 18.3 per cent of the vote in the Reichstag election only two months earlier).

Table 1.4. *Elections to the Nationalrat 1930: Vienna (1927 results in brackets).*

	SDAP	CSP[a]	NWB[b]	HB	Others
Wien-Innen-Ost	46 (46)	30 (50)	16 (0.3)	3	5 (4)
Wien-Innen-West	44 (45)	32 (50)	15 (0.2)	4	5 (5)
Wien-Nordwest	50 (51)	27 (44)	14 (0.3)	3	6 (5)
Wien-Nordost	67 (67)	20 (28)	7 (0.3)	1	5 (5)
Wien-Südost	67 (69)	20 (29)	8 (0.1)	2	3 (2)
Wien-Südwest	61 (61)	23 (36)	10 (0.3)	2	4 (3)
Wien-West	66 (68)	21 (29)	8 (0.2)	1	4 (3)

[a] The 1927 figures refer to the *Einheitsliste* ('Unity List') of bourgeois parties, i.e. include much of the German nationalist vote in that election).
[b] In 1930 NWB = *Nationaler Wirtschaftsblock und Landbund* (National Economic Bloc and Agrarian League). The 1927 figures refer to votes for the *Landbund für Österreich* (Agrarian League for Austria).
HB = *Heimatblock.*
Source: *Statistisches Handbuch* (Vienna, 1931), pp. 209–10.

The *Heimatblock* did especially poorly in Vienna. There its average vote was 2 per cent, rising to 3 per cent or 4 per cent in the more prosperous inner districts and middle-class suburbia, and falling to 1 per cent or 2 per cent in the more outlying working-class areas (see table 1.4). The most striking feature of the election in Vienna, however, was the defection of middle-class voters from the CSP to Schober's National Economic Bloc, which paved the way for Nazi gains later.[61]

The *Heimatblock* fared better in the provinces. In Upper Austria, for example, it won 8.3 per cent of the total vote (11.4 per cent in Linz) and it seems to have attracted almost 40,000 votes from the mainstream clerical and nationalist parties, whose share fell sharply.[62] It scored its biggest successes in industrial upper Styria, however, where it won 17 per cent of the vote. Here the CSP vote again fell sharply, to 20 per cent. The SDAP also lost more support here than elsewhere; its share of the vote fell from 50 per cent to 45 per cent. Electoral support for the *Heimatblock* fell off rapidly. It was still ahead of the Nazis the following year in provincial elections in Upper Austria, but disappeared from the scene after an abortive *putsch* by the Styrian *Heimwehr* leader Walter Pfrimer in 1931.[63]

The Nazi electoral breakthrough came later, but was more impressive. No more parliamentary elections were held, of course, before the suspension of the *Nationalrat*, but between 1931 and 1933 regional and local elections were held virtually everywhere in Austria. In 1931 there was a

Landtag election in Upper Austria, and in 1932 elections were held to the Vienna city council and *Landtage* in Lower Austria, Salzburg and Vorarlberg. In addition local elections were held the same year in Styria (except Graz), and Carinthia (except Klagenfurt), and in a handful of other municipalities, including Krems and St. Pölten, two of Austria's larger provincial towns. Finally, a city council election was held in Innsbruck in April 1933. Virtually the entire electorate went to the polls once more at some point before the abolition of local government elections in 1933.

These were important elections in that a pattern of Nazi gains was established which seemed to echo, albeit belatedly, the experience of the Reich. The party had won around 3 per cent of votes cast in 1930. In 1931 it won 3.5 per cent in Upper Austria, while in Linz itself it did better. Nevertheless it was the Social Democrats who won the day in Hitler's home town, winning over half the votes there in the *Landtag* (50.8 per cent) and in simultaneous elections to the city council.[64]

The elections of the following year involved three quarters of the electorate voting at one level or another: half the entire population of Austria lived in Vienna and Lower Austria alone. The results show that support for the Nazis had risen to 10–15 per cent, and was particularly strong in towns. The real political outcome of the elections was a very clear one: the non-clerical Right was virtually eliminated. In provincial diets and town councils throughout the country the German nationalists, the Agrarian League and a whole range of smaller parties were replaced by Nazis.

More importantly, the Christian Social Party lost enough, and sufficiently decisive seats for the aggregate of the election results to have important political consequences. The party lost control of the Lower Austrian diet, where it had taken absolute majorities for granted, and its cumulative losses in the three *Landtag* elections in April cost it control of the *Bundesrat*, the upper house of the Austrian parliament.[65] Finally, the Nazis' astonishing success (41 per cent) in 1933 in Innsbruck, capital of the devoutly Roman Catholic Tyrol, was swiftly followed by an announcement, at the Christian Social Party's conference in Salzburg in May of that year, that the government intended to prohibit local government elections until 31 October, supposedly to avoid the economic losses incurred by holding elections during the tourist season.[66]

Where did support for the Nazis come from? The turnout in the regional and local elections was lower than in 1930, so that on the whole new voters in Austria did not play the role they had in Germany. The exception was the municipal election in Innsbruck in 1933, later than the others, and the last significant election. Here, where the Nazis won 41 per cent of the vote, nearly half their new votes seemed to have come from new voters. In fact these were not new registrations, but German Nationalists who had abstained in 1931. Much of the remainder came from those who had continued to vote for the German Nationalists in 1931.[67] Votes for the Nazis, then, clearly came from supporters of other parties. The Social Democratic Party seems to have maintained its support remarkably well, and particularly in Vienna, Lower Austria and Carinthia, whose electorates accounted for 80 per cent of those voting in 1932.[68]

Vienna is important not only because it had the largest constituency, but because it also had the largest Nazi vote in 1932. But the marginality of the Left's losses there, and the manifest collapse of the bourgeois parties, was so stark that there has been little scope for controversy. The SDAP won some 10,000 votes fewer in 1932 than in the previous council election in 1927, while the Communists had won an extra 14,292. The Social Democrats' share of the vote had declined from 60.3 per cent in 1927 to 59 per cent (exactly the same proportion as in 1930). The party gained an extra seat on the council, the Christian Social Party and the German Nationalists lost 16 seats between them, and the Nazis won 15.

There was a particularly clear continuity in support for the German Nationalists and support for the Nazis, as might have been expected (see table 1.5). The German Nationalists had never done particularly well in the capital, but had had relatively high levels of support in the fourth and eighteenth districts, where many white-collar workers lived. These were also the districts where the greatest support in extra votes came from the Catholic *Lager*, which had been able to rely on at least a third of the vote in Vienna in the 1920s, but had won only 24 per cent in 1930. In 1932 the governing party of Austria could rely on the support of only a fifth of voters in the capital city. This collapse was the more remarkable given the relative weakness, historically, of German nationalism in Vienna. Clearly the same claims cannot be made for the ideological immunity of Catholic communities in Austria as for those in the more diverse confessional landscape of Germany: to be a Catholic here was little more than to be an Austrian. Yet Vienna had been the home of an extraordinarily successful political Catholicism, which had now crumbled in the face of political competition. Support for Hitler in Catholic Vienna was higher than anywhere else in Austria in 1932, while Protestant Berliners were among the Führer's least enthusiastic followers in Germany.

The Social Democratic vote was resilient in the most important contests outside Vienna. In Upper Austria, the share of votes for the SDAP

Table 1.5. *Support for German nationalism and Nazism in Vienna, 1919–1932 (percentage of total votes cast).*

District		1919*	1923*	1930†	1932*
1	Innere Stadt	5.1	3.6	1.9	17.6
2	Leopoldstadt	3.5	3.4	2.4	16.7
3	Landstraße	7.6	6.8	2.7	23.4
4	Wieden	14.6	10.4	3.8	31.0
5	Margareten	5.8	5.0	2.4	19.6
6	Mariahilf	7.1	6.8	2.9	23.5
7	Neubau	7.9	7.2	3.4	24.9
8	Josefstadt	9.5	9.3	3.3	27.9
9	Alsergrund	7.0	5.9	2.8	21.2
10	Favoriten	-	2.4	1.3	10.0
11	Simmering	-	2.3	0.7	7.3
12	Meidling	4.2	3.6	1.5	14.1
13	Hietzing	7.1	5.8	2.2	18.1
14	Rudolfsheim	2.0	2.8	1.4	13.0
15	Fünfhaus	3.6	5.2	2.4	18.4
16	Ottakring	2.5	2.4	1.4	12.0
17	Hernals	3.5	3.4	2.6	17.0
18	Währing	18.8	11.9	4.4	28.1
19	Döbling	8.6	6.8	3.4	21.5
20	Brigittenau	2.1	2.2	1.6	10.6
21	Floridsdorf	5.1	3.7	2.4	12.1
Vienna		5.4	4.9	2.3	17.4

* municipal election
† parliamentary election
Source: Maren Seliger and Karl Ucakar, *Wien. Politische Geschichte 1740–1934* (Vienna, 1985), vol. II.

in 1931 (28 per cent) was virtually unchanged from 1930 (28.4 per cent), and had increased since the previous election to the *Landtag* in 1925 (26 per cent). In Lower Austria the following year the SDAP lost 20,000 votes, but its share of the total vote fell only marginally, from 35.7 per cent to 34.7 per cent, and Communist gains accounted for more than half of this loss. In municipal elections in Carinthia, where the Nazis won 12.3 per cent of the vote, the SDAP remained the most popular single party, and won almost 1,300 more votes than in 1928 (and 39 more council seats). The Communists, too, won 2,000 more votes and 27 seats.[69]

In all these provinces the electoral upheavals of the early 1930s were on the Right. Apart from the rapid eclipse of the *Heimatblock*, the most salient feature was the obliteration of the German Nationalists as a political force distinct from the Nazis, the collapse of the Agrarian League and the decline of a whole range of other small groups purporting to represent sectional economic interests – such as Carinthia's intriguingly named Non-Marxist Business Party. As a consequence, the Christian Social Party regained some support initially, particularly in Upper Austria in 1931 and in Carinthia. In Lower Austria, on the other hand, where the *Heimatblock* and the German Nationalists lost over 105,000 votes between them, the CSP clawed back less than 2,000, while the Nazis gained over 76,000. Many of the Nazi gains probably came from the *Heimatblock*, although it has been noted that the Upper Austrian *Heimwehr* was much less pro-Nazi than the Styrian *Heimatschutz*.[70]

In Salzburg the Nazis took all the seats held by the German Nationalists (including that held by the one remaining elected Nazi from the so-called Schulz party, the original Austrian Nazis), and one each from the SDAP and the CSP. Both the major parties lost votes (the Social Democrats 6,696, and the Christian Social Party 11,359). In Vorarlberg the Nazis managed to win a seat each from the Agrarian League and the Socialists (the party blamed the Communists, whose gains accounted for over half the Socialist losses). Here the Christian Socialists hung on to their apparently unassailable two thirds majority. Even the German Nationalists and Agrarian League managed to keep a seat each, although the 6,400 votes the three parties lost between them presumably furnished the greater part of the 7,150 gained by the Nazis.[71]

As expected, the SDAP recorded its heaviest losses in the municipal elections in industrial Upper Styria. The Styrian *Heimatschutz* had effectively gone over to the Nazis after the unsuccessful Pfrimer *putsch* of September 1931, and managers and technicians at the Alpine Montan in Donawitz also switched their political allegiance.[72] Where previously workers had been forced to choose between unemployment and membership of the *Heimwehr*, the company now preferred to employ Nazis, and the NSDAP made substantial gains in towns like Leoben, Eisenerz and Donawitz itself. The KPÖ also made gains, although on a much smaller scale, and in fact the Social Democrats also gained seats in a number of Styrian municipalities, including Gröbming and Mariazell, where they had been hitherto unrepresented. It has been argued that a correlation can be established between Nazi gains and SDAP losses outside Vienna.[73] This in itself is uncontroversial, provided that a sense of perspective is retained; the only generalisation that can reasonably be made is that there was a defection of voters of landslide proportions from the parties of the non-Nazi right to the NSDAP. This haemorrhage of support from the CSP to the Nazis helped determine the political course on which the the Dollfuss government was to embark.

Civil war and the establishment of dictatorship
1932–1934

In May 1932 the government resigned following the departure of the
German nationalists from the coalition. The new government, a coalition drawn from the Christian Social Party, the Agrarian League and
the *Heimatblock*, and led by Engelbert Dollfuss, had a majority of one
in the *Nationalrat*. Co-operation with the SDAP was unthinkable, not
least because it was anticipated that this would precipitate further losses
to the Nazis, binding the two major parties in a 'Grand Coalition' of
indefinite duration.[74] With the example in mind of Heinrich Brüning's
circumvention of the German Reichstag by the use of presidential
decrees, the new chancellor looked for a similar means of circumventing
the *Nationalrat*.[75] He found it in a War Economy Enabling Act of 1917,
which had never been repealed, and which enabled government not only
without parliament, but without resort to the President's 'strictly circumscribed' power to issue emergency decrees. The law was first used
on 1 October to pass an order (*Verordnung*) making members of the
Creditanstalt liable for the bank's losses, and with retroactive force.[76] It
was this decree which was used to suspend local elections the following
year.

The War Economy Enabling Act was most useful, however, in the
suspension of parliament itself. The Social Democrats and German
Nationalists joined forces in March 1933 to prevent the government
punishing striking railway workers with disproportionate severity, but
when Karl Renner, the chairman of the *Nationalrat*, declared the motion
for leniency carried, his decision was vehemently challenged by the
government.[77] Renner resigned, and his own resignation was followed
by that of his two deputies. For Dollfuss the opportunity to institute a
more authoritarian system of government was not to be missed. The
much repeated fallacy that parliament had somehow suspended itself
was rejected by most people outside the government at the time,[78] and
was belied when the second deputy chairman, on finding that there was
no provision for him to resign, defied Dollfuss and President Miklas
(who had backed the chancellor) and attempted to convene parliament,
but was forcibly prevented from doing so.[79] The Dollfuss government,
although originally elected to power, had now effectively seized it
unconstitutionally from above, and backed up its action with the threat
of armed force.[80] Within days the government had banned public political meetings, ostensibly as a response to developments in Germany,
and amended the press laws; and the following month a draft decree
'protecting employers against work stoppages (*Arbeitseinstellungen*)' was

presented to the cabinet. It was proposed that this decree, like the other measures, be enacted under provisions of the War Economy Enabling Act.[81] Outside parliament, in conflict after conflict with workers and labour organisations, the *Heimwehr* could be confident that government and security forces would generally be indulgent, if not encouraging, while the *Schutzbund* was held back both by the authorities' partisanship and by its own leaders' insistence on legality. Following the suspension of parliamentary government, the labour movement was driven further onto the defensive. Government policy was deliberately confrontational, and it is difficult to draw a line between provocation on the part of the state security services and provocation by the paramilitary wing of the government coalition. Both police and *Heimwehr* were used to intimidate workers during the railway strike of March 1933.

The response of the hesitant SDAP leadership, caught between its own fears of a civil war which it felt the workers would inevitably lose and the demands of the rank and file for decisive action, was to name four specific measures, each of which the party would counter with an immediate general strike: the dissolution of the party itself; the dissolution of the Free Trade Unions; interference with the autonomy of Vienna;[82] or the promulgation of a fascist constitution.[83] The government was now able to proceed with its 'salami tactics' of undermining the strength of the labour movement little by little, and provoking conflict while avoiding the specific measures which might give rise to united resistance from the Left.

Matters came to a head in February 1934. Dollfuss had come under renewed pressure from Mussolini to establish his provisional dictatorship on a more permanent footing through constitutional reforms replacing parliamentary democracy with a corporate state. At the beginning of February police arrested the leaders of the Social Democrats' paramilitary organisation, the *Republikaner Schutzbund* (Republican Defence League). The public security minister, Vienna *Heimwehr* leader Emil Fey, had also instituted provocative searches for *Schutzbund* weaponry. At the same time *Heimwehr* leaders in the provinces attempted to mount a rolling *coup d'état*.[84]

National leaders of the labour movement still counselled caution, while many in the rank and file of the party saw it as a last chance to act. On 12 February 1934, after duly warning the national leaders of the party (Otto Bauer), *Schutzbund* (Theodor Körner) and Free Trade Unions (Johann Schorsch), Richard Bernaschek and *Schutzbund* men in Linz carried out their threat of meeting any further provocation – whether a weapons search or the arrest of any party or *Schutzbund* official – with armed resistance.[85]

Fighting broke out in Linz, and the Vienna *Schutzbund* demonstrated support by attacking the police station in Simmering. Power workers cut off the electricity supply and the trams came to a standstill. A general strike was belatedly and reluctantly called, but it was incomplete and ineffective. The British press reported that even in Vienna many people continued to go to work, and that essential services were maintained, and a British foreign correspondent noted that workers were confused, ill-informed and uncertain what to do.[86]

In the capital there was not so much a major conflict between workers and security forces as a series of armed clashes in working-class districts, with police attacking *Schutzbund* positions, often with military support.[87] Resistance was probably stronger than the government side expected. Much of the working-class district of Simmering was still under *Schutz-bund* control by 14 February, and order was not restored in Floridsdorf for a further two days.[88]

The conflict was by no means restricted to Vienna. Fighting was particularly intense in Styria, but there was little hope of success against the overwhelming forces of the government without a general strike. There was some limited response to the strike call here, but the failure in particular of most railway workers to join the strike hastened the defeat of the *Schutzbund*. The conflict was particularly intense in the provincial capital, Graz, and at Bruck an der Mur, an industrial town in Upper Styria, where *Schutzbund* men led by Kolomann Wallisch opened fire on police breaking a strike. The workers were dislodged from their positions and dispersed only with the deployment of artillery and mortars; the fighting in this part of Styria was perhaps among the fiercest in the civil war.[89]

The Workers' Club in Linz, where the conflict had started, was taken by security forces within hours, and the fighting was over within a day, except in the Urfahr district on the left bank of the Danube, where the *Schutzbund* held out until the following morning.[90] There was also fighting in Steyr, a nearby industrial town noted for the strong Social Democratic sympathies of its working class. Workers at the *Steyrwerke* went on strike, cleared the factory and occupied the telephone exchange. The bitterest fighting concentrated around the barracks and the Ennsleithen housing blocks, and again the *Schutzbund* was defeated in the end only by the use of heavy artillery.[91]

Outside the urban centres of Upper Austria preparations were made for resistance but they came to little: railway stations and post offices were occupied, the gendarmerie was disarmed and workers issued with arms instead. In some cases the workers held out for up to a week.[92]

Essential services were maintained in Linz, and again, the trains ran. The very arrival of the first trains in the provinces was an indication in itself, in the absence of other reliable information, of the failure of a nationwide general strike. The (almost) punctual arrival of the 11.00 a.m. train from Vienna in the small railway town of Attnang Puchheim alerted striking railwaymen to the failure of the strike in a number of key towns along its route, including Vienna, St. Pölten and Linz.[93]

By 17 February the fighting was over. In Vienna alone 131 civilians were killed, including 25 women and children, and a further 358 were wounded. On the government side there were 55 dead and 251 wounded.[94] The combined forces of military, police and *Heimwehr* broke all resistance within days by simple superiority in numbers and sheer firepower, most cynically deployed in the artillery bombardment of Vienna council flats. Whether a general strike would have altered the outcome much is debatable, and in any case most workers were reluctant to take the risk. Workers' collective and individual financial security had already been undermined by the depression and the government had made it clear that politically unreliable workers would lose their jobs. They were not encouraged by the lack of confidence of the hesitant party leadership, and were ill-prepared to fight, unable even to locate or obtain the weapons hidden by the *Schutzbund* for such an eventuality.[95]

The establishment of a dictatorship in Austria was a long and piecemeal process. Many conservative leaders in Austria, among them Ignaz Seipel, the CSP's most important leader, and the dominant political figure of the 1920s, simply never accepted parliamentary democracy or the legitimacy of the parties of the Left, and alternatives were frequently discussed by the right-wing intelligentsia.[96] The turning point was the string of political crises of the late 1920s and early 1930s, when the threat to the Republic came not so much from political violence as from the government's response: the partisan deployment of state security forces in close collusion with the militant fascist wing of the governing party. It was a course which culminated in the suspension of the constitution and political rights, and the establishment of a one-party state.

Dictatorship and opposition 1934–1938

The SDAP was dissolved on 12 February, and within a fortnight over two thousand of its members had been arrested. Summary courts were set up and nine death sentences were carried out almost immediately in the capital. Kolomann Wallisch was arrested and hanged on the same day in Styria. Others, including the majority of the national leadership, fled abroad, where the *Auslandsorganisation österreichischer Sozialisten* (ALÖS) was formed.[97] Both *Die Arbeiterzeitung* and *Der Kampf* continued to be published in Czechoslovakia and smuggled into Austria.

Government persecution continued long after the immediate aftermath of the fighting. Steps were taken to exclude any potential Social Democratic sympathisers from the legal processes, including defence lawyers and jurors, and the deterrent nature of the justice meted out was made clear. When the summary courts had finished their business, the ordinary courts settled down to deal with the cases referred to them, and these were followed by proceedings against the party and *Schutzbund* leaders, which went on into 1935.[98]

Immediate steps were taken to reform those aspects of the republican constitution the Right had always found irksome. The Vienna City Council and Senate were dissolved on 12 February, the mayor dismissed and a federal commissioner appointed to take charge of the city.[99] A new, arguably fascist, constitution was promulgated on 1 May.[100]

The new regime brought immediate and tangible gains to employers at the expense of a further deterioration in working-class living standards. Firms quickly took advantage of the absence of trade unions and the weak bargaining position of the workforce to enforce wage cuts on their workforces. By July a hundred collective wage agreements had been broken by employers in Vienna alone, and wages fell on average between 4 per cent and 8 per cent.[101]

Workers' experience under the Austrofascist regime foreshadowed that under the Nazis. For most active resistance or any illegal political activity remained out of the question, and labour leaders advised caution, rather than heroics. The main objective of Social Democratic strategy was to maintain contacts but keep a low profile, recalling the tactics of the party's illegal years during the late nineteenth century, and this established an approach which continued after 1938. The majority of both the leadership and the rank and file regarded further armed resistance as futile, but more active resistance to the new regime also persisted nevertheless, and proved to be a force for disintegration within the labour movement. Illegal trade union and political activities continued underground, and middle and lower ranking functionaries of the SDAP came together and formed the Revolutionary Socialists (RS).[102]

The threat of disintegration was posed most clearly by the defection of political activists to other parties. Despite adopting a consciously more radical position than the SDAP, the Revolutionary Socialists faced competition for the loyalty of disaffected and radicalised socialists. Some *Schutzbund* members went over to the KPÖ, which flourished now as it never had as a legal party. The communist paper *Rote Fahne* claimed in March that KPÖ membership in Vienna had more than doubled, and that of the Communist Youth League had increased tenfold, while in nine districts of Vienna the Social Democratic *Rote Falken* formations had gone over to the Communists collectively. In Wiener Neustadt fly-sheets were distributed by local Social Democrat functionaries enjoining loyalty to the party, and warning against defections to the Communists and the Nazis.[103]

While it is not disputed that a considerable number of Socialists went over to the KPÖ, the question of defections to the Nazis has been more controversial. The party clearly thought such a danger existed, and the *Arbeiterzeitung* carried a warning to 'young comrades' not to join the Nazis 'in order to take revenge on the clericofascist hangmen': Hitler's regime was not only far more brutal than that of his Austrian imitator, but there was a danger that a Nazi dictatorship would find a broader basis of support in society than the Austrofascists; behind Dollfuss, on the other hand, stood nothing more than a few thousand aristocrats, capitalists and priests; a Hitler dictatorship in Austria would be more enduring than that of Dollfuss and Fey.[104]

Assessments of the scale of defections to the Nazis vary. Willibald Holzer refers to short-term co-operation between illegal *Schutzbund* units and Nazi party members 'here and there', a desperate measure prompted by defeat and the solidarity of shared persecution.[105] Gerhard Botz has estimated that in western Austria and Carinthia up to a third of *Schutzbund* members switched their support to the Nazis, while a much smaller proportion of Viennese members did so. It is difficult to establish with accuracy the number of such conversions, the motives behind them, or their durability. There are simply no Nazi Party membership statistics for 1934 from which it is possible to establish that there were defections from the Socialist Party, however marginal. NSDAP membership figures for 1933 show an increase in the proportion of workers in the party, but a breakdown of membership by occupational group cannot reveal the former political commitments of new members, and it seems likely that many working-class Conservatives of long standing joined the party as part of the exodus of defections from the crumbling parties of the non-Nazi Right.[106]

A further threat to the maintenance of a Social Democratic *Lager* was posed by the attempts of the Austrofascist regime to integrate workers into the new order. There were few converts, however, from the Social Democrats to the *Heimwehr* after 1934, and the latter remained very much a rural organisation. Participation in the government's own 'Unity Union' (*Einheitsgewerkschaft*) held some appeal to those trade-unionists and activists who thought that a degree of autonomy in the organisation of labour might be regained through such an accommodation with the government. These hopes were disappointed when Dollfuss and his Social Affairs Minister, Odo Neustädter-Stürmer, rejected socialist proposals for internal democracy within the union. Illegal trade-unionists, supported by the Revolutionary Socialists, now called for a boycott of the government union, which was then extended to other government organisations and institutions in the summer of 1934, when workers' leaders did not expect the 'corporate state' to last. After the assassination of Dollfuss in July, and a wave of arrests in January 1935, it became increasingly clear that a swift end to the dictatorship was not to be expected.[107]

Communists and Revolutionary Socialists undertook what resistance they could, sometimes working together, as in the latter half of 1934. Much of their activity anticipated that of the KPÖ after 1938: conspiratorial organisation in small groups; the distribution of propaganda and the collection of donations for the wives and families of imprisoned comrades by the relief organisations *Sozialistische Arbeiterhilfe* and *Rote Hilfe*. None of these activities were as difficult or as dangerous at this stage as they were to become later.

Illegal trade-unionists engaged in similar activities on the shop floor, and the *Einheitsgewerkschaft* (EG) clearly had difficulties in industry. The *Arbeiterzeitung* reported a number of cases in 1935 of resistance to the union. In a textile factory in Kleinmünchen workers left the EG en masse, following management attempts to appoint Christian Socialist shop stewards instead of former Social Democrats. In a nearby metal works a former Social Democrat was appointed an EG shop steward 'although he [was] no more a member ... than the rest of the workforce.'[108]

Workers in the tobacco factory at Linz were the accidental beneficiaries of rivalry between 'Christian' and *Heimwehr* elements within the EG, which led to a decree that nobody in the factory was to be disadvantaged by refusing EG membership. As a result women workers who had been demoted from the second to the lowest wage grade had their wages restored, and 250 women who had joined the EG under extreme pressure cancelled their membership.[109]

Workers were also often ready to take collective action against the widespread wage cuts introduced under the new regime. Workers at the car factory in Steyr had their old levels of pay restored after a strike of only a few hours in May 1934.[110] The Revolutionary Socialists, in an attempt to harness spontaneous resistance in industry, concentrated increasingly on industrial agitation, and a strike in two Vienna car factories (Fiat and Saurer in Floridsdorf) early in 1936, in support of a claim for a 15 per cent wage increase, was an indication that workers were once again prepared to take the initiative in industrial relations. The strike was quickly put down by the authorities, but the tactic of short strikes came to be increasingly exploited by workers in support of more wage claims as a modest improvement in Austria's economic performance became apparent. The Revolutionary Socialists saw in such industrial disputes a means towards weakening the political system; shop stewards on the other hand were more interested in winning realistic concessions within the system, and were only prepared to co-operate with activists to a limited extent.[111]

There was a qualitative difference between the Austrofascist dictatorship, which left some scope for illegal organisation, and the Nazi regime which was to follow. In 1937 the Gestapo in Passau reported to Munich – a foretaste of the surveillance to come – a convention of trade-unionists and Socialists at Ebensee which would have been unthinkable a year later. But ultimately, no formal political concessions were made by the government towards organised labour, and this remained the case when Austria was threatened with imminent invasion by Nazi Germany. Last minute secret negotiations between Schuschnigg and the underground movement in March 1938 came too late. Shop stewards demanded the lifting of restrictions before they could guarantee working-class support for Schuschnigg, and this was confirmed at the meeting of illegal trade-unionists which the government permitted in Floridsdorf on 7 March: although they recognised that Nazism was a greater evil than the Schuschnigg regime, they could not persuade the people they represented to throw their support behind the chancellor without a radical change of policy.[112] Schuschnigg reluctantly agreed to the demands put before him, but less than a week later, on 11 March, German troops had occupied Austria.

2 Economic integration and political opposition between the Anschluss and the war

The German annexation of Austria constituted the third major upheaval in the country's political system in twenty years. During the eighteen months between the invasion and the outbreak of war the new regime overturned both the remaining republican structures and the newer 'corporate' arrangements and laid the foundations for the permanent administrative, political and economic integration of Austria into the German Reich.[1]

There was no military resistance to the annexation: quite apart from the Chancellor's reluctance to order the army to open fire on German soldiers there was no shortage of sound reasons for failing to resist the German occupation. Austria's international isolation, and the indifference of the western democracies to the annexation were important external factors influencing Schuschnigg's decision. Among domestic reasons perhaps most important was the ambivalent national identity of many Austrians, and the strength of pro-Anschluss feeling that had followed the end of the First World War. Even by 1938 the sense of being an Austrian citizen was by no means always incompatible with a sense of German *national* identity, particularly for the German nationalist constituency, of course, but also – if in different senses – for other Austrians. Austro-Marxist thinking had accepted 'national unification' as a necessary precondition for the socialist transformation of a greater Germany, and the SDAP had been in favour of Anschluss immediately after the First World War, when the prospects for a socialist 'greater Germany' had seemed particularly auspicious. The party leadership continued until 1943 to adhere to the goal of national reunification within a democratic Germany, and for the social democratic Left the political cleavages within Austria were nominally still perceived as internal to a greater German (or international) political framework which transcended the Austro-German border. This prompted Karl Renner, for example, to think in terms of class divisions between the labour movement and fascism, be it clerical ('black') or nationalist ('brown') rather than national divisions between Austrians and Germans.[2] Roman

Catholics might have harboured lingering anxieties about domination by Protestant Prussia but, as we have seen, the clerical-conservative leadership which represented this constituency seems to have been even more afraid of collaboration with the Left than annexation by Germany. Here too, class interests seem to have been more persuasive than an Austrian national interest.[3]

This did not mean that the Nazis would not face opposition, and the industrial working class constituted an important, latently oppositional group. The new regime's primary concern was to prevent open industrial or political conflict, and in this at least it was successful, as it had been in Germany, where the threat of political opposition had been practically non-existent since 1933. The suppression of the organised labour movement, trade unions and political parties alike, was a process which was now repeated in Austria, in so far as it was still necessary after the events of 1934.[4] The task was made much easier by the existence of extensive police files on the political Left, compiled since the 1920s,[5] and the occupation was immediately followed by yet another wave of arrests of workers' leaders and left-wing activists. Some, of course, had already fled; others now attempted to do so and succeeded; but many were arrested – at home, on the platform of the *Ostbahnhof* waiting for the night express to Prague, or after being turned back at the frontier by the Czech police.

The violent suppression of overt political opposition was only one aspect of the new regime's strategy. A complementary aspect – and stated aim – was the integration of the majority of workers into the 'national community', and this entailed constructing a measure of popular consensus in support of the regime among the working class. Whether propaganda reflected policy, and the Nazi regime genuinely sought, or expected to win working-class support is open to question. Certainly the propaganda effort in the first weeks after the Anschluss was considerable. The purpose was to maximise support for the new regime in the forthcoming plebiscite on the 're-unification of Austria with the German Reich', scheduled for 10 April. The campaign directed at industrial workers and the Left was dominated by two themes: the shared persecution of Nazis and Socialists at the hands of the Dollfuss-Schuschnigg dictatorship, and the promise of economic recovery and employment. The measures taken in the short term were largely cosmetic. The price of gas was reduced by a few Groschen; benefits for the long-term unemployed, abolished by the 'Corporate State', were restored; and one-off bonuses were paid to a number of workers. Many of the Viennese workers who found jobs in the first month of Nazi rule did so in the course of a 'special programme', organised by the new

Nazi mayor of Vienna, Hermann Neubacher. Many were Socialists and Communists dismissed for political reasons by the old regime, and their reinstatement was clearly intended as a political gesture. Neubacher himself had been appointed for his past experience of dealing with the old social democratic city administration as manager of a concern owned by the council. His campaign to win over the workers was characterised by a mixture of promises (of reconciliation and future prosperity) and threats (of punishment for incorrigible elements), all couched in the tones of the ostensibly 'straight-talking' manager addressing a workforce which he affects to believe is basically 'sound', but has been led astray by a minority of disruptive agitators.[6] The Nazis, of course, had raised this affectation of managerial rhetoric to the level of official ideology and although it was a line prompted more by wishful thinking than accurate observation of social reality, it did reflect the mixture of coercion and paternalistic consensus-building which characterised the Nazi approach to the problem of integrating labour into the 'national community'. Nor was this a novel approach. It was a more emphatic restatement of the labour policy of the Corporate State, the articulation, in fact, of a set of assumptions which had been adopted in varying degrees since the origins of the labour movement, and it elicited different responses from different quarters.

Problems of political resistance 1938–1939

The response of the two principal political groups within the labour movement differed considerably. The social democratic camp, now represented by the Revolutionary Socialists (RS) immediately recognised the qualitative difference between the repressive methods of the Corporate State and the brutality of the Gestapo. They abandoned all organised oppositional activity, provisionally for three months, but effectively for an indefinite period. This was also the recommendation of the exiled social democratic leadership in Paris. *Der sozialistische Kampf* argued that the German experience of the Nazis showed that even small scale opposition was futile and dangerous, and warned that anybody touting fly sheets or newspapers was 'either a fool or a spy'. It would take months before anything more could be attempted than the maintenance of contacts between individuals.[7]

The Communist Party (KPÖ), on the other hand, was uncompromising in continuing its resistance activity, and gained more recruits from like-minded Socialists who had no organisation of their own. Failure to secure the co-operation of other anti-Nazi groups did not deter communist leaders from using the party organisation as a vehicle for active anti-Nazi resistance.[8] The party was an experienced conspiratorial organisation already practised in clandestine operations: it concentrated on recruitment, the dissemination of illegal propaganda and the collection of contributions for a relief fund. Members were also encouraged to infiltrate and sabotage Nazi organisations, although Communists were aware that they were known to the Gestapo, and that their arrest might endanger other individual comrades, if not the whole fragile network of contacts in Austria and abroad.

Communist activists therefore refrained from conspicuously adopting the role of leader or agitator in industrial disputes, and many went underground altogether. The party itself took 'protective measures' to ensure the security of the network and the safety of individual members. It dispensed with the services of known activists and paid functionaries, and insisted on the smallest, tightest possible form of organisation. It came to consist of a network of small local cells arranged in a vertical communications-and-command structure: cells were not to contact each other, and individuals were not even to know the identity of other members outside the group.[9] As a result, activists were isolated not only from each other, but also from the working-class communities which contained the movement's potential mass base.

Direct involvement with the resistance was a relative rarity. The resignation which had come from past experience, and particularly from the defeat of 1934 was a psychological obstacle for many. Nevertheless the KPÖ had expanded its ranks in the mid nineteen-thirties and continued to do so under the Nazis, particularly among the young, and it had attracted many former Social Democrats. Although usually led by Communists, many cells consisted entirely of Socialists who had gone over to the KPÖ in the absence of an organisation of their own, but nevertheless preferred not to mix with Communists.[10]

This is not to say, however, that the party's opposition to the Nazis was at odds with working-class opinion, or even that its activities were entirely outside the working-class community. Most of the party's activity took place in the public and private places of Vienna's outer industrial suburbia and in similar communities in smaller towns outside the capital. It was here, largely on the factory floor that collections were made for the dependants of imprisoned activists, and it was in bars and shops, markets and trams, that whispering propaganda and rumour-mongering were most widespread.

Relief organisations served to mobilise working class support for the resistance movement from beyond the core of committed activists. Indeed the socialist relief organisation, *Sozialistische Arbeiterhilfe* (SAH) was something of a substitute for a resistance organisation proper, and the first trial at the *Volksgerichtshof* in Vienna, in April 1939, was directed against its leadership.[11] *Rote Hilfe*, too, the relief organisation run by the KPÖ, was an important part of the activities of the communist resistance. Apart from providing financial help to the families of those imprisoned or executed by the Nazis, the contributions were used to finance the entire organisation, and were ostensibly the party's only source of income. Members of communist cells in the Graz *Puchwerke* regularly paid Rpf.15, and in St. Pölten RM 1,000 was collected by a *Rote Hilfe* organisation within a matter of fifteen months.[12] The Nazi authorities, for their part, took the activities of the relief funds seriously and charged contributors with membership of a subversive organisation involved in high treason.

Communist activists were also assiduous in originating rumours that put the regime in a bad light and fuelled popular disaffection or anxiety. On the other hand, such rumours often scarcely needed the benefit of a fervid communist imagination. The SD reported that in Favoriten, a working-class district of Vienna, rumours were being spread about the mistreatment of Jews, internal party wranglings, disagreement between members of the government, and so on – all of which, of course, was more or less true. The security services often saw local communist agitation where it was neither present nor necessary, and especially after the outbreak of war many 'rumours' originated from the broadcasts of the BBC World Service or Radio Moscow, which were heard by many people not otherwise involved in oppositional activity.[13]

Following the initial repressive measures of the spring there was little evidence of direct political opposition or conspiratorial activity in the early summer of 1938. The Gestapo monitored closely the activities of its political opponents, and those of communist activists in particular. It seems to have been relatively successful in gaining information by a variety of means, including the seizure of printed material, interrogation, and perhaps most successfully, the infiltration of communist ranks with Gestapo spies. The Gestapo also kept a close eye on the activities of the Social Democrats – Vienna's former masters appeared under the rubric 'other Marxist movement'.[14] In addition the SD reported to the Reich Security Head Office (*Reichssicherheitshauptamt*, RSHA) in Berlin on popular morale.

All these reports reflect a period of relative calm in 'working class circles'. The more optimistic reports interpreted the manifest lack of oppositional activity as evidence of open-mindedness, and some reporters regretted that so many workers were maligned as opponents.[15] Such interpretations of the popular mood were balanced by the more cynical judgements of others, who argued that refraining from underground activity was merely expediency on the part of workers, some of whom, at least, were only too eager to join the Nazi bandwagon: former anti-Nazis from both the Right and Left alike 'were only too grateful if they could get into the *Sturmabteilung* [the stormtroopers, SA] or the Nazi motor corps', and took every opportunity to curse the '*Systemzeit*'.[16]

Such oppositional incidents as the regime's reporters were able to find in the spring and summer of 1938 were relatively minor. There were complaints that Communists in the northern suburbs of Vienna were taking advantage of the relative leniency(!) of the Gestapo, and the regime's general policy towards the working class. The catalogue of minor peccadilloes which accompanies this complaint is revealing not because it suggests a hotbed of subterranean subversion, but because it provides a benchmark for the sensitivities of the local Nazis who had reported the 'incidents', and some sense of what constituted a political threat to the bureaucrats who recorded them.

In Währing, for example, communist songs had been sung in a public bar, and although the names of all participants had been written down by an affronted SS *Obersturmführer*, the case was not followed up by the Gestapo because subsequently 'all the participants unanimously declared that they had sung nationalist songs'. In Döbling an SA bar had been daubed with the slogan '*Heil Moskau*' and a number of communist fly-sheets had been found.[17] Such graffiti were neither unusual nor restricted to Döbling. The Gestapo regularly recorded the appearance of communist flysheets on the streets of Vienna, and there does not seem to have been any alarm on the part of the authorities.

The situation outside the capital varied from province to province, but nowhere was there evidence of concerted political activity during the spring and early summer of 1938. The Gestapo in Graz had found that many denunciations in industrial Upper Styria were based on remarks which indicated not so much political opposition as justified economic grievances. They recognised that in the prevailing economic circumstances unrest and rumour were inevitable, and that stoppages might well occur without political agitation or trade-union organisation.[18]

Reports from other provinces suggested an even lower level of political activity: beyond the industrial centres of Vienna and Upper Styria there were relatively few industrial workers, and even fewer who lived in the homogeneous working-class communities characteristic of the capital.[19] Nor were economic conditions as severe here as they were in manufacturing and heavy industrial areas. Dissent was either more rarely felt or more seldom voiced. Scattered incidents were reported from Carinthia of agricultural labourers and men working on road construction sites who made 'communist remarks' under the influence of alcohol. Hammer and sickle graffiti had also been found occasionally scrawled on the walls of houses or in lavatories, but there was little sympathy for that sort of thing among the population as a whole. The report from Klagenfurt went on to note that Carinthia was hardly the most likely place for a communist movement to develop: there were almost no industrial workers, and such communist cells as had existed had been broken up as a result of the activities of the DAF.[20] Reports from the west of Austria reflected a similar situation. There had been some political graffiti in Salzburg, but this was attributed to individuals rather than organised action, and in the Tyrol and Vorarlberg there had been no signs whatever of Marxist or communist activity – nor was any being planned, according to 'reliable sources'.[21]

If there was no conspicuously visible agitation during the summer of 1938, this did not mean that no conspiratorial activity was taking place. We know from the accounts of resistance activists themselves, from court records and from other surveillance reports by the same security services, that groups were formed, detected and their members arrested. Active involvement in such groups, furthermore, was confined to a committed few, who were failing to attract wider support, even among former Social Democrats, Communists or trade-unionists.

By September, however, the initial enthusiasm which accompanied the Anschluss among some sections of the population was beginning to wear off, not least among Austrian Nazis themselves,[22] and oppositional political activity was threatening to spread beyond the narrow conspiratorial elite. In Vienna the Revolutionary Socialists (RS) had been increasingly active, particularly in the fifth and twelfth districts, and the illegal Free Trade Unions had intensified their activity in many larger firms, notably in Floridsdorf, where membership fees and donations had been collected.[23]

There had been serious breaches of industrial discipline and strikes at the *Steyrwerke* in Upper Austria and the Alpine Montan in Upper Styria. The security services suspected sabotage behind the increasing number of breakdowns in industrial machinery, and the suspicion was strengthened by the simultaneous increase in absenteeism rates due to illnesses with no external symptoms (such as rheumatic pain).[24] In addition, the tense international situation had encouraged open dissent and criticism, primarily of the Reich's foreign policy, but increasingly of the regime generally. This was particularly the case in Upper Austria, which had a long border with Czechoslovakia.

The response of the regime was to order a further round of arrests. On 27 September Heydrich ordered 'preventive measures' to be taken against Socialists and Communists in Austria:

All leading functionaries of the KPD and SPD [sic!], in so far as it can be proved that they have continued to take part in activities hostile to the state, are to be taken into custody at once.[25]

As a result of this directive 42 people were arrested in Styria, 47 in Upper Austria, 51 in Carinthia and 11 in Salzburg. The Gestapo in Innsbruck had already made a number of arrests before Heydrich's order,[26] and the Vienna Gestapo had established the identities of 80 functionaries and 150 other activists, but refrained from making immediate arrests for fear of alerting its other suspects.[27]

Foreign political successes probably did as much to take the wind out of the sails of the resistance as repressive measures. With the resolution of the Czech crisis in Germany's favour much of the anxiety and uncertainty which activists had been unable to exploit disappeared. The occupation of the Sudetenland, and subsequently of Bohemia, Moravia and the Memelland, disarmed the government's critics somewhat. A report from Upper Austria recorded the 'dejection and . . . indifference' with which Social Democrats had observed these developments.[28] Social democratic activity, it seemed was now almost entirely restricted to exchanges of news and meetings in coffee houses and bars.[29]

The Communist Party was more resilient and determined, and its activity received correspondingly greater attention. More arrests followed in November and December 1938,[30] and an important offensive against the Styrian section of the party was undertaken by the Gestapo in Graz between December 1938 and March 1939. Significantly, communist activity seemed to be concentrated in Graz, where the leadership had its base; from the Upper Styrian industrial belt there was no sign of communist activity apart from a few drunken outbursts.[31]

Resistance activists, then, never managed to build a mass movement. The prospect of work after the economic insecurity of the 1930s had given rise to a widespread acceptance of the Anschluss. Repeated attempts were made to exploit disaffection in industry, but most disruption arose in response to economic grievances and political agitators, constrained by the necessity of secrecy, were unable to assume leadership and direct this discontent into political channels. Austrian workers themselves were wary of political involvement and confrontation with the forces of the state. In 1934, the social democratic labour movement in Austria had been numerically stronger than any in Europe – the

Republican Defence League had outnumbered the army – and it had been beaten into submission within a matter of days. Since then its property had been confiscated, its leaders had fled or been rendered ineffectual, its organisation had fragmented and it had lost both confidence and unity of purpose. In the intervening years persistent unemployment had further impoverished individuals, families and communities. Finally, the degree of state coercion and surveillance exercised by the Nazis was unmistakably greater than that of the 1930s. For these reasons, all attempts at collective political or industrial action were bound to be stillborn.

Unkept promises and incipient disaffection: problems of economic integration

Economic considerations were central to the German decision to annex Austria, and undoubtedly important to the timing of the invasion. Strategic and ideological considerations were also important, of course: the Anschluss strengthened the central European core of Germany's proposed European 'new order', effected a semi-encirclement of Czechoslovakia, and opened the way for the domination of the Balkans. In addition, some six million 'Germans' were brought 'home to the Reich'. It also brought immediate and tangible gains in gold, currency reserves, natural resources and labour, all much needed by the hard-pressed German economy. Economic arguments for the incorporation of Austria had gained in strength and currency as the Reich's own resources had been depleted. A number of institutions had assessed the potential economic benefits of Anschluss: Austria had a range of valuable mineral deposits, including oil and iron ore; Germany's timber requirements would be almost entirely met; hydro-electricity could be exploited to cover some of Germany's energy requirements; and the Austrian steel industry would be of particular value to the German war effort. Other immediate shortages could be covered by imports paid for by Vienna's accumulated gold and currency reserves. In addition Austria's half million unemployed would ease the Reich's labour shortages.[32]

A number of leading Nazis, including Hitler, came to Vienna during the plebiscite campaign to raise morale and mobilise support with speeches about the economic reconstruction of Austria. One of the most important was that of Goering, who spoke on 26 March, and listed a number of general measures which would revitalise the Austrian economy: capital investment, the removal of customs barriers, military and civilian construction programmes, the expansion of the arms industry, the development of hydro-electricity, the expansion and rationalisation

Table 2.1. *Unemployment in Austria, 1924–1938.*

	% unemployed	% change over previous year
1924	8.4	
1925	9.9	+17.0
1926	11.0	+10.9
1927	9.8	−11.1
1928	8.3	−15.7
1929	8.8	+4.9
1930	11.1	+26.6
1931	15.4	+37.4
1932	21.7	+40.1
1933	25.9	+19.0
1934	25.2	−2.2
1935	24.1	−5.5
1936	24.1	—
1937	21.7	−9.9
1938	12.9	−40.5

Source: Butschek, *Die österreichische Wirtschaft*, p. 60.

of timber production, copper-mining (in Carinthia and the Tyrol), oil production (in the Vienna Basin) and various programmes to improve agricultural output, including drainage works.[33] The most important single project, however, was in heavy industry. The new '*Hermann Goering Werke*', hitherto planned for Franconia, would now be built in Linz. This would be the 'most modern plant yet built' and would provide thousands of jobs in construction (starting in May) and afterwards in the works themselves. There would also be motorways between Munich, Salzburg and Vienna, and a number of smaller projects.[34]

The fulfilment of economic promises was, however, more difficult than Austrians were led to believe. Certainly, unemployment fell much more rapidly in 1938 than in the previous four years. The number of those out of work in Austria had been falling since 1934, as the world economy had recovered from the slump, but it had done so almost falteringly, and remained at over 20 per cent of the workforce at the end of 1937 (table 2.1). Nevertheless, Austria's unemployed labour could not all be deployed immediately, and for a variety of reasons: the Austrian unemployed were largely inexperienced or deskilled after years out of work; Austrian plants and machinery were old and outdated; and skilled workers could not be transferred to the Reich without severe disruption of the home economy and far-reaching social and political repercussions. In addition, there were all the problems of integrating two independent economies: the introduction of the German currency and taxation system, and the adjustment of Austrian wages and prices to German levels.[35] Above all full employment came most slowly to those regions which had been hardest hit. In January 1938 45 per cent of Austria's unemployed were Viennese; by December this figure had risen to 59 per cent.

Paradoxically, many of the difficulties experienced in reducing Austrian unemployment arose from the strains this placed on the already stretched German labour market. Call up to the Wehrmacht during the period of tension preceding the Anschluss had aggravated the labour shortage in German industry, and the problem returned with the recurrent international crises of 1938 and 1939. In addition, the shortage of skilled workers among the Austrian unemployed was so great that some German workers had to be transferred to Austria to work on the 'reconstruction programme' there. It was extremely difficult to find skilled German workers who could be released for such work, and this was bound to affect the rate at which reconstruction, and the attendant absorption of unskilled Austrian labour, could proceed. Furthermore, the possibility of transferring unskilled Austrians to the Reich was also limited, and the process was fraught with difficulties.

Austrians had gone to Germany in increasing numbers to find work even before the Anschluss. The trend had started almost as soon as labour shortages had become apparent in Germany, and 41,169 had left for the Reich during the year from April 1936 to March 1937. A further 69,063 followed during the subsequent twelve months.[36] The process naturally continued and accelerated after the occupation, but the perceived urgency of the situation prompted the authorities to put haste before other considerations, so that problems and resentments quickly arose. A particular source of grievance was the indiscriminate allocation of workers to Germany without any special consideration of domestic circumstances. An SD reporter referred pointedly to emotional scenes at the *Westbahnhof*, and noted the repercussions of bureaucratic insensitivity:

Those who refuse to go to the Altreich have their benefit stopped, and are told they are a work-shy rabble. The unscrupulousness of officials in the labour exchanges is generalised by the unemployed. . . and there are rumours among the working class that anybody who refuses a job three times will be sent to Dachau. In such circles the coercion and terror is considered worse than under Schuschnigg.[37]

Apart from the effect on the morale of the workers, compulsory transfer was an issue which oppositional agitators could easily exploit, and disruptions in the labour supply occurred when Austrian workers found that their experience in Germany did not match up to expectations, left their jobs and returned home.[38] Sopade reports from German industry describe the growing disillusionment of initially enthusiastic Austrian workers: the reports suggest that some of them were Nazis, who had been promised well-paid jobs in Germany before the Anschluss. Wages in one case were 30 per cent lower than expected, generally below the local average, and often insufficient for workers to be able to send money to their families. They were unused to the pace of work in German industry and consequently disadvantaged by a piece rate system of payment. Protests elicited minimal concessions at best, in one case a bawling out by the management, and generally arrest by the Gestapo. Some left secretly, without notice or permission, applying later in writing for the transfer of their papers. Others had their families secure them jobs at home in Vienna factories.[39]

Those returning could expect little better in Austria, however, as some of them already knew from the disillusioned letters they had received from their families. Economic adjustment had proved rather one-sided: while prices had risen quickly enough wages were still 30 per cent lower in Austria than in Germany, and the difference was even greater in the case of public sector workers.

On 27 May *Gauleiter* Bürckel, Reich Commissioner for the reunification of Austria with the German Reich, ordered a general wages and prices freeze, and the Reich Trustee of Labour for Austria, Alfred Proksch, was assigned the task of setting new wage levels. But the necessity of avoiding general wage inflation, and of examining the pay structure of each industry individually, prevented any real progress. In a report at the end of August, Proksch noted that Austrian wages were still lower than those in Germany. There were a number of reasons for this: the technical backwardness of Austrian industry, poor productivity, the limited market for Austrian goods and, not least, the high level of employers' national insurance contributions. Wages were relatively high in mining, the chemicals industry and construction, and particularly low in textiles and clothing, where employers did not benefit from lucrative government contracts. The wages of agricultural workers were still often below the level of unemployment benefit. Austria's integration into the Reich's rearmament economy could, of course, only serve to widen such differentials between priority economic sectors and those less privileged.

In most cases Proksch was optimistic that wages had either improved and were equal to those of the *Altreich*, or were fast approaching parity. He noted that the problem of massive underpayment which had been widespread in the textile industry, particularly among homeworkers, had now been overcome, and that some RM 200,000 of back wages had been paid.[40] The problem was by no means solved, however, and take-home pay had been further reduced by the increase in deductions from pay packets since the Anschluss. Workers complained that while nominal wages were usually the same as before the Anschluss, they had effectively been cut by such extra deductions.[41] The introduction of German income tax in Austria on 1 February 1939 was particularly resented, and unleashed a wave of industrial unrest.

Government authorities and employers were agreed that wages could not be raised in line with those in Germany without a corresponding rise in productivity to *Altreich* levels. On the other hand labour trustees could only use their power to freeze wages (granted by an order of 28 June 1938) at the cost of making the government unpopular. It was also clear that skilled labour was already becoming scarce, and that employers were prepared to raise wages in order to poach the labour they needed. Intervention by the employer to prevent this gave the impression that the government was acting to maximise the employers' profits at the expense of the employee.[42]

It is clear that the authorities were aware of the dangers of a situation in which Communists had been able to exploit growing disaffection 'for their own purposes',[43] and their reactions were cautious. Careful distinctions were made between political activity and genuine discontent arising from economic grievances. A Gestapo report from Graz singled out the 'unsettled' economic situation as the most important reason for working-class discontent in Styria during the summer of 1938,[44] and the SD's report on the German economy in 1938 drew particular attention to the situation in Austria:

There has been no general improvement in the wage levels of Austrian workers and [clerical] employees. In some branches . . . there was no need for adjustment as wage levels were not below those of the Altreich. In others this adjustment has been carried out, if only with difficulty, but price inflation has more than cancelled out the gains . . . The new wage and salary rates are on the whole lower than those announced in the propaganda. Yet . . . prices have risen, and DAF contributions are higher than former union dues, and taxes and deductions are higher than before.[45]

Integration into the German rearmament economy brought a measure of expansion which lifted Austria out of its economic stagnation, and generated expectations which won the new regime a degree of consent, support, or even enthusiastic acclamation in the short term. Popular approval was founded on inflated promises which seemed to be guaranteed by the limited initial measures for relief of the most acute poverty – particularly among the long-term unemployed – and the publication of grander designs for the future. Yet the process of economic integration proved to be less straightforwardly beneficial than had been widely believed. Economic modernisation proved to be double-edged, bringing not only employment and welcome – if limited and paternalistic – welfarism, but also a tightening of industrial discipline. Workers finding their wage levels increasingly undermined by inflation and employers reluctant to raise them without corresponding gains in productivity resorted to a variety of strategies to improve their position. The nature and development of these strategies was determined by the new industrial relations context, made up as it was of a mixture of extreme repression and full employment.

Popular disappointment and developments in labour discipline

The turning point in popular attitudes to the Anschluss dated from the summer of 1938. The change was gradual, but affected all regions and social groups in one way or another. It reflected frustrated expectations rather than any real change in circumstances for the worse: the Nazis had simply failed to deliver what they had promised.[46] By midsummer, the manufactured euphoria of the plebiscite campaign was largely dissipated, and it was also becoming clearer to industrial workers that the economic changes which were taking place did not automatically bring jobs – there were still 113,655 unemployed in August, 87,751 of them in Vienna.

In Upper Styria, which had experienced particular hardship, the morale of the industrial workforce was deteriorating rapidly, and in August the miners of the Erzberg began a strike which within a few days threatened other sections of the Alpine Montan and the Styrian sections of the Böhlerwerke. The strike was an isolated incident and was quickly put down by an SA division of 150 men, but was serious enough to revive memories of 1918.[47]

Reports from the *Steyrwerke* were most disturbing. The factory was traditionally a Social Democratic stronghold and had experienced an upsurge in oral propaganda and political agitation. The situation had deteriorated further after the arrival of several hundred Viennese workers. There had been no punishable offences, but a report from the works in August claimed that former Social Democrats had been able to exploit their position on the shop floor by making sure that 'Marxists' who had been unable to get a job in the *Steyrwerke* for years were 'now given preference over National Socialists'. This was because it was often a Social Democrat who was in charge of hiring and firing. The master in one section, for example was 'an old red big-wig', who made sure that he was 'surrounded by his red friends'. Nazis were given the worst jobs and there were some sections of the *Steyrwerke* where only 'red comrades' were taken on or tolerated. It was of particular concern to this reporter that some of the new employees were men returning from the Soviet Union, who were taken on 'without any consideration of their political reliability.'[48]

A further report (from the *Werkschutzleiter* of the *Steyrwerke*) went to the heart of the problem. The town itself was still a communist stronghold, he said, and the arrival of rather dubious outsiders to cover shortages of skilled labour in the expanding *Steyrwerke* had only made matters worse. Not only were many of the new employees politically unreliable, they were not even skilled and had to be trained on their arrival. To throw out all the Communists would mean closing down the factory altogether, and they could not be dismissed until more skilled workers were available.[49] Labour shortages had removed the threat of dismissal and although the Gestapo might intervene in extreme cases, it was difficult for the authorities to act if the political activity was not restricted to a minority, but found a resonance among a workforce with long social democratic traditions, as in Steyr. It was also difficult to justify intervention which might fail to isolate and remove a purely political problem, while nevertheless disrupting production. Except in cases where political agitators encouraged industrial sabotage it was wiser to tolerate the political affront for the time being, despite the aggrieved resentment of local Nazis.

This tolerance was increasingly tested in the autumn of 1938. On 20 September the SS in Steyr reported that industrial unrest had increased markedly in recent weeks. Party leaders were openly insulted, fights were provoked with Nazis, and there had been repeated and numerous instances of refusal to work (*Arbeitsverweigerungen*).[50] The Gestapo in Vienna confirmed that the observations made in Steyr were true of all industrial regions of Austria, and that oral and even printed propaganda was also on the increase.[51] The authorities attributed these difficulties to the particularly tense international situation during the summer and the ability of agitators to exploit economic grievances.

The crackdown on political opposition ordered by Heydrich a week later, and the end of the Czech crisis, helped remove the most visible expressions of political opposition, but the underlying problem of defining a new relationship between industrial labour, employers and the state was not resolved so easily. Friction in industrial relations persisted, and took a variety of forms.

The clearest expression of industrial conflict was a strike, and although they were by no means common, strikes were not unheard of in the Third Reich.[52] The authorities rarely described them as such: the most common designations were 'strike attempts' (*Streikversuche*), 'refusal to work' (*Arbeitsverweigerungen*) and 'interruptions of work' (*Arbeitsunterbrechungen*), and these were relatively accurate as descriptions of industrial action which was quickly truncated by the intervention of the Gestapo. Strike attempts in pursuit of wage claims had become increasingly common in Germany in the mid 1930s, and to a lesser extent in Austria during the last months of the Corporate State.[53] Spontaneous stoppages continued to occur in Austria after 1938, although such organised direct confrontation was more dangerous than under Schuschnigg. Many such stoppages were defensive and sought to protect existing wage agreements and conditions against the attempts of employers to take advantage of the new balance of power in industrial relations by cutting both hourly and piece work rates. They were generally localised responses to perceived chicanery or injustice on the part of local employers. Offensive strikes in support of wage demands or in response to the local implementation of unpopular government measures were less common. Stoppages were also generally short, often lasting less than one hour, were often limited to one plant or even one shop, and involved very small numbers of workers, or even individuals.[54] They were not strikes in the formal sense, nor were they conceived as such and there was rarely any danger of them being politicised or of a strike wave spreading even locally, still less regionally or nationally as, for example, during the First World War.

One of the commonest causes of such stoppages was piece rate working. Many inexperienced workers found that they were unable to earn a living wage on existing piece rates, and employers were trying to improve productivity by reducing them. Workers downed tools in a Vienna metal works after the arrival on the shop floor of German engineers with stop watches.[55]

Trade-unionist practices persisted in workers' approaches to industrial relations conflicts. In one instance, again a dispute over piece rates, production ground to a halt while workers elected a deputation to Bürckel.[56] Welders in metal works responded to a cut in hourly wage rates of 15 Groschen by forcing the Nazi chairman of the works council to listen to their grievances at a meeting of some two hundred workers. Discussion during the meeting went beyond the proposed wage cuts and the demand was raised for the payment of public holidays. The same Nazi functionary had voted against the introduction of such payments, and he was called upon to justify his position. As he attempted to do so one worker called out: 'If the *Obmann* does not represent the workers he can go to the devil.' Demands were then made that the German Labour Front (*Deutsche Arbeitsfront*, DAF) convene a meeting, which its leaders declined to do.[57] In another large metal works such holiday payments were introduced after three delegations had gone to the National Socialist Factory Cell Organisation (*Nationalsozialistische Betriebsorganisation*, NSBO).[58]

The consequences for workers' wages of the piece rate system during a period of industrial modernisation were revealed at the Hemp, Jute and Textile Company of Neufeld an der Leitha in the Burgenland, when production fell from 100 metres to 30 metres per hour, and wages fell correspondingly from RM 40 – already a low wage – to RM 10 per week. The manager of the factory refused to make any concessions and the all-woman workforce went on strike. The local Nazi Party leadership in Eisenstadt, the Labour Front and the Trustee of Labour all became involved in the dispute and the women were assured of a 60 per cent supplement and the introduction of new more efficient machinery. The manager was replaced.[59] The following year the women went on strike again, this time for a real wage increase, which was conceded by the management.[60] Industrial disputes seldom led to strikes, however, and such strikes as there were elicited few real concessions. The eighteen months between the Anschluss and the war were characterised less by widespread industrial militancy and direct confrontation with employers than by sporadic industrial unrest. Social Democrats in exile in Paris were sceptical about reports they received from within Austria of 'open mutinies' in factories and, more commonly, on new construction sites, although they reported them.[61] The authorities were quick to move, and although the Gestapo in particular was often overly keen to see political motivation where there was none, its agents also recognised that there were real grievances arising from the problems of economic integration. Concluding a report on a short strike at a spinning mill in Pottendorf in February 1939, the Vienna Gestapo noted that discontent was widespread in industry, and arose from the high levels of deductions from wages and the erosion of the purchasing power of wages by inflation.

This unrest increased after the introduction of German income tax in Austria on 1 February 1939, when strikes took on a more explicitly political content. The tax reform, of course, was irreversible, and employers sought to resolve the tension by making concessions in other areas; the management of the Krause machine works in Brigittenau, for example made concessions on breaks.[62] Other firms, of course, were not in a position to compensate workers for higher taxes, and it became clear that the regime itself would have to act to restore order in industry, and the deployment of troops and SS men was reported in working-class districts such as Floridsdorf and Steyr.[63]

Direct confrontations were merely the most obvious symptom of a more widespread disaffection and decline in workers' morale, reflected in a disturbing decline in industrial productivity. An economic report to Bürckel on the situation in Viennese industry in June 1939 indicated that this went beyond levels which could be ascribed to structural causes: complaints had been received of reductions in productivity of between 20 and 30 per cent. The extent of the phenomenon was disputed: the industrial section of the Chamber of Trade reported that it was a general development, while the Labour Front argued that there were only isolated cases. Clearly, some of the reduction was attributable to the re-employment of relatively inexperienced and poorly skilled workers. It was acknowledged, however, that workers' morale had been undermined by the new tax system and the point was also made that 'the fear of unemployment [had] disappeared'. If the introduction of the new tax system was the reason for poor productivity and rising absenteeism, then clearly there was an intentional protest. At this point, however, the reporter was prepared to accept the argument that falling productivity was not a general phenomenon and had largely been brought about by changes in the composition of the workforce and the extension of working hours.[64]

Other observers were less circumspect. The general Reich Security Head Office (Reichssicherheitshauptamt, RSHA) report on the situation in Austria during 1938 put disproportionately high sickness rates in the same category as sabotage, insubordination and 'whispering propaganda'. The report noted that the introduction of the Four Year Plan and the restructuring of the economy had created an environment in which illegal communist or Marxist (i.e. social democratic) activity was able to flourish. Industrial accidents and similar incidents reinforced suspicions that the cause was not so much chance or negligence but deliberate sabotage on the part of Communists and Marxists. It was noteworthy, it went on, that at the end of September sickness rates had reached enormous levels in vital industries as well as in industry 'generally'. In the Wienerberg brickworks, currently working exclusively for the Wehrmacht, sickness rates had risen to 25 per cent of the workforce compared with 3 per cent the previous year. The suspicion that this was deliberate sabotage was reinforced by the Gestapo's discovery of 30 leading and middle-ranking members of opposition groups, and a further 150 people involved in illegal activity.[65]

Workers themselves were often only too eager to make the reasons for absenteeism and falling productivity clear, and to resume normal working when their aims had been achieved. The workers of one large Vienna factory reacted to a management refusal to increase wages with the expressed intention of matching performance to wages ('*Wie der Lohn, so die Leistung*') and there was such a dramatic slowdown in work that the management had been forced to capitulate. Similarly the distribution of protective clothing in a chemicals works was achieved by a massive increase in numbers reporting sick.[66]

After February 1939 there was no longer an argument for seeing such problems as 'isolated cases'. Workers were reported to be working 'passively' in a number of Vienna factories in direct response to the introduction of German income tax. In any event, it was clear by the end of June 1939 that falling productivity was not an isolated phenomenon, and the fall in industrial productivity was estimated at 20–30 per cent.[67] The *Gau* economic adviser for Vienna wrote that almost all branches of industry were complaining of problems of this sort, which were 'often political in character'. A 'serial pattern of illness' was to be identified among workers at the Siemens-Schuckert cable works in Leopoldau. Here too the authorities were dealing with a problem which was difficult to prove. Employers, afraid of losing their workers, were reluctant to take energetic action.[68]

Although the extent and nature of absenteeism are difficult to assess, it was sufficiently widespread to cause official concern. Moreover, it was associated variously with both political agitation and protest at economic grievances. The emphasis often depended on the function of the agency which monitored it: Gestapo reporters were more inclined to look for subversive elements, economists and bureaucrats for structural problems arising from economic adjustment. Certainly, the phenomenon was prompted by real or perceived economic grievances associated with economic change, which workers sought to redress. While the political situation closed off the possibility of direct industrial confrontation, the developing economic situation increasingly opened up other, more covert ways of airing protest and forcing concessions which were equally long-established.

Such strategies were characteristic of the re-ordered industrial relations of the Third Reich during the short period of relatively normal conditions between recovery from the slump and the outbreak of war, a period which was compressed in Austria into little more than a year. The attempt of the new regime to build an industrial (or political) consensus was largely restricted to a not unfamiliar rhetorical mixture which cajoled and threatened simultaneously. Official propaganda encouraged class reconciliation within a national community, and invited 'decent' workers to distance themselves from persistent offenders against the community's general interests, traitors who would have to be isolated and punished. Yet neither the rather hackneyed depiction of workers' leaders as Marxist pied pipers working in the interests of a 'racial' enemy (whether Jewish, Soviet or both) nor the necessarily idealistic notion of social harmony built on self-sacrifice was likely to square entirely with workers' own experience. The most persuasive appeal was to self-interest (dressed up as 'common sense'). The new regime would modernise and expand industry, bringing economic growth and expansion that would ultimately benefit all Austrians.

Economic modernisation, of course, would have to be paid for by higher productivity and higher taxation, and the new (largely cosmetic) welfare schemes would have to be financed by bigger deductions from wages, generating more resentment and grumbling. The ultimate destination of such deductions was widely believed to be the coffers of monopolistic party bureaucracies such as the DAF and NSBO than organisations genuinely working for the interests of the labour force. In addition, wages were further eroded by the price inflation which was the concomitant of full employment, economic growth and integration into the German economy.

Germany's own domestic economic problems had been replicated very quickly in Austria. Workers chose to exploit their stronger position on the labour market in whatever way they could in their attempt to maintain real wage levels and working conditions. Their ability to do so was, of course, constrained by the removal of their right to organise collectively or to withdraw their labour in support of their claims, and they acknowledged this. Employers, for their part, also acknowledged that little had changed fundamentally in their relationship with the workforce. The Nazis had dealt them a much stronger hand and the Gestapo was there to guarantee good industrial discipline. Employers paid lip service to the notion of a 'factory community' and the associated corporatist ideology propagated by the regime but relied on the more or less open threat of force to foster and maintain industrial discipline.

3 The war economy and the changing workforce 1939–1945

In terms of its economic objectives the Anschluss was very much a success. For Germany's part, the relief it brought to the depleted labour market in the Reich was a particularly welcome bonus, while Austrians benefited from the rapid fall in unemployment: the number of those out of work in Austria fell by 76 per cent in 1939 to only 3.2 per cent of the workforce. By October of that year there were already fewer than 50,000 out of work in Austria (although there were a further 40,000 on short time). By 1941 there were only 3,000 Austrians still without jobs.[1]

By 1939 then, Austria was sufficiently integrated into the Reich to share all the features of the latter's 'overheated' war economy. Very soon there were the same shortages of labour and raw materials in the 'Alpine and Danubian *Gaue*' as in the *Altreich*, and these were further exacerbated by the introduction of conscription. Between 1939 and 1940 the number of people employed in Austrian industry declined by 10,000 (2.1 per cent). The loss of labour was not even, however, and this small net decline disguised a more significant shift in resources from consumer goods to capital goods. The consumer goods sector, which had already suffered closures and lay-offs, contracted further with the outbreak of war. Its workforce declined by 14.4 per cent, while the numbers employed in the primary sector and in heavy industry rose by 6.8 per cent and 7.1 per cent respectively.[2]

One of the effects of this shift in resources was to create isolated cases of new unemployment, particularly in communities dependent on one industry, such as the hard-hit textiles branch. More than twenty textiles mills had been closed throughout Austria by November 1939, and the ensuing unemployment caused severe hardship to the communities affected. Although the problems of such communities elicited little sympathy from economic managers whose task increasingly involved dealing with shortages rather than surpluses of labour, the authorities were often sensitive to the possible political repercussions.[3]

The Nazis, of course, were well aware that the exploitation of Austria's labour and capital resources would have only a limited and short-

term effect on the Reich's shortages, and it was fully expected that
further territorial expansion would be necessary to consolidate the
Greater German core of the Nazi new economic order before the decisive war for 'Lebensraum' in the east could be waged. The incorporation
of Austria was therefore swiftly followed by the annexation of the Sudetenland (parts of which were incorporated into the new *Gaue* of Upper
and Lower Danube).[4] The following year Bohemia and Moravia were
also brought under German control as a 'Reich Protectorate', and the
greater part of the Czech industrial economy was thereby placed at the
disposal of the Reich.[5] Although Czech gold reserves, armaments and
industrial resources were important acquisitions for Germany, the
exploitation of Czech labour reserves was also a consideration. In 1936
and 1937 there had already been twice as many Czechs as Austrians
working in the *Altreich*. In 1938 Czechs still formed the largest single
national group of foreign workers there, and were over a quarter of the
total.[6]

Austria, as an integral part of the Reich, now also began to receive
Czech and Slovak workers to make up labour shortfalls in its industries.
Vienna already had a significant Czech minority, largely the result of
economic migration to the Habsburg capital before the First World
War. This community now expanded rapidly. According to the 1939
census there were 56,248 Czechs and Slovaks in Vienna in 1939, an
increase of almost 42 per cent over the 1934 census.[7] They formed the
largest single national or linguistic minority in the capital, comprising
some 60 per cent of all those identified as such minorities. The Viennese
Czechs' perception of their own nationality was rather problematic: only
around a third (35.3 per cent) acknowledged their Czech nationality,
while the rest claimed German nationality although for the most part
they identified Czech as their mother tongue.[8]

New Czech workers arriving after the Anschluss were, of course,
unambiguously more foreign. Unlike their predecessors who had arrived
in a Vienna arguably more at ease with its ethnic mix, they were also
arriving in a modified political climate, characterised by a much sharper
awareness of 'racial' difference. Despite the prejudice that was rife in
Vienna, however, the Czechs' perceived temperamental similarities to
the Germans themselves, and particularly their 'efficiency' and technical
skills, won them a respect as members of the workforce which was not
accorded to later waves of foreign workers arriving in Austria.[9] Moreover, the 1939 census reinforced existing ambiguous perceptions of
nationality by inviting appropriate respondents to classify themselves as
bilingual, not least in the hope of identifying suitable candidates for
Germanisation ('*Umvolkung*').[10]

The invasion of Poland had a dramatic impact on the Austrian labour force, and one which was twofold. Firstly, in precipitating the formal outbreak of war with Britain and France the invasion prompted further conscription to the armed forces, thereby placing further strains on the labour market. By the end of 1940 industrial employment in Austria had fallen by 10,000 (2.1 per cent). This happened throughout the Reich, of course, and various measures were introduced to alleviate the worst effects of the shortages.[11] Skilled workers were recalled from the Wehrmacht, or seconded back to industry, and conscription orders were frozen for certain age groups. Other groups of workers, in specially designated factories (*Spezialbetriebe*) were exempt from conscription.[12]

None of these measures was particularly successful. In Austria the local situation was further aggravated by the continuing drain of workers to the *Altreich*.[13] The Austrian branch of the Ministry of Labour Supply was particularly insistent on this point: the office faced the combined pressures of seasonal demand for labour from agriculture and the construction industry, and the loss of men both to the armed forces and to the *Altreich*.[14]

Austria also fared differently from the *Altreich* in other ways. Firstly, although conscription reduced the employed population by more or less the same proportion as in the Reich as a whole, Austria lost relatively fewer industrial workers, arguably because its emergent industrial capacity enjoyed a sort of protected status.[15] Secondly, initial attempts to secure the release of skilled workers from the Wehrmacht had been more successful than in Germany: 40 per cent had returned by Christmas (compared with a quarter in the Reich as a whole), and 62 per cent by February 1940. This was still far from adequate, however, and the Defence Economy Inspectorate claimed that 'despite the instructions from the OKW ... considerable difficulties [had] been made by the units involved.'[16]

It was impossible to square the circle: men had to be recruited to the armed forces to fight the war, and they were also needed in essential industries on the 'home front', where their work was vital to the war economy. No amount of taking up slack from the consumer sector or non-essential firms, nor attempts to impose rigid controls on conscription and allocation of skilled labour would provide the number of workers necessary. If new sources of labour were not found, then the productivity of the existing industrial workforce would have to be increased, and this might well prompt the political confrontation with the working class which the regime feared, and believed to have been instrumental in the downfall and military defeat of the German Empire in 1918.[17]

The alternative to forcing higher productivity from the existing work-force was to exploit new sources of labour, and there were two possibil-ities: women and foreigners. (Some of the foreigners would also be women, but Nazi race theorists believed that only the women of 'superior' races differed sufficiently from men to warrant different treatment.)[18] Either solution would compromise the ideological objec-tives of the regime: to recruit women would be to undermine in many respects Nazi policies towards women; and to deploy more foreigners in the Reich's expanding industrial cities would compound the problem of accelerating urbanisation with that of increasing the 'racial' hetero-geneity of the working population of the Reich. The deployment of foreign labour on the land, on the other hand, would undermine the notion of a quasi-mystic relationship between blood and soil promoted by the regime's own propaganda. In addition there would be inevitable resentment on the part of German workers at the import of cheap for-eign labour. Nevertheless the 'temporary' deployment of large numbers of foreigners in German industry and agriculture was perceived in all quarters to be far preferable to the employment of German women.[19]

Securing a supply of foreign labour

It was in the context of the Polish campaign – something of a test case, and a turning point in the development of labour supply policy under the Nazis – that important decisions were made about how labour short-ages would be covered during the war. Before the outbreak of war the employment of foreigners in the Reich had been on a limited scale and had been seen as a temporary measure. The need to address the impli-cations of the policy had thereby been avoided.[20] The defeat of Poland, however, was the first opportunity to press large numbers of foreign workers into the service of German industry and agriculture, and brought the issue to a head.[21] Poles did not enjoy even the modicum of (relative) tolerance extended to the Czechs, and there were reser-vations about their employment in the Reich in large numbers. In the event such reservations were set aside on the understanding that even this new influx of foreign labour would be a temporary phenomenon, and national pride was satisfied by the institutionalisation of racial dis-crimination. Objections to the large-scale employment of Polish labour had been as much economic as ideological in any case: before Sep-tember 1939 the Poles had still been foreigners, and had been inclined to send a part of their wages home to their families. Now that their families too lived within the borders of Greater Germany this drain on resources was no longer a consideration.[22] The cost of labour was further reduced by the immediate transfer of Polish prisoners of war to the Reich, where they were rapidly put to work on the land. The total number of Polish prisoners of war was relatively small, however, compared with the demand for labour in the Reich and the reserves of civilian labour in Poland.

Nazi leaders – Hitler, Himmler, Darré and Frank – were quick to appreciate the changed situation. Whatever threat was posed to the Reich's 'racial purity' by the mass importation of foreign labour was outweighed by the economic advantages. In any case Poles would not be assimilated into German society but would remain itinerant workers, deployed as necessary within the Reich, but with domiciles in the *Generalgouvernement*.[23] Nor were the benefits only economic. The exploitation of foreign labour would permit the repeal of the War Economy Decrees and a relaxation of the tension they had caused among Germany's indigenous industrial workforce.[24] To this extent the war and the exploitation of occupied Europe contributed to the resolution of Germany's potentially explosive domestic political problems. The point has been made that without foreign labour, a more intensive exploitation of German labour would have been necessary during the war.[25] The Nazi regime was relieved not to have to ask the Germans to make sacrifices.

Poland was a watershed. Once it was admitted that 'racially inferior' Poles were indispensable to the war economy and were to be set to work there without any prior 'racial' selection, a significant concession had been made to the demands of economic pragmatists over the possible objections of ideological purists. This did not mean that Polish workers were treated by any means with fairness or respect. They were subject to a harsh and discriminatory policy of racial segregation within the Reich, and as hundreds of thousands of Poles were brought to Germany the regime found it necessary to formulate guidelines to regulate their position. A series of decrees promulgated in 1940 provided for the harsher punishment of Poles in cases of indiscipline or 'breach of contract', and for the death sentence in cases of sexual intercourse with Germans.[26] The provisions of these so-called '*Polenerlasse*' (Polish Decrees) reflected all the lingering reservations about the exercise.

This influx of Polish workers into the Reich also made its impact on Austria. In November 1939 the Defence Economy Inspectorate (*Wehrwirtschaftsinspektion*) for Defence District XVII (Vienna, Lower Danube and Upper Danube) reported that the arrival of 250 workers a week from Poland and Slovakia was helping to relieve local labour shortages, and there were by then 7,000 prisoners of war in Austria.[27]

Table 3.1. *Foreign workers in the* 'Ostmarkgaue', 25 April 1941.

Labour office district	Foreign	% of total
Vienna-Lower Danube	50,385	5.3%
Upper Danube	24,904	9.6%
Styria-Carinthia	41,858	11.5%
Alpenland	11,583	6.2%
Total	128,730	8.1%

Source: Hans Pfahlmann, *Fremdarbeiter und Kriegsgefangene* p. 126.

Although there were proportionately more foreigners in Austria's labour force than in other parts of the Reich, however, Poles were relatively under-represented. Detailed and accurate statistics about the number of foreign workers in the Reich, their countries of origin and their deployment were first collected in January, and then again in April 1941. On 25 April there were almost 130,000 foreign workers in Austria (table 3.1). Only Pomerania (16.4 per cent) and Lower Saxony (13.9 per cent) had a higher proportion of foreign workers than Styria and Carinthia (11.6 per cent). The proportion of foreigners in Austria was over 8 per cent, as against a Reich average of 6.6 per cent.[28]

Austria's foreign workforce was more heterogeneous than that of the Reich as a whole. In April 1941 only 32 per cent of Austria's increasingly foreign labour force were Poles, compared with 60 per cent in the whole Reich.[29] Nevertheless, there were 40,928 of them, and they were still the largest single national group. The numbers of workers from eastern and south-eastern Europe, on the other hand, were above average for the Reich. There were 22,180 Slovaks, 20,594 Yugoslavs, 8,258 Hungarians and 3,414 Bulgarians.[30]

Between a third and a half of all prisoners of war put to work in Austria were employed on the land, where they undeniably made an impact on Austrian society. Austrian agricultural workers were immediately suspicious of the cheap competition: Poles were paid between 50 per cent and 85 per cent of the wages of indigenous workers. By the spring of 1940 there were reports from Vienna of widespread conflicts in the Austrian countryside between farmers and agricultural workers over the issue of the use of Polish labour, and between Austrian workers and the Poles themselves. It was assumed that such conflicts were the principal cause of Poles leaving their jobs.[31] The sense of grievance was compounded when local people felt disadvantaged by a combination of the regime's labour policies. In December 1939, for example, Sudeten Germans in the newly annexed parts of Czechoslovakia complained that

Table 3.2. *Labour shortages in Upper Danube, Winter 1940–1941.*

Month	Vacancies*	New workers	Prisoners of war	Foreign civilians
October 1940	48,288	9,245	723	592
November	33,609	15,236	3,858	1,818
December	29,719	8,256	1,432	636
January 1941	17,949	9,592	1,414	440
February	21,916	7,300	759	150
March	32,083	8,374	1,355	381
April	46,344	13,871	2,865	3,691

*On the first day of the month.
Source: RW21–38/5; RW21–38/6.

local people were being allocated to jobs in other parts of Upper Danube and even as far away as the Rhineland, while local jobs were being taken by Czechs and Poles.[32]

The government responded to such reports – which came from all parts of the Reich – by imposing a compensatory tax on employers, so that the cost of employing Poles was the same or only marginally less than the cost of employing Germans. This, it was hoped, would prevent employers, particularly farmers, dismissing their workers on trivial or contrived grounds in order to employ cheaper foreign labour.[33]

Agriculture absorbed a hefty proportion of all foreign workers in Austria: 38.5 per cent in Defence District XVII and 46.1 per cent in Defence District XVIII (covering 'Alpenland', Salzburg, Styria and Carinthia) by 1941.[34] The ambitious construction projects begun after the Anschluss also absorbed a large number, so that the supply of foreign labour was never enough, and was rarely drafted directly into the arms industries.[35]

Seasonal fluctuations in demand for outdoor labour meant, of course, that more foreigners were available to industry in winter. The number of unfilled vacancies in Upper Danube, for example, began to decline after the harvest in 1940 and reached a low point after Christmas. Even then, however, nearly eighteen thousand jobs remained unfilled, and in the new year the demand for labour, especially seasonal labour began to increase again (table 3.2). The number of unfilled vacancies increased by 85 per cent between the end of January and the end of March, the demand for skilled building workers by 168 per cent. By the end of April there were over 50,000 vacant jobs. In this context of rapidly expanding demand the prisoners of war (mainly Frenchmen) allocated to the *Gau* made little impact, and the number of foreign civilians was almost marginal.[36] Even workers allocated to the defence sector might be diverted

at short notice as the need arose. Five hundred prisoners of war promised to the Graz labour office for the Styrian arms industry in the
autumn of 1940 had been sent by the Todt Organisation to Villach to
work on motorway construction.[37] The demand for foreign labour and
the deployment of prisoners of war in the domestic economy does not
seem to have been satisfied by Germany's successful campaigns and
territorial acquisitions in 1941. The number of foreigners in designated
defence industries ('*Rüstungsbetrieben*') in Defence District XVII
increased from 2,063 to 8,824 during that year, and the number of prisoners of war from 1,207 to 4,181. This was still not enough and the
Armaments Inspectorate suggested that firms be allowed to recruit foreigners directly.[38]

Prisoners of war and concentration camp prisoners apart, the recruitment of foreign labour for the Reich had been largely based on a voluntary programme before the war in the East. An element of force was
introduced after the Polish campaign, in that all able-bodied persons in
the *Generalgouvernement* between the ages of eighteen and sixty (later
extended to 14–16 year-olds) were subject to compulsory public labour
from 26 October 1939, unless they could prove they were otherwise in
useful employment.[39] Further force in the recruitment of Polish labour
seemed to be obviated by the swift success of the campaigns in the
west in 1940. Again, the resources of the occupied territories, including
labour, were subjected to systematic plunder.[40] In the west, however,
there was little compulsion until 1942. In the first instance the Germans
put prisoners of war to work on the land, and otherwise recruited selec-
tively. Propaganda was used to attract skilled workers from the west,
where unemployment was rising, to jobs in the Reich.[41]

The situation was altered by the failure of the invasion of the
Soviet Union. Between 1942 and 1944 over three and a half million
men throughout the Reich were newly conscripted into the Wehrmacht, and many of these were men in reserved occupations. Despite
resistance to conscription on the part of both workers and
employers – a coincidence of interest which contributed to smoother
industrial relations – the male workforce of the Reich fell by over a
million between the end of 1941 and the summer of 1945.[42] Reports
on labour supply described a situation which changed relatively little
in its essentials: it was always bad, and invariably getting worse. The
chronic shortages, in so far as they were covered at all, continued to
be covered by foreign labour.

This involved something of a reversal of policy on the employment of
Russians in the Reich. Initially, the regime's expectations of a swift victory had led it to foresee millions of 'superfluous' Soviet citizens, who

would either have to be forced east or left to die. The Russian population would be decimated rather than recruited to work in the Reich, and this was in any case the fate of thousands of Russian prisoners of war.[43] In the event of course, there was no swift victory: industry found itself without the demobilised German soldiers it had expected, and was struggling to maintain output for the protracted conflict. Hitler's prohibition of the recruitment of Russian labour was relaxed only weeks after the invasion,[44] and by the end of the summer it was increasingly accepted that large numbers of Russians would have to be put to work in the Reich, although there were still reservations, and it was accepted that the policy would be withdrawn should a 'racial danger' to the German people emerge. By the end of October the mass deployment of Russians in the Reich had been accepted.[45] There could, of course, be no question of voluntary recruitment in the Soviet Union, and the Russians – like the Poles before them – were paid low wages, with employers paying an extra tax to the government.[46]

The recruitment of Soviet labour fluctuated. The first transports from Galicia, the Bialystok region and the Baltic, along with 5,000 miners from Krivoi Rog, left for Germany at the end of 1941. There was a sharp increase in the numbers recruited during 1942, something of a decline in 1943, and a further sharp increase in 1944.[47] Foreign labour continued to be the preferred solution to Germany's shortages of workers, a point which Hitler himself made forcefully to Fritz Sauckel in 1942,[48] and Soviet workers ('*Ostarbeiter*') came to dominate numerically.[49]

Despite persistent complaints from industry of labour shortages, the numbers of foreign workers more than made up for the shortage of indigenous workers in those industries and areas where they were most needed. In Upper Danube, where Austrian industry was expanding fastest, the total number of workers in the armaments industry increased by 22 per cent during 1941, that of prisoners of war by 120 per cent and that of foreign workers by 473 per cent.[50] By 1942 thousands of Russians were arriving every month in Upper Austria alone: 3,656 in July; 2,618 in August; 1,480 in September, 1,225 in October and 1,915 in November. Often, over half of these were women:[51] the workforce of Austria's arms industries increasingly consisted of foreign (especially Soviet) women, overseen by a dwindling number of skilled Austrian male workers.

If the total workforce increased, the supply of labour nevertheless consistently failed to cover demand. In the summer of 1942 over half the demand for industrial labour in Upper Danube was unmet, and although the proportion of foreign workers in the labour force of the arms works had risen from 28.6 per cent to 38.8 per cent between Sep-

Table 3.3. *Foreign workers in Upper Danube, 1942–1944.*

		Total workforce	Foreigners
December	1942	303,011	174,858 (57.7%)
March	1943	332,270	189,305 (57.0%)
June	1943	335,169	185,599 (55.7%)
September	1943	338,840	186,018 (54.9%)
December	1943	337,020	182,794 (54.2%)
March	1944	334,719	180,705 (54.0%)
June	1944	332,069	176,354 (53.1%)

Source: Slapnicka, *Oberdonau*, p. 162.

tember and December 1942,[52] the authorities receiving foreign workers were sceptical to the point of dismissiveness about the impact they made.[53] For political reasons, the difficulties of the situation were emphasised, the usefulness of remedial measures understated, to avoid the transfer of workers to regions which seemed to be more hard-pressed, or at least made a better case. Certainly, the influx of foreigners into Upper Danube slowed, stabilised and even declined in the middle of the war. As the tide of war turned it became increasingly difficult to recruit foreign labour at all (table 3.3).

Foreigners, including prisoners of war and prisoners from concentration camps, were indispensable to the maintenance of wartime industrial production. In Austria their labour was not only central to the economic boom which was the result of Nazi construction projects and the expansion of the industrial economy, but laid the infrastructural basis of Austria's post-war economic success.[54] Until the last year of the war the indigenous workforce was spared the intensity of exploitation (or the necessity of self-sacrifice) which might have prompted working class resistance on a larger or more threatening scale. The fragile social peace which was maintained within the Reich (including Austria), was achieved not through the creation of a 'national community' but by the first steps towards a new European political and economic order, where class conflict within Germany would always be bought off by the subordination of the European economy to German interests, and the intensified exploitation of 'inferior' peoples.

Women

Given the reluctance of the regime to provoke class conflict, and the very limited efficacy of the various measures designed to return workers from the forces to vital industries, the only alternative to the exploitation of foreigners was the mobilisation of more German women for war work. At the time of the Anschluss the absolute number of German women in paid employment in the visible economy was greater than ever before.

After the Nazis came to power in 1933, many of the women who had been cheaper to employ during the depression were displaced by men as a consequence of Nazi policies aimed at reducing unemployment figures (married women leaving the workforce to make way for men would not generally be added to the statistics). From 1936, however, the employment of women had increased quite sharply as a result of the rearmament boom and accompanying labour shortages. In 1939, 36.2 per cent of German women were in paid employment, and women, in turn, constituted 35.8 per cent of the workforce.[55] Women were also increasingly employed in industrial work. German women, it has been argued, were mobilised for what was effectively war work even before the outbreak of war itself, and to a greater extent than in other industrial states.[56] By 1939, the argument continues, women constituted a greater proportion of the German workforce than of the British, and even by 1943 the proportion of women in the British workforce was still far smaller than the proportion employed in Germany; smaller, in fact, than the proportion of women in the German workforce in 1939.[57]

A comparison with the USSR, on the other hand, reveals a rather different picture. In 1940, on the eve of the German invasion, 41 per cent of Soviet industrial workers were women, compared with 26.2 per cent of those in Germany. By 1943 women's share in industrial employment in the Soviet Union had risen to 53 per cent, in the Reich, German (as opposed to foreign) women workers accounted for only 26.5 per cent of the workforce. In the 'Alpine and Danube *Gaue*' the proportion of Austrian women in the workforce had fallen from 27.7 per cent to 24.8 per cent.[58] The Soviet government was, of course, less wary than the German of demanding total commitment to the war effort, and particularly after the German invasion and the experience of occupation it was more likely to get it. In addition, the ideological and cultural context was rather different in the USSR. The official ideology was nominally progressive in its attitude to women (however much the reality of women's experience may have fallen short of the promise), and the social upheavals which accompanied and followed war and revolution had, arguably, eroded popular cultural objections to women working.

In Germany both ideology and popular attitudes to women's work were more conservative, or so it has been assumed. More recent research presents a more complex picture.[59] Nazi policies towards

women were neither monolithic nor unambiguously conservative. Dif-
ferentiated attitudes towards women (expressed most radically in the
regime's eugenic preoccupations) were also present in attitudes to
women's work. Although excluded from positions of any power or real
responsibility,[60] women were encouraged to take up 'feminine' occupations compatible with the 'social' or 'nurturing' role of the woman in
the family and society. For reasons of economic expediency, the
exclusion of women from the workforce was less forceful than might
have been expected. Women's work was piously condemned in public
while large numbers of women were assiduously recruited to the industrial workforce. This, of course, was not unusual in itself (although the
Nazis' public ideological objections to women's work were more
emphatic than most). Women were not prevented from working, merely
paid less, and offered inducements to stay at home and have children.
Many working-class women, of course, had no choice but to go to work:
the household budget depended on the individual woman's wages, as
much as the national economy needed the cheap labour of women collectively. The German Labour Front took pains to ensure that working-
class women would be able to combine the fulfilment of their domestic
duties with semi-skilled industrial work, continuing a trend encouraged
by employers during the Weimar Republic.[61]

If women were recruited into industry during the war, they were
encouraged to leave paid employment afterwards to make room for
demobilised men.[62] Similarly, if women were politicised by the revolution of 1918, their material and social position was advanced only
superficially and temporarily by the welfare measures of the First
Republic. The 'modernisation' of the Austrian economy during the
1920s meant that more women who might in the past have stopped
work when they married or started having children were now returning
to employment as working wives and mothers, and the average age of
women in employment after World War I was generally higher. The
gradual introduction of more modern methods of production meant that
unskilled labour – especially women – could be employed more exten-
sively. For women, then, the 'modernisation' of the economy often
entailed poorly paid unskilled short-time work, and a continuing
responsibility for domestic work even when men were unemployed.[63]

In the depression in particular, women were employed short-time on
low wages as men were laid off, and as unemployment benefits expired
women often became solely responsible for the family's income, while
continuing to remain responsible for housework and child care as well.
As the deflationary economic policies of Dollfuss and Schuschnigg prolonged the effects of the depression in Austria, however, women were

gradually squeezed out of the workforce again as unemployment forced men's wages down. While unemployment among men fell between 1933 and 1938, albeit slowly and in fits and starts, the number of unemployed women continued to rise until the Anschluss.[64]

The return to full employment between the Anschluss and the war was effected by the extension of Germany's 'war economy in peace time' to Austria. The expansion in the female share of employment in Austria was sluggish. Some women were absorbed into the expanding war economy, others lost their jobs in the contracting consumer goods sector, and as we have seen, the textiles industry was particularly affected by short-term structural unemployment. Nevertheless levels of unemployment among men and women had more or less converged by February 1939, although women's unemployment remained rather higher than that of men in Vienna.[65]

As in other parts of the Reich, the recruitment of women to the workforce during the war was not without problems, and these became immediately evident with the introduction of the War Economy Decrees of September 1939. Almost at once a Tyrolean textile firm with an almost exclusively female workforce and an outstanding government contract for 20,000 metres of cloth for field uniforms reported widespread refusals to work the new ten-hour day. The women clearly had the sympathy of the local authorities in both Innsbruck and Salzburg, who accepted that the war had also made women's domestic duties more demanding, and agreed that the ten-hour day only be introduced in those departments where there were severe production bottlenecks.[66]

In March 1940 the authorities in Graz reported that there were now more women on the books of labour offices than could be employed, and that there had been an 8 per cent increase in the number of women workers. Nevertheless, there were jobs for women of certain types (for example, in offices) which could not be filled, while there were other types of job (unskilled manual work in the Upper Styrian steel industry) which could in theory be covered by women, but were unsuitable because they involved shift work.[67] By May 1940 the number of women in the industrial workforce had actually declined (see table 3.4).

Employers and the local authorities responsible for the arms economy seem to have been optimistic about the recruitment of women at the beginning of the war. The *Rüstungskommando* in Linz specified a local demand for female labour in the last quarter of 1940 which was a third of the total demand. In the event only a third of the total demand was met, and the proportion of women in the workforce remained more or less the same.[68] Nevertheless women were recruited, and were trained

Table 3.4. *Austrian industrial workforce, 1941–1944.*

	All	Austrian women	Foreign workers Men	Women	Prisoners of war
1939	535,959	147,263 (27.5%)	4,208	1,014	
1940	527,061	146,170 (27.7%)	11,902	1,470	1,513
1941	553,442	151,779 (27.4%)	29,988	4,558	20,904
1942	579,424	150,546 (26.0%)	46,200	11,944	27,724
1943	673,729	167,376 (24.8%)	93,400	36,860	37,983
1944	735,022	185,340 (25.2%)	162,302	43,549	54,705

Source: Wagenführ, *Die deutsche Industrie im Kriege*, pp. 139f, cited in Freund und Perz, 'Fremdarbeiter', p. 345.

in skilled manual jobs. In September 1940 more women than men were being trained in skilled manual work at the *Steyrwerke*.[69]

Young women were drafted into the Reich Labour Service (*Reichsarbeitsdienst der weiblichen Jugend*, RADwJ) from October 1938. Any single woman between the ages of 17 and 25 who was not already employed, in education or needed on a family farm could be drafted into the labour service, and after the outbreak of war the number of such recruits was repeatedly raised (in 1939, 1940 and 1941) and the grounds for exemption reduced. It was emphasised, however, that such employment was temporary, and these young women would find their true role within marriage after the completion of their service.[70]

More generally, women, no less than men, were subject to labour conscription laws. In practice the regime was aware of the possible repercussions on morale, and was inclined to tread carefully. At the beginning of the war conscripted women were generally either single or already employed elsewhere. Nevertheless, conscription generated resistance, especially where it involved movement away from home, or allocation to an employer with a bad reputation. Women conscripts from Bregenz who were to be drafted to jobs in Germany in 1939 had to be brought forcibly to the labour exchange by the police.[71]

The recruitment of women into the industrial labour force was a policy which also generated new class resentments. There was an acute awareness in working-class communities that middle-class women were not only able to avoid work, but even retained female domestic servants during the war.[72] The regime's observers conceded that differences in the treatment of working-class and middle-class women were responsible for declining morale among those women already in the workforce.[73] Despite propaganda and high profile transports of young middle-class women to the *Altreich*, the impression of class bias could not be dispelled.[74]

Working women increasingly felt that a general labour service should be introduced for all women between the ages of 16 and 40 without family responsibilities. It was also felt that if some women were to be exempted from work, the distinction should be made between soldiers' wives and others. The authorities took these complaints and suggestions seriously, although the response was only to exhort more middle-class women to do their duty (and to 're-educate' those soldiers who considered it improper for their wives to work).[75] By June 1941 (in a report dated a few days after the invasion of the USSR) SD observers drew attention to increasingly poor industrial discipline among the female workforce, and a rise in female absenteeism on the grounds of fatigue and pressing domestic duties.[76]

The regime finally resorted to a more coercive approach to the mobilisation of labour in the wake of the defeat at Stalingrad. By the 'Decree Concerning the Registration of Men and Women for Work for the Defence of the Reich' of 13 January 1943 all men between the ages of 16 and 65 and women between the ages of 17 and 45 were to register for work at labour offices. The only women exempted were mothers of one child under school age or two children under fourteen, and pregnant women.[77] The move was welcomed in working-class circles,[78] where responses to the decree reflected popular opinion in general, in so far as interest was focused on the attempt to recruit more women into the labour force. In one part of the Reich women volunteers had to be turned away.[79]

Whatever initial success the measure had in the first few weeks soon died away. By the summer there were reports from Austria that attempts to recruit women had run into the sands, and that the same particular problems cropped up again and again: 'training, accommodation and domestic circumstances'.[80] Women used the provisions of the decree as excuses to leave employment, and of those who did register for work and were allocated jobs, few remained in employment for long. Those who did were often relatively indifferent to industrial discipline and preoccupied with domestic concerns, and their unpredictable absenteeism proved to be disruptive.[81]

Although there was a sharp increase in the number of women in the German industrial workforce in 1943 and 1944, the growth in female employment did not keep pace with the overall growth in industrial employment, which was largely fuelled by the intensified exploitation of foreign workers and prisoners of war; and the growth in female employ-

Table 3.5. *Women's share of industrial employment: Austria and the Reich, 1939–1944.*

	Industrial Employment (1,000s)		Women Employed (1,000s)		Female Share of Employment (%)	
	Reich	Austria	Reich	Austria	Reich	Austria
1939	101,38	536	2,504	147	24.7	27.5
1940	9,238	527	2,425	146	26.2	27.7
1941	9,598	553	2,469	152	25.7	27.4
1942	9,151	579	2,370	150	25.9	26.0
1943	9,530	673	2,429	167	25.5	24.8
1944	9,650	735	2,377	185	24.6	25.2

Source: Wagenführ, *Die deutsche Industrie im Kriege*, pp. 139f, cited in Freund and Perz, 'Fremdarbeiter', p. 345.

ment overall concealed a much sharper rise in the number of foreign women in industry than of native German or Austrian women. In this respect the situation in Austria differed little from that of the Reich as a whole (see tables 3.4 and 3.5). In 1943 Austrian women in the industrial workforce were outnumbered by foreigners and prisoners of war for the first time.

This did not mean that the number of women recruited into industry in the last two full years of the war was not substantial, and the pattern of recruitment remained the same: it was above all working-class women who were recruited for the war effort. The failure of the 'total war' measures to redress perceived injustices in the recruitment of female labour refuelled criticism of the regime at a time when its military reverses were already undermining popular morale.[82] In particular, the requirement for female domestic servants to register for work – a clause which had been given a great deal of publicity in the press – had become a mockery. 'Everywhere', it was reported by the SD in April 1943, 'there is bitter discussion of cases of the better off or childless households – or those with few children – still hanging on to housemaids who are felt to be unnecessary, and this is having a very adverse effect on women already in the workforce.'[83]

Nevertheless, it was only with the introduction of the 'total war' measures in 1943 that the authorities were able to announce an improvement, particularly in the high-priority arms industries. In 1943 the authorities in Lower Danube reported that the 'quota of women' had exceeded 30 per cent in the first quarter of the year.[84]

By 31 March 1943, 182,064 Austrian women had registered for employment as a result of the Decree for the Defence of the Reich of

January 1943, half of them in Vienna or Lower Danube. Of these 88,982 registrations (48.9 per cent) were processed and 71,922 (39.5 per cent of the original registrations) were found eligible for work. Even fewer (51,527) were actually employed. Agriculture took 14,456 (28.0 per cent) of the new female recruits, the arms industries 15,543 (30.2 per cent), and clerical work 10,926 (21.2 per cent).[85]

Women were frequently over-stretched by the combination of domestic responsibilities and paid employment. At best this affected work discipline and productivity, at worst (from the perspective of employers and the state) it forced them to make a choice between the two, and the commitment to domestic responsibilities was often greater, particularly where young children were involved. After the 1943 decree such choices ran up against the 'total war' measures, and absentee women workers were charged with 'breach of contract' and brought to court. The case of a kitchen assistant from the Eisenwerke Oberdonau in Linz is typical. She had left her job in Linz and taken casual work on farms before finding another job in her home town of St. Florian, about ten kilometres south of the city. She refused to accept any job in Linz on the grounds that she had an eight year old son to look after. The labour office had little sympathy with this argument, and referred to the introduction in January 1943 of the obligation of women with only one child over school age to report for work.[86]

All the usual problems were exacerbated in the case of working mothers: their husbands would either be employed or at the front, in which case the expectation that they put work before the children generated enormous resentment. If they were unmarried (as many young mothers in provincial Austria were) a move away from the community would involve them in difficulties of all kinds: loss of support from members of the extended family, difficulties in finding accommodation in the towns (especially for a young woman with an illegitimate child), and difficulties in arranging child care for the hours when children were not at school and the mother was still working. Employers were not always willing or able to be flexible in their approach to working hours, and in any case many of the problems were outside the competence of either employers or the state. Getting workers from the countryside into Linz (or other industrial towns), for example, was a general problem: quite apart from anything else workers might pay a disproportionate amount for public transport.[87] Nor was this a problem for urban employers alone: farmers complained of the shortage of experienced milkmaids who could get to work on time, many had to walk miles across the countryside to get to the dairy where they were employed.[88]

Of the 44,311 women newly employed in Austria as a result of the decree, 4,263 had one or more children under the age of fourteen (women with two children under fourteen, or any children under school age were exempt).[89] A substantial proportion of these working mothers had not previously worked the forty-eight hour week which was now expected of them.[90]

Thousands of Austrian women were mobilised for war work, and others were effectively transferred from consumer goods industries or other 'non-essential' work to jobs related to the war effort. Paid employment often involved considerable difficulty for the women themselves, particularly for the wives of serving soldiers, for single mothers and for women living in communities remote from their place of employment. These difficulties often compounded the resentment already felt by the wives of servicemen, and by working-class women who felt that too little was being done to bring better-off women into the workforce.

If more women were not recruited the objections were pragmatic and political as much as ideological. Few women were trained in the skills needed in the arms and arms-related industries, and although many underwent retraining (as, for example in the *Steyrwerke*), the recruitment and training of women with industrial skills could not be undertaken quickly enough, as Hitler himself told Fritz Sauckel, when he proposed to extend the recruitment of women.[91] Ever wary of the spread of working-class disaffection, the regime was cautious in its attempts to impose sacrifice on the working class. The spread of a popular belief that working-class women were being compelled to work despite real domestic difficulties, while middle-class women with no real domestic responsibilities retained housemaids, was viewed with concern by the authorities.

Above all, however, more women were not recruited because early decisions were taken to exploit foreign labour in order to make up the shortfalls in German industry. If the number of women in the Austrian industrial labour force increased by more than half (56.6 per cent) during the war, the number of foreign workers quadrupled and the number of prisoners of war doubled. This too generated political and industrial relations problems, but they were of a different kind to the ones the regime was trying to avoid, and different, generally more coercive solutions were applied to them. The solution was an unsatisfactory one. Despite the massive exploitation of slave labour from the whole of Europe, but above all from the USSR, the Reich failed to mobilise an industrial capacity to match, still less out-pace, that of the Allies in a long war.

4   Work discipline in the war economy

Some of the most important changes determining industrial relations and work discipline in the Third Reich had already been effected before the outbreak of the war.[1] By September 1939 the conditions that prevailed in Austrian industry were those that had been shaped in the *Altreich* since 1933. Austrian workers, no less than Germans, had experienced a 'reordering of class relations' (in so far as this had not already happened before the Anschluss). Similarly, economic integration had produced the rearmament boom and labour shortages which Germany had already experienced for two years or more. These new conditions meant that, even without trade unions, workers in many industries were again in a position to bargain for higher wages and better conditions. Their bargaining position was, of course, more circumscribed than it had been when full employment had first been achieved in Germany, because measures had been taken to regulate both wages and labour mobility.[2]

Even before the war the reorientation of the economy towards rearmament had meant that the state increasingly had become industry's most important customer and would have to foot a large part of the bill for any increase in wages. Controls on wages and labour mobility had been imposed in 1938, but these were circumvented by workers and employers alike: the former were happy to leave their jobs for better paid employment; the latter were prepared to poach them rather than lose lucrative government contracts for want of skilled labour. This created inflationary pressures which tighter controls on labour mobility were intended to curb. Whether it involved breach of employment contract or failure to go through the correct bureaucratic procedures and obtain permission from the local labour office, 'job changing' (*Arbeitsplatzwechsel*), remained a persistent problem throughout the war.[3]

Labour shortages had also created other problems. Above all, the removal of the threat of dismissal had given rise to greater indiscipline on the shop floor. Nothing overtly political, or even collective, could be attempted of course. Close surveillance, frequent intervention by the Gestapo and the severity of exemplary punishments made sure of that. Instances of insubordination, such as incidents of refusal to work (*Arbeitsverweigerungen*) or take up a job allocated through the civil conscription programme, were sporadic, brief and small-scale. Other types of perceived industrial 'indiscipline' involved larger numbers of workers for longer periods of time. Rates of sickness and absenteeism fluctuated, but frequently reached unacceptable levels, whether they were intended as a protest against particular policies or simply constituted what has been called 'workers' resistance to work'.[4] Less tangible discipline problems, such as indifference, sloppiness, go-slows, or insolence, also recurred frequently in the endless streams of reports compiled by a range of Nazi bureaucrats. What was politics or protest, what was self-interest or indifference, and what was little more than the self-righteous rage of minor party apparatchiks at the unwillingness of workers to sacrifice more for Führer and fatherland, is not always easy to determine.

At the level of policy-making, however, the distorted mythologies of November 1918 were an important determinant of government attitudes to the working class during the Second World War.[5] Where the government could avoid demanding undue sacrifices it did so. Relatively draconian measures were introduced in September 1939, but were quickly withdrawn, and the military successes of the next three years did much to extend and reinforce a popular consensus behind the regime. It was neither an all-embracing consensus nor a very stable one, especially in working-class circles, where the economic pressures of war were felt first and most keenly;[6] but German victories dispelled the anxieties that had preceded the war and generated a popular euphoria from which even committed anti-Nazis found it difficult to distance themselves.[7] Morale was generally good, according to some SD reporters in Austria, even during the difficult days of October 1939. The war had demoralised the regime's opponents as much as it had heartened its supporters. Communists, especially rank and file activists, had been disarmed by the Hitler-Stalin pact, and were reluctant to accept its implications.

It was not until the invasion of the Soviet Union that war began to intrude into the everyday experience of German civilians. It was not the beginning of the war, but 1941 that marked a watershed, when 'normality', it was later recalled, gave way to the abnormalities of shortages, bombing raids, and the loss of husbands, sons and brothers in action.[8]

In addition the regime itself was more determined to direct its resources more purposefully, and this was realised in Speer's success in increasing armaments production. Raw materials and labour were released from capital projects which had either been completed or suspended, but gains were also made by the application of more rational procedures to management, production, storage and distribution.[9] Automated production was expanded, workers were de-skilled and although per capita productivity in the German armaments industries rose rapidly, real net industrial wages fell as pressure was put on employers (by means of a fixed-price system of contracts) to contain wages costs.[10] Although attempts to introduce piece-rate working foundered against opposition from both the workforce and the Trustees of Labour, and although both employers and the state were increasingly aware of the importance of the 'social wage' in compensating workers for the declining value of take-home pay, long hours, deteriorating conditions and shortages of consumer goods, the industrial peace was kept as much by threats, surveillance and coercion as through the judicious distribution of rewards. Labour shortages persisted, of course, but the threat of unemployment had been replaced by the more serious threat of withdrawal of reserved status, conscription and a probable posting to the eastern front.[11] The position of industrial workers deteriorated, and with it their morale. The victories of the early war years had not only compensated for material sacrifices, but had also made sense of them. Deprivation and self-sacrifice seemed increasingly gratuitous once the tide of the war had turned.

War economy measures

Indiscipline and industrial protest found its most dramatic focus when, in September 1939, a series of measures was introduced to meet the expected demands of the war economy. The provisions of the War Economy Decree of 4 September suspended industrial safety regulations, abolished paid holidays and bonuses for overtime and shift work, and sought to reduce wages. In addition there was to be more civil conscription and an end to restrictions on the length of the working week.[12] Any savings from these measures were to be paid to the state rather than retained by the employer. Workers, as the Vienna SD office pointed out in its report to Berlin, did not always appreciate this point.[13]

These measures were not taken without reservations, particularly about the effects they might have on workers' morale. The consequences of the measures have been well documented. The War Economy Decree provoked a wave of disaffection throughout Germany's industrial workforce during the autumn of 1939.[14] The measures provoked similar disaffection in Austria. There too, workers complained about the loss of overtime bonuses which they suspected went straight into the employers' pockets. With so many people working away from home, the abolition of cheap weekend fares was a further cause for concern.[15] By the end of October the Vienna SD reported a general deterioration in the mood of the workforce. Disparaging comments and minor incidents were common, the Communist Party was unusually active, and some workers had refused to pay their DAF dues. The reasons were ostensibly material: workers complained that the combination of overtime and poor diet was making them ill, and there had been an increase in numbers reporting sick. Many people had complained that soldiers were so much better fed than civilians that they were sending parcels home to their families, containing the food they could not eat themselves. Turning the regime's rhetoric to their own advantage, workers made the point that 'work on the home front' was also important and that they too were expected to give their all. In response to these complaints, the DAF duly set about making arrangements for the establishment of works canteens and the distribution of a 'hearty meal' for workers, but the SD reporter was more sceptical about the broader reasons for all the trouble, and suggested that, with less exciting news from the front to distract workers, they had lapsed into their selfish habit of putting themselves first.[16]

Despite the focus for disaffection which the War Economy Decree provided, dissatisfaction usually arose from a combination of individual factors, which included rationing, shortages, and other day-to-day grievances, along with the effects of the new measures whether it was pressure to work overtime without pay, or the suspension by some firms of traditional holidays. (The first public holiday to be affected was 1 November, as a minor holiday an easy target for management economies, but an important one for many Austrians.)[17] In addition, problems already apparent before the promulgation of the Decree, persisted throughout these months. Redundancies continued to be announced. In some cases, as in the textiles industry, for example, this was due to the restructuring of the economy, in others it was due to shortages of raw materials.[18] Even arms works were running at only 75 per cent of capacity in October, and Semperit had been forced to relinquish a quarter of its workforce. Short-time workers, on a thirty-two-hour week, might earn as little as a quarter of full-time wages, and complaints about low wages and rising prices were persistent.[19]

Such disaffection, as several reports made clear, was concentrated in larger industrial towns, above all in Vienna, but also in Styria and in Linz. Not unexpectedly, rural provinces were generally quieter. There was much less sympathy in the countryside for the oppositional carping that was common in the capital. When a 'whingeing Communist' was killed by a 'couple of blows' from an SS man in the Tyrol, the incident

attracted no public interest, (and since 'self-defence was clearly established' no arrest was made). It was reported from Carinthia that morale
there was particularly good, and here, as in Upper Austria, the local
mood seems to have been improved by the arrival of foreign workers.
In some rural districts there seems to have been little awareness of what
was going on in the outside world. Alpine villagers, it was reported,
were totally unsympathetic to all the new measures, even the ones
favourable to them. Attempts to apply the new regulations were found-
ering against complete lack of comprehension, and people were reacting
as if they were being terrorised.[20]

The widespread collective sense of disaffection of the autumn of 1939
was made up of very specific and reasoned grievances: if there was a
passive resistance to the War Economy Decree, it was often the very
practical resistance to a series of hastily conceived measures whose
implementation had been too brisk to make allowances for anomalies.
The consequence was that a great deal of patriotic sympathy which the
regime might otherwise have exploited was rapidly dissipated.

Above all it was felt that the measures had been imposed without due
consideration of some of the local difficulties and anomalies that might
arise. There was a strong sense that the measures had given rise to some
specific injustices, and this feeling was shared by a number of institutions and individuals within the regime. DAF officials could not help
but be aware of feelings on the shop floor, and rank and file functionaries of the Nazi Party and its associations were acutely conscious of the
importance of maintaining a degree of popular support.[21] 'Anti-social'
attempts by employers to exploit the situation were denounced not only
in propaganda but even in the regime's internal reports. Thus there was
a tacit acceptance, for example, that there was a certain common sense
in the refusal of Styrian miners to work every Sunday, and a residual
good will in their agreeing to work every other.[22]

More generally, a number of observers in the Nazi administration
in Vienna were sensitive to the particular grievances of Austrian workers. Prices were still rising more rapidly in Austria than wages; and
further cuts in wages, or even the loss of bonuses would seriously
damage morale. Transport workers in Vienna, and those employed
in public utilities argued that, for them, the loss of bonus payments
was particularly unjust. Night work and Sunday shifts were essential
in these public services, and the bonuses were, in part, a compensation for the incidental costs of working outside normal hours. Furthermore, far from being a windfall from the armaments boom, such
bonuses had operated for years, so that their abolition now would
effectively mean a 10 per cent wage cut. In public transport there

were over seventeen different wage grades, and the amount of overtime payable was the result of a particularly complicated mathematical calculation. If the war economy measures were to be applied rigorously, transport workers would, in some cases, receive less for overtime than for normal working: 'A one-sided burden for precisely those who perform the most responsible services' and one that would be perceived as 'an unfair hardship', it was argued in a request to Bürckel for the introduction of special regulations.[23]

Bürckel accepted this argument, and wrote to Hitler on 2 October, pleading the case not only of workers employed by the Vienna municipality, but of Austrian workers generally. Supporting his case with reference to the success of his political work both in Vienna and in the Saarland before that, he suggested that this progress might now be jeopardised by a general reduction in Austrian wage levels.[24] His case was supported by economists in the *Gau* administration, who emphasised the particular difficulties of the local economy. If prices could not be reduced, then it would be very difficult to keep wages at their present level, still less implement the automatic and indiscriminate wage cuts that were now being introduced, unless other measures were taken to get round the problem. The DAF, for example, had recommended that an expansion in the number of works canteens selling decent food at reasonable prices might do something to appease disgruntled workers.[25]

By the end of October it was clear that the war economy measures were unpopular throughout the Reich, and reporters from Austria too detected a discernible deterioration in popular morale, particularly in Vienna, where there was also a marked increase in oppositional political activity. Communist flysheets attacking Hitler and calling for sabotage in munitions works had been found in the Leopoldstadt, in the *Aurerwerke*, and in the railway works in Simmering.[26]

Disaffection was translated into indiscipline in a number of ways. The Vienna Gestapo reported a rash of 'refusals to work' (*Arbeitsverweigerungen*), particularly on construction sites. Not really strikes in the proper sense, and never referred to as such, these incidents generally involved a handful of workers refusing to do a particular job, or making a clear protest in response to real or perceived chicanery on the part of employers. The term also included refusals to work overtime, a practice which became understandably widespread in the absence of bonuses. To turn down a Sunday shift because there was no overtime for it would once, of course, have been wholly uncontroversial. To do so now risked arrest by the Gestapo, as in the case of two workers at the *Ostdeutsche Glaswerke* in Brunn am Gebirge.[27]

Pressure to work at weekends was particularly resented by workers separated from their families. Such workers had frequently been guaranteed free weekends with pay in their contracts, and many of them were foreigners, for whom such guarantees had been a condition of their taking up employment in the Reich in the first place, and who were also beyond any patriotic appeals for self-sacrifice. Such workers were doubly hit by the suspension of weekend bonuses and holiday pay, and many of them took the law into their own hands. It was reported in October that many building workers were taking weekend leave without permission anyway;[28] others, including Austrians working away from home in northern Germany, were feigning illness.[29]

Certainly, sickness rates rose sharply when the War Economy Decree came into force, and had reached 20 per cent in Floridsdorf by the end of October. Some of this increase was no doubt down to poorer diet, longer hours and harder work. The working day had been increased to ten or twelve hours, and the working week to 54 hours, and there had long been complaints about the murderous rate of work expected under the new industrial regime.[30]

The Reich Insurance Office undertook an investigation into absenteeism whose results were reported shortly before Christmas 1939. The office came to the conclusion that an absentee rate of 2 per cent of the workforce was justifiable and to be expected under normal conditions. A slightly higher rate might be expected at the present as a result of longer shifts, the use of untrained workers, the increased pace of work, public transport difficulties and so on. Taking these factors into account a rate of 4 per cent or 4½ per cent might be justified, but not the 7 per cent to 10 per cent that was currently common (and, presumably, not the 20 per cent that had been recorded among some groups of workers in Vienna during the autumn). The urgency of action to deal with the problem could not be overstated: a 1 per cent absenteeism rate represented the loss of 20,000 man shifts at a cost of RM 60,000 a day. Several possible explanations for the phenomenon were suggested. The first supposed a greater resistance to work as the work itself became harder; the second that doctors had not been sufficiently conscious of their patriotic duties when examining sick workers, and had too generously agreed to sick leave or the extension of sick leave. And then the life assurance institute had recently taken over the company doctor service in Austria, and the administrative teething difficulties that had followed had impaired the efficiency of the system. Conscription was also a problem, which had given rise to manpower difficulties in both the medical profession and in insurance agencies, and the loss of personnel by insurance agencies was exacerbated by the petrol shortage, which slowed down the remaining insurance agents on their rounds. Finally it was suggested that political organisations, above all the DAF, had been remiss in their 'educational' work on this matter.[31]

Persistent absenteeism was not the only discipline problem, and by early November it was clear that something had to be done to remedy a situation that seemed to be threatening the level of productivity not in Austria alone, of course, but in the Reich as a whole. On 10 November it was decided to reintroduce bonuses for overtime and Sunday shifts, despite objections that this would lead to inflation.[32]

The government attempted to offset the consequent loss of revenue by adjusting tax thresholds, but this step was also more difficult than anticipated to implement. It created a tax trap for some workers, who found themselves in a higher tax bracket, which wiped out their overtime earnings. This in turn provoked a fresh wave of resentment and unwillingness to work.[33]

As the government made more and more concessions, however, the mood of the workers began to relax. The limiting of the working day to ten hours, and the reintroduction of statutory holidays and night shift bonuses had led to 'general satisfaction', it was reported at the end of November. These concessions were welcomed not only by the workforce, but by the employers as well. Not only had employers derived no direct benefit from the measures, they had also borne the brunt of absenteeism and other labour discipline problems. The suspension of paid holidays, where employers had gained directly, was another matter, and they opposed their reinstatement. Firms were afraid that the backlog of holidays would be expensive, and lead to production difficulties, but it was this concession in particular, along with the decision to pay Christmas bonuses, that decisively improved worker morale.[34]

The measures in the War Economy Decree had provoked particularly strong reactions, and their repeal did much to appease the industrial workforce. Indiscipline was not entirely eradicated, but the authorities were confident, in the wake of the retreat from the draconian measures of September 1939, that they could build on the improved mood of the workforce.

Refusing to work: insubordination and breach of contract in the war economy

Various authorities responsible for monitoring discipline in the workplace were vigilant throughout the war. Whether politically motivated or not, breaches of discipline were potentially disruptive. The range of misdemeanours that interested the authorities, and which were

categorised as 'indiscipline' in the sheaves of internal reports compiled
by the regime remained much the same throughout the war: 'slacking'
(*Arbeitsbummelei*); insubordination and refusal to work; absenteeism and
feigned illness; and unauthorised changes of employment.

Discipline problems were particularly persistent among those relatively well-defined categories of workers who were new to the industrial
workforce, or whose employment was directed in some way, rather than
freely chosen: foreign workers and labour conscripts; women and young
people; and agricultural workers entering the workforce for the first
time.

Some of the complaints directed against these 'undisciplined' groups
of workers were based on rather predictable generational or class prejudice. There was no discipline among young industrial workers in Styria,
industrialists complained to the Armaments Command (*Rüstungskommando*) in Graz; the authorities, putting this down to the conflicting
demands of the parental home, the Hitler Youth and training courses,
despaired of ever rearing a new generation of technically competent
young workers. Similarly, there was indignation when the Böhler company of Upper Styria managed to engage the services of only one or
two of the 500 working-class women nominated by the Nazi women's
organisation (*NS-Frauenschaft*) as eligible for industrial work in an exercise whose purpose, apparently, was to expose childless women receiving family support payments.[35] In Vienna, similarly, a number of firms
complained that workers allocated to them simply refused to take the
job, and it seemed that both refusal to work and absenteeism were a
particular problem among newly employed workers and civilian labour
conscripts.[36]

High sickness rates proved not to be merely a temporary phenomenon
occasioned by the draconian measures of 1939. They had risen sharply
in Austrian industry from the beginning of 1940, and the rate of absenteeism, at over 7 per cent of the male workforce, was reckoned to be
$1\frac{1}{2}$ per cent higher on average in Austria than in Germany. By October
1940 there were reports of delays in the construction of new industrial
capacity as a result of permanently high sickness levels.[37] In Upper Austria it reached 20 per cent of the workforce in February.[38]

Confronted with what seemed like wilfully disruptive indiscipline on
the part of the workforce, some senior officials urged deterrent measures. Friedrich Gärtner in the Vienna branch of the Reich Labour Ministry, for example, reprimanded presidents of provincial courts and
public prosecutors for their leniency in dealing with cases of breach of
employment contract, and emphasised that civil conscription had the
same significance as military conscription. Offences against the labour

laws, he insisted, should be punished with exemplary sentences, and offenders – whether workers or employers – should be arrested and imprisoned as soon as the offence was known.[39]

Increasingly, such 'offenders' did come up before the local courts. The authorities themselves were always prepared to ascribe the worst motives to absenteeism and breach of contract, and they ranged from fecklessness to political subversion. They noted the incitements of the Communists and the Allies to sabotage and disruption; they looked for ringleaders and evidence of collective action, but more often than not they failed to find it. Defendants in cases brought for breach of contract (including prolonged absences from work) offered a variety of reasons for their behaviour. Illness was the most frequent justification for long periods of absence, and women in particular also cited child care responsibilities or other pressing family or domestic circumstances. Men were more inclined to voice their dissatisfaction with wages or conditions in the workplace itself, or with what they felt to be an inappropriate use of their skills.

An assistant painter in the *Steyrwerke*, for example, who had been persistently absent from work between April and December 1939, explained that as a trained painter he was 'annoyed' to be employed as an unskilled worker, for which he received less pay.[40] Specific grievances were also cited by a building worker at Wayss and Freytag in Linz. Between starting work on 5 February 1940 and his last shift on 11 April – after which he had failed to turn up at all – he had been at work only twelve days. On two of these days he had worked only five hours, and on another only two hours. He explained his absence from 7 March to 7 April by illness, but his other absences were unexcused. Although he claimed that an inflamed throat had kept him away from work, he added that he had not enjoyed working for the firm because the wages (Rpf. 64 per hour) were so low, and because he was mistreated by his superiors. Then, evidently feeling that these were insufficient or unconvincing grounds, he added that as a Tyrolean he had yearned for the mountains, and in June had gone to Sillian in the Tyrol for a week.[41]

The cases brought against workers for breaches of contract reveal very little beyond confused excuses relating to the individual. While some evidence suggests a correlation between absenteeism among former peasants and periods of peak demand for agricultural labour in rural areas,[42] it is generally difficult to see any pattern in such behaviour. Collective action seems to have been rare, but did occasionally occur. A typical case took place in a Vienna firm in the spring of 1940, when a section of the workforce downed tools for two hours following changes in the wages system. The strike was attributed to the management's failure to explain the new system, and work was resumed within a couple of hours, but the incident was an illustration of the latent capacity for collective action, which might surface if the workforce felt threatened.[43]

Control of labour was intensified during the war. According to the Second Decree on Breach of Contract of 1942, the duties of the worker were to turn up for work; not to refuse overtime, night shifts, Sunday or holiday work; not to take time off, leave one's job, turn up late or behave in an undisciplined manner; not to terminate the employment contract prematurely, and not to demand disproportionately high wages. The employer's duties were not to terminate the employment contract without due cause; not to poach workers from other firms for higher wages or by offering better conditions; and to report all offences against labour laws to the authorities.[44]

Penalties were imposed in five stages. The first stage involved a disciplinary penalty imposed by the employer, which could be a warning, a reprimand or a fine of up to 500 Reichsmarks. The second stage involved a disciplinary penalty imposed by the local representative of the Reich Trustee of Labour (later also by the courts): again, a warning, a reprimand, and a fine, this time of up to RM 1,000. The third stage required a report to the district magistrate or local chief of police, week-end detention or three to seven days in custody in more serious cases, penalties which were imposed by the district magistrate. The fourth stage required a report to the police, arrest, and referral to the Gestapo, who imposed a custodial sentence or a term in a 'work education camp'. Alternatively, a report might be made directly to the Commander of the Security Police, generally leading to a prison sentence.[45]

Needless to say, workers were not always aware, either of their duties under this legislation, or of the disproportionate nature of the penalties they might incur for neglecting them. Nor was there any unified policy on what offence, precisely, might incur what penalty until December 1943, when an order was made enabling employers to penalise offences against labour discipline. Minor offences, such as one day's unpunctuality, might be penalised with a warning, while more serious offences could incur a money fine of up to a week's wages. If an internal penalty was insufficient, the case was to be referred to the labour office in the case of Germans, and to the police department responsible in the case of foreign workers.

Disciplinary offences increased during the last years of the war, as popular morale deteriorated and civilians found themselves increasingly subject to the dislocations and material deprivations they had hitherto been spared.[46] The preference of the authorities was for as many offences as possible to be dealt with internally by employers, in order to avoid the courts becoming jammed with cases; public prosecutors and court presidents received a circular from the Justice Ministry outlining cases in which court proceedings should be instigated, and making the point that they should be undertaken in only the most exceptional cases, as the most extreme form of deterrent.

Nevertheless, there was a sharp increase in cases coming before the courts.[47] Whether workers were deliberately flouting the law and how far they were ignorant of it, or even indifferent to it, is unclear from the records of such cases. Clearly, however, many people were increasingly inclined to reorder their priorities, and many of the defendants in labour discipline cases cited pressing domestic or other circumstances among their reasons for not turning up to work. Frequently, too, difficulties might have been avoided if the authorities had shown a greater willingness to take domestic circumstances into account when allocating jobs. In February 1943, for example an unskilled eighteen-year-old labourer from Gallneukirchen was allocated to a firm in Linz, but worked for only two weeks before persistently failing to turn up despite repeated reprimands. In his defence the youth claimed that it cost him more to travel to work than he earned, and although he was instructed to return to work, failed to do so. The case was passed on to the chief public prosecutor, and it was ascertained that he had been similarly reprimanded two years previously, and had spent a year in a remand home.[48]

Illness continued to be the most common reason given for absence from work, and many of the cases that came before the courts involved people who actually had a doctor's note. Many had no medical certification, however, and their cases frequently revealed a whole range of other contributory circumstances. A construction worker from Linz, for example, claimed that he had suffered from stomach pains, and returned to his village in the Burgenland. His wife had been ill, too, with gall stones, and had been unable to look after their small allotment, so he had stayed in the Burgenland, taking on two new jobs – as a parish official and on a farm. (His daughter, despite the labour shortages, was employed as a housemaid in Vienna.) Eventually he had returned to Linz and resumed his job as a construction worker, apparently without any penalty being imposed.[49]

Outside Vienna, of course, many Austrian workers lived in small rural communities, where they often either farmed some land themselves, or helped with the harvest. For such workers a local job was important, and attempts to transfer them to the expanding munitions works in nearby towns were not always successful. A worker in a furniture business in Krummau, for example, who had been told by the Labour Office that he was to be transferred to Steyr, was instructed to report to the *Steyrwerke* during the harvest and, since there was nobody else at home to get it in, he simply did not turn up for work.[50] As many similar cases were to show, it proved simply impractical to try to reorder the labour market in the countryside in the face of established custom.

For those workers who did take up new jobs, either in nearby towns or further afield, finding accommodation was always a problem, and many new recruits ended up in hastily erected or converted 'barracks'. 'After the accommodation problems, I have no further interest in working [at the shipyards] and I'll see to it that the Labour Office has me released', one worker told the authorities, while another declared: 'I'm not going back to Nuremberg, because I've nowhere to live there. I'd rather be locked up.'[51]

Other frequent complaints included mistreatment by superiors, cold or poor food and the hard work (especially among women). Those who abandoned their jobs entirely often referred to an accumulation of problems. A German worker at the *Eisenwerke Oberdonau*, for example, returned to Bavaria because his wife had just given birth to a seventh child and could not cope on her own. He managed to get a job in Munich, claiming that his wages at the *Eisenwerke Oberdonau* had been insufficient to keep his wife and family in Munich and pay for accommodation in Linz; furthermore, his work in Linz had been unskilled, whereas in Munich he had a job as a qualified stone-mason. Finally, he added that he did not like living in Linz because Reich Germans were unpopular with local people.[52] The frequency of such cases suggests that the regime had underestimated the unwillingness of people to be uprooted and separated from their families. They also resented being allocated to jobs which they did not want, and which did not make full use of their skills – an increasing problem as more and more production lines were rationalised.

The *Eisenwerke Oberdonau* was one of many large concerns which established relatively efficient internal procedures for dealing with labour discipline problems. By 1943 the company's employees formed the largest single group of offenders charged with breach of contract in Upper Austria and, although their motives remained obscure, it is striking that by 1944 the majority of the offenders had already been penalised for similar offences, often several times.

The organisation of labour discipline in the *Eisenwerke Oberdonau* was well-established by 1943. At fairly regular intervals between the end of April and mid-November of that year the company held five internal 'summary courts' (*Schnellgerichte*) for breaches of labour discipline. These five sessions dealt with a total of 188 offenders of eighteen different nationalities. A third of these were French, and 16 per cent were Czech. 'Germans' (9 per cent) constituted the third largest national group.[53] Discipline was a much greater problem among foreign workers than among the Austrians themselves. By 1943 there were twice as many foreign workers as Austrians in Upper Austria, but absenteeism rates among foreign workers at the *Eisenwerke Oberdonau* were three or four times as high, and foreigners were up to ten times more likely to be penalised.[54] Increasingly, towards the end of the war, foreign workers failed to return from holidays at home. Austrians and Reich Germans were also inclined to do the same, of course, but the scale of this type of desertion by foreign workers was much greater, and had implications for industrial productivity: the Nibelungen works, for example, lost three hundred workers in this way in just three months, and the problem was exacerbated by the fact that most of the successful deserters were Czechs, who were among the most skilled members of the foreign workforce.[55]

Work discipline among foreign workers

The experience at the *Eisenwerke* was reflected throughout Austria and indeed the Reich. In the first six months of 1941 the Gestapo identified 5,699 breaches of labour discipline in the Vienna police district (which also covered Lower Austria), and made 1,667 arrests, of whom 7.6 per cent were 'German citizens'. The vast majority of all the offences were committed by Poles, many of whom were young fugitive agricultural workers.[56]

In December 1941 a third of all labour offences in the Greater German Reich were committed by Poles, but the proportion was generally higher in Austria (see table 4.1), and in the east of the Reich generally, in districts with or near substantial Polish populations, such as Breslau, Oppeln or even Frankfurt an der Oder.[57]

After the invasion of the USSR, Soviet workers rapidly became both the largest single foreign nationality in the workforce, and the most frequently arrested for labour discipline offences. In November 1942 the Gestapo made 1,640 arrests in Vienna and Lower Austria. Of these 1,254 (76 per cent) were for work stoppages (*Arbeitsniederlegungen*), and of these in turn the majority by far were east Europeans: 729 (58 per cent) were Soviets ('*Ostarbeiter*'); 244 (19 per cent) were Poles; 158 (13 per cent) were from the Balkans, and one was from the Baltic. Only 62 (5 per cent) of those arrested were German. Of those arrested, over a quarter were sent to a work education camp, and just over 5 per cent received formal warnings.

Table 4.1. *Gestapo arrests for labour discipline offences: Vienna and Lower Austria, January–June 1941.*

Nationality		Proportion of total (%)
German	126	(7.6)
Polish	1,208	(72.5)
Slovak	140	(8.4)
Czech*	54	(3.2)
Hungarian	49	(2.9)
Bulgarian	37	(2.2)
Ukrainian	27	(1.6)
Other	26	(1.6)

* i.e. from Bohemia and Moravia.
Source: DÖW 5732d.

Soviet and east European workers together accounted for the overwhelming majority – over 80 per cent of arrests for labour discipline offences in Vienna and Lower Austria during the later years of the war (see table 4.2). Indeed, two thirds of all activities undertaken by Gestapo officers throughout the Reich in the first nine months of 1943 were related to discipline problems among foreign workers, above all among Soviet and Polish workers, and the punishments they received were generally much harder than those received by Germans.[58] In the wake of the German defeat at Stalingrad, of course, labour discipline among Soviet workers had deteriorated further. In February 1943 the Rothmüller company in Vienna's Twentieth District reported a steep drop in the productivity of its thirty-one Soviet workers, who were increasingly unwilling to obey the foreman's instructions.[59] Foreign workers were also generally more assertive in their relations with German civilians. Both Poles and Soviets refused to wear the badges identifying them as foreign workers. Employers complained that Soviet workers left the camps in which they were lodged in the evenings, and local people complained of public houses full of drunken foreigners. The Czechs refused to speak German or use the 'Hitler' greeting as they had formerly done, and Polish workers demanded holidays, and even insisted on the right to have relationships with German women.[60]

It was rare, however, that developments in work discipline were officially attributed to direct political motivation. The authorities knew of Communist attempts to incite sabotage, and they suspected that such incitement did have some effect. In September 1941, for example, the Armaments Inspectorate reported that productivity had fallen during a three-week period of pirate radio broadcasts encouraging Czech workers

Table 4.2 *Arrests for work stoppages in Vienna and Lower Austria, February 1943–March 1944.*

	All	All arrests	German labour	Soviet	Eastern Europe
February 1943	2,097	1,634	48 (3%)	790 (48%)	713 (44%)
March	2,223	1,729	68 (4%)	774 (45%)	768 (44%)
May	2,122	1,654	65 (4%)	822 (50%)	632 (38%)
July	2,051	1,641	65 (4%)	866 (53%)	591 (36%)
August	2,143	1,817	61 (3%)	892 (49%)	650 (36%)
September	2,262	1,840	65 (4%)	840 (46%)	673 (37%)
October	2,347	1,821	42 (2%)	844 (46%)	715 (39%)
November	1,999	1,496	35 (2%)	487 (33%)	739 (49%)
December	1,758	1,354	31 (2%)	538 (40%)	581 (43%)
January 1944	2,086	1,502	18 (2%)	606 (40%)	639 (43%)
February	2,423	1,813	44 (2%)	789 (44%)	683 (38%)
March	2,656	2,071	47 (2%)	1,074 (51%)	736 (36%)

East Europeans were from Bohemia-Moravia, the Baltic, Poland and the Balkans. The percentage figures refer to the proportion per nationality of all labour stoppages.
Source: DÖW 5743a–5743d; 8477–8749.

to sabotage industry.[61] Although the authorities were aware of the implications of such incidents, however, it was difficult, in individual cases, for them to prove any clear intention to undermine the war economy. Mass arrests of foreign workers could only have the counter-productive effect of undermining production further.[62] Nor could ringleaders be identified and arrested, in the hope of breaking up a political movement; where there was an active oppositional intention behind indiscipline it arose from a collective and tacit resolution to undertake passive resistance. All that it was possible for the authorities to do was to attempt to deter others by making an example of those who were 'particularly unwilling to work' (*arbeitsunwillig*).[63] In the case of German workers, especially women, the regime was forced to proceed even more cautiously: only one worker in 10,000 was arrested for a labour discipline offence in Germany in 1943, and if more women came to the attention of the Gestapo it was because employers felt that forcing women to work was too sensitive an issue to be dealt with internally.[64]

Sabotage and resistance

During the early years of the war the caution of the authorities was even extended to responses to deliberate acts of sabotage. Although it eventually became very clear that covert sabotage was a widespread and systematic response to the suppression of legitimate forms of protest, 'industrial accidents' were for a long time classified by the Gestapo under the rubric 'other' (*Sonstiges*) at the end of their daily reports.[65] At the end of May 1941 three very different cases came to the attention of the Vienna Gestapo at the same time. On 23 May the safety valves of a steam engine were found to be deliberately blocked, a personal act of revenge or even a practical joke was suspected, but not industrial sabotage, since the loss of the engine would have had only a limited effect on production. The next day 200,000 hand grenades exploded at a munitions store in Lower Austria, burning down entirely a nearby barracks which had been used to store machines, damaging several other buildings and causing total damage costing RM 150,000 to RM 200,000. The cause of the explosion was unknown. On the same day there were two train crashes in Lower Austria, resulting in the death of an inspector on one train, the destruction of several goods wagons and an eight-hour interruption in rail traffic. Again the Gestapo recorded that no indications of sabotage had yet been established.[66]

The number of accidents possibly originating in sabotage increased after the outbreak of war, and an average of three per week were being reported in Vienna and Lower Austria by 1941. In addition, unusually high levels of frequency of certain types of 'accident' suggested a pattern: fires, including the burning of hay stacks (in season); faults with industrial machinery, which were often traced to a (literal) spanner – or other object – in the works; and above all railway accidents. The latter were the most frequently reported, the most suspicious, and the most dramatic of 'industrial accidents'. The most successful sabotage went undetected or was difficult to attribute. Sabotage by railway workers did not always mean a train crash, for example, and where police found evidence of incitement in underground propaganda, it suggested wasting time rather than causing derailments or collisions; and there were, of course, other possibilities, as effective as they were subtle, such as the switching of destination plates on rolling stock.[67]

But there was, in the end, an extraordinary number of derailments, many of them with disproportionately serious consequences. In September 1941, for example, an engine shunting rolling stock derailed at Vienna's Leopoldau station, which was not an unusually serious accident in itself; but the derailment took place next to five wagons of petrol and two of hay, all of which were engulfed by a fire which had spread from the derailed locomotive. In other cases suspicions of sabotage were confirmed when the saboteurs themselves were more or less caught in the act, as at Breitenstein in June 1941, where two suspicious persons were observed on the railway track in the middle of the night at a place where explosives were later discovered.[68]

Transport workers were particularly well represented in active underground resistance groups. Many railway workers belonged to communist cells, and there was an extensive network of such cells on the *Reichsbahn*. In Vienna there were such groups at all the main stations, and at the railway workshops in Floridsdorf and Simmering. A further network was based around the *Reichsbahn* at St. Pölten in Lower Austria, the first major station on the line west out of Vienna. Activists at St. Pölten also had contact with cells in the municipal public transport system, and the network was extended into the countryside by the rural post buses, gaining footholds in places such as Krems and Waidhofen. When the network was detected by the Gestapo and broken up at the end of 1941, 166 members had been discovered in Vienna and Lower Austria, of whom 70 had been arrested.[69]

Municipal transport workers in both St. Pölten and Vienna were also often involved with the Communist Party. Tram drivers were identified as a troublesome lot, and suspicions were expressed shortly after the outbreak of war that the increase in tram crashes in Vienna – 18 in one evening in October 1939, was more likely to be due to sabotage than the blackout and staff shortages, as the drivers themselves claimed.[70]

Less frequently, there was quite open industrial sabotage. In one case a man was arrested for spitting a mouthful of water into a vat of liquid nitrogen, rendering both vat and contents unusable. He was charged with damaging war material. Even where the act of sabotage was not so demonstrative, it was not always difficult to find somebody with a motive: the worker suspected of damaging a centrifuge in a Schwechat factory, for example, had received his call-up papers the same day.[71]

Unexplained industrial accidents persisted, and by the autumn of 1942 the Gestapo had moved it to the top of its daily agenda and was taking it much more seriously. Sabotage was now sabotage regardless of the level of political consciousness, and 'personal acts of revenge' might easily lead to an arrest, as in the case of a 17-year old apprentice at Simmering-Graz-Pauker in Vienna, who was arrested in October for causing RM 350 damage to a lathe after being punished with unpaid overtime for failing to return on time from a holiday. On the same day an electrician was arrested by the Kripo in Mödling after causing an explosion and injuring a colleague by 'unnecessarily' switching on a 6,000 volt electric current. What might once have been negligence was now suspected sabotage.[72] Similarly, an unskilled worker in Engerau was arrested a week later for failing to remove a broken screw from one machine tool, and misusing another to such an extent that two to three weeks of production was lost. In fact sabotage now covered a range of behaviour and motivation, A Slovak worker was charged with sabotage after cutting up machine fan-belts to make shoe leather,[73] and an electrician from the *Semperit-Werke* was arrested in April 1943 for refusing to extinguish a motor which had caught fire during his meal break.[74]

Fires, especially in the countryside, caused extensive material damage. At Oberpullendorf, in Lower Austria a fire destroyed animal feed stocks, agricultural equipment and farm vehicles,[75] and in May 1943 a saw mill in Lower Austria which supplied timber to the SS was also destroyed by fire, and the damage was estimated at RM 1,800,000. A Czech driver was arrested on suspicion after other workers said they had seen him in the vicinity beforehand: their testimony seems to exclude the possibility of much sympathy or solidarity among the rest of the workforce.[76]

Devastating fires were not restricted to the agricultural sector, however. In July 1943 a bakery at Lillienfeld was burned down causing an estimated RM 100,000 damage, and French or Belgian workers were arrested on suspicion of arson.[77] Here, too, the meaning of sabotage was often clearly extended to include negligence. A fire in a Schwechat factory in September 1943 destroyed an entire machine shop, complete with all its equipment and semi-finished products. The cost of the damage was estimated at RM 325,000 and an electrician from the works was blamed because he had not attended to a faulty light switch which had been brought to his attention.[78] If evidence were needed that a concerted campaign of arson was behind such fires it was provided by a schoolboy in the rural district of Scheibbs who found seven bottles of highly inflammable liquid, with a note attached saying that they were to be used to burn 'German' material or set fire to factories working for the Germans, and instructions on how to use them effectively.[79]

Rounding up the usual suspects seemed to have little effect. Despite a crackdown on local communist groups the Gestapo were repeatedly

called in to investigate sabotage in the aircraft industry in Wiener Neustadt. A number of workers were arrested in the latter half of 1943,
principally from the Austrian Aircraft Engine Works (*Flugmotorenwerke
Ostmark*). The charge was often one of causing minor damage, and the
estimated cost relatively modest; but the sabotage of an electric cable,
for example, could and did put machinery out of action for a considerable time, as in June 1943 when an electrical fault resulting from sabotage disabled two machine tools for 20 hours. On this occasion,
unusually, a mature, skilled Austrian worker was arrested.[80] Most arrests
for suspected sabotage were of foreign workers, and increasingly so
towards the end of the war; it was not only that foreigners dominated
the industrial workforce, but also that Germany's military misfortunes
gave a more cogent purpose to their sabotage. Sporadic acts of malicious
damage, in protest against conditions and treatment, putting cables or
machinery out of action gave way to sabotage of the planes themselves.[81]

What had been sporadic acts of industrial sabotage now increasingly
seemed to be politically motivated. Two young Czechs were arrested at
the *Flugmotorenwerke* in Wiener Neudorf in November 1943 for causing
minor damage estimated at a cost of RM 1,600; a French worker was
arrested the next day, also for causing minor damage (the cost, curi-
ously, was estimated at exactly the same sum). Two days later, another
French worker was arrested, and finally a Czech mechanic was charged
with causing damage which had led to the loss of a hundred aircraft
engines.[82] An element of political symbolism in this wave of protest is
suggested by the timing of the incidents on or around 7 November, 'the
anniversary of the Proletarian revolution, of the establishment of the
Dictatorship of the Proletariat', as workers in the nearby Enzensfeld
metal works were reminded by flysheets distributed at the time.[83]

Nevertheless, the motives and the degree of political intention in cases
of ostensible sabotage are difficult to assess. A Czech worker was
arrested in September 1943 for starting up a machine into which somebody had thrown a piece of scrap metal (again at the *Flugmotorenwerke*),
and the Gestapo merely commented that since there had been several
similar cases the damage was probably caused deliberately.[84]

In many cases it was difficult to say whether accident, staff shortages,
indifference or intended sabotage had been instrumental. Sabotage is,
after all, intentionally invisible by definition. In other cases, of course,
there was no ambiguity: a shovel in the works in the case of a Czech
worker in a Lower Austrian sugar refinery.[85]

Certainly, there were fewer arrests for sabotage than reported incidents, and fewer still were charged with the offence, rarely more than
one a month in Vienna and Lower Danube during 1943.[86] For those

who were, and especially for foreign workers, the punishments were of 'exemplary brutality';[87] and of course, many of the suspected saboteurs in Austria were foreigners, above all Czechs.

Both the Allies and the Communist Party hoped to be able to exploit the disaffection of foreign workers and Allied radio broadcasts encouraged them to stop work, sabotage their machinery, leave the cities and form resistance bands in the country.[88] Although there was no sudden wave of resistance in response to such broadcasts, national resistance groups were built up by foreign workers. The most active were Czech, Polish and other east European workers. The Vienna Gestapo rounded up a number of Serb resisters at the beginning of 1943, and established the existence of two important national resistance groups in the autumn of that year. One was the 'Eastern Workers' Anti-Hitler Movement'. which already had members among Soviet workers in Vienna and Lower Danube. The movement's programme declared its intention to overthrow the 'Hitler government', to perpetrate acts of sabotage, to form partisan units, and to 'erect an Austrian state on a socialist-communist basis'. This would be achieved largely through terrorist groups which would dispose of leading politicians and businessmen, blow up targets of military importance; production for the war was to be 'crippled' by the disruption of work in industry.

At the same time the Gestapo discovered a Ukrainian nationalist group whose principal objective was the establishment of an independent Ukrainian state, and the 'annihilation' of foreign colonisation of the land. (Interestingly, the new Ukrainian state would be a one-party nationalist dictatorship, which would return the land to private ownership, but retain central government control over nationalised industries.) A number of these Ukrainian nationalists were arrested by the Gestapo at the beginning of the following year. By the spring of 1944 the Gestapo was also aware of Dutch, Norwegian and above all French involvement in national resistance movements.

Agitation and unrest among foreigners anywhere in occupied Austria paled into insignificance, however, in comparison with the partisan activity in 'South Carinthia', 'Lower Styria' and 'Upper Carniola'. These districts, formerly part of Slovenia, had been incorporated directly into the Reich after the defeat of Yugoslavia in 1941,[89] and their annexation had brought the guerrilla warfare seen in many parts of occupied Europe into the Reich itself.[90]

The partisans were for the most part Slovenes, although there was some involvement on the part of Austrian Communists from Styria and Carinthia; and their activities remained very much restricted to the newly incorporated districts of 1941, although there were some operations in linguistically mixed districts in the south of Austrian Carinthia. Partisan activities did not become the overriding concern of the local authorities, but they presented a persistent problem, meriting particular attention in every report submitted between 1941 and the end of the war by the authorities supervising the local armaments industries.[91] The guerrillas disrupted the local economy in a number of ways. Gangs of armed men raided the villages, rounding up local men for service in the resistance (such expeditions were referred to by the Nazi authorities as 'forced recruitments': *Zwangsrekrutierungen*); farms, shops and offices were plundered for supplies; and factories, power lines, railways and other installations attacked or sabotaged. The 'recruitment' exercises exacerbated the labour shortages and discipline problems experienced by the industries of the area, and the sabotage threatened supply lines from the Balkans. In short, the activities of the partisan gangs threatened to undermine the economic rationale of the annexation. In addition they also threatened to carry the instability of the new territories into Styria and Carinthia proper.[92]

Here in south-eastern Austria the activity of Austrian Communists was as often as not directed from Ljubljana or Belgrade as from Vienna, and there were strong links between the KPÖ and the communist-dominated Slovene Liberation Front (*Osvobodilna fronta*, OF). Communist partisans were operating successfully during the last months of the war both in Styria and elsewhere, notably in the Salzkammergut.[93]

Communist guerrilla warfare was one fragment of an Austrian resistance movement which drew closer together in the last years of the war. It never became a convincingly national resistance, however, despite the tremendous reinforcement of a separate sense of Austrian national identity effected by the occupation of Austria (and more forcefully by the defeat of Nazi Germany in the war). The Gestapo distinguished quite clearly between communist or Marxist (i.e. social democratic) resistance and the 'reactionary' resistance of legitimists and Roman Catholics (both clergy and laity) which was particularly important in Austria, and frequently regarded as a greater threat than the resistance of the Left, particularly in the countryside.

In numerical terms, however, the Communist Party was by far the most significant anti-Nazi resistance movement in Austria during the war. Active political resistance was not a mass movement, but working-class support far outstripped that of other social groups, and its wider resonance in working-class communities was more extensive still. Active members of the communist resistance persisted with their underground activities: principally the recruitment of new members, the dissemination of propaganda and the collection of donations for the relief fund.[94] And while the relief funds appealed directly and successfully to a sense of solidarity within working-class communities, political slogans and dissident graffiti found on factory walls, although generally originated by the Communist Party, were widely used as offensive shorthand protests by other workers. Although they attributed them to the activities of marginalised political activists, the authorities were aware that such slogans were also used as expressions of resentment or frustration by non-political workers. 'Heil Hitler!' became 'Heil Stalin!' and 'Hitler verrecke!' recalled 'Juda verrecke': anti-Nazi slogans referred, whether unwittingly or with conscious sarcasm, to the Nazis' own sloganeering.

Whatever indications there are of a continued political antipathy to Nazism, however, there was no political rebellion. More importantly, workers were compelled to adopt covert strategies in order to oppose attempts by employers and state to re-order class relations in industry at their expense. In this conflict, unspoken as it was in public, workers had two advantages: their bargaining power in what was increasingly a seller's market in labour; and the Nazis' own nervousness of incurring widespread popular antagonism during the war. This enabled them to win limited concessions. Ultimately, however, such 'functional' resistance to Nazi policy was marginal to the concerns of both industry and of the regime itself, when compared with the difficulties of labour and raw materials shortages, and the emergencies of the war.

5 Popular opinion and political protest in working-class communities

Much of the discussion in the preceding chapters has shown that the concept of the *Betriebsgemeinschaft* ('factory community'), which was at the centre of Nazi industrial relations policy, was little more than an artificial construct used by Nazi ideology and propaganda to cover the persistent underlying conflicts in industrial relations during the Third Reich. In this respect the experience of Austria was not significantly different from that of the rest of 'Greater Germany'. The relationship between employers and workers was a tense one, and the decisive factor in maintaining industrial peace was repression. The *'Betriebsgemeinschaft'* was, of course, merely an extension of the more general ideological construct of the *Volksgemeinschaft* ('national community'), and relations in the workplace reflected similar relationships outside.

The aim of the 'national community' (as of the 'factory community'), was to transcend, or more realistically, to neutralise social conflicts and create a society whose first loyalty would be to the racially determined nation (*Volk*) rather than to any particular interest. Existing loyalties to class, confession and region presented natural barriers to the creation of such a community and to the development of the *völkisch* consciousness which would sustain it, and the regime sought to break them down, not least by discouraging the development of any form of solidaristic association within working-class communities. Of course, the restrictions on freedom of expression and assembly which this entailed were not limited either to the industrial working class or to the political Left, but it was from this quarter that serious opposition was most feared: workers, in view of their numbers, cohesion and political sympathies, were still potentially Nazism's most serious opponents. Other than in official propaganda the 'national community' never became any more of a reality than the 'factory community', but an uneasy social peace was maintained, and remained more or less intact even during the war. The basis of this precarious stability is much more elusive. It is difficult to say whether it reflected a general consensus in support of the regime punctuated only by sporadic outbursts of dissent, or whether a broader opposition, suggestive of a general rejection of Nazism, was simply suppressed by force or by the threat of force.[1]

What follows is an attempt to assess what was revealed by the extensive surveillance of working-class communities undertaken by the regime and its agents. The Nazis, like others before them, suppressed public opinion but then found it necessary to eavesdrop on the silenced with the aid of police spy networks and civilian informants willing to denounce their neighbours in a tradition established and developed over a number of centuries by a variety of modern political systems.[2] A number of agencies was concerned with the surveillance of opinion, either in order to suppress dissent, as in the case of the Gestapo, or to assess the popular mood and civilian morale, as in the case of the SD and the judicial authorities. The result of their observations is at best an approximation of popular attitudes, weighted towards the opinions of those who volunteered them most readily in public, and determined by a number of incidental factors. The most vociferous political opinions were most likely to be heard in public houses, one of the most important public spaces occupied by working-class men; but in this context they were often unlikely to be either as moderate or as cogently argued as they might have been.[3] Opinions expressed in shops and markets, mainly but not only by women, were often related more directly to everyday issues, such as prices, food shortages and the other deprivations of wartime. Public transport was often also a forum for the exchange of opinion.

Although we may be able to sketch the salient features of political opinion and social attitudes in working-class communities, we should always be aware that attitudes changed, and that in any case the rejection of particular policies did not necessarily mean the rejection of *all* government policy or even of the Nazi *Weltanschauung* in general, still less of the government as such. Full employment notwithstanding, the focus of much of the resentment among workers and their families was generated by material grievances and although older workers may have generalised such issues into a more comprehensive disagreement with the government and its politics, they were not necessarily ready to question constituted authority fundamentally. Similarly, although there was a wide measure of sympathy and support for the Communists, and provocatively pro-Soviet comparisons were often made with the workers' lot in Russia, this did not mean that there was significant support for a revolutionary upheaval of society on the Bolshevik model. 'Heil Stalin!' could be as bogus as 'Heil Hitler!', albeit in a different way.

It will not be surprising, either, that many of the Nazis' social and cultural values were shared by much broader sections of the population than actively supported the regime. Many people otherwise opposed to the Nazis on political grounds nevertheless shared their antipathy to a whole range of 'community aliens' (*Gemeinschaftsfremde*) who were persecuted by the regime, but were already stigmatised to some degree by society (such as 'asocials' or homosexuals).[4] Casual anti-semitism clearly extended far beyond the Nazi movement, as did Nazi attitudes to the role of women, abortion, sexual promiscuity and a whole range of issues. Nor were the petty bigotries which society shared with the Nazis primarily 'popular' prejudices, characteristic only or largely of peasant or working-class milieus. They were vigorously promoted by conservative political parties and associations, churches, academics and schoolteachers, and sustained by the manufactured anxieties of broad sections of society about the 'enemy within'. Regime and society could agree on the limits of a notional *Volksgemeinschaft* by identifying the same 'misfits'.

Class relations in industry were reinforced, not transcended, and this naturally bore on workers' experience of the Third Reich as a whole. Workers were contained by, rather than integrated into, the new political order;[5] and despite propaganda to the contrary, few of the Nazi leaders themselves would have claimed that class conflict had been eliminated, rather than suppressed. Despite the apparent social changes of the Third Reich, the lives of most ordinary people were dominated by material considerations (wages, working conditions and the cost of living), and by the war.

At the same time there was no public discussion of the reality of everyday life. If perceptions of reality and attitudes to society changed, they did so to the extent that public perceptions, and society's image of itself, were monopolised and distorted by the official mass media. The Nazi propaganda machine, failing to come to terms with social conflict, talked about something else – the achievements of the Führer, perhaps, or military successes. It was a recognition of this absence of real public opinion that the regime felt it necessary to have regular and meticulous reports on popular opinion and attitudes, and popular reaction to its own propaganda.[6]

The subject of this chapter is dissenting opinion and oppositional behaviour, often unintentional, in the working-class community. The importance of this kind of dissent was its passive function as a barrier to the Nazi claim to total rule, its role in preserving the relative ideological immunity (*Resistenz*) of a community, in the face of attempts to impose Nazi values.[7] It reflected not only the persistent sense of a working-class community, but the growing sense too of a separate Austrian identity, which reinforced the resistance of Austrian workers to integration into any kind of 'Greater German' national community.

Anti-Nazi propaganda and dissenting opinion

The Nazi regime's effective monopoly of the mass media – press, radio and cinema newsreel – prevented any possibility of a free public opinion in Austria between 1938 and 1945.[8] However, this monopoly did not go unchallenged. In the case of the press, the challenge was an active one, and was mounted largely by the Communist Party and its *Lit-Apparat*.[9] The challenge to the more important Nazi control of the wireless was more passive. People listened to a variety of foreign radio stations in defiance of the law: Radio Moscow and the BBC were perhaps the most popular, but people in western Austria could receive signals from Beromünster in Switzerland and, before the fall of France, the French '*Österreichischer Freiheitssender*': indeed, the local police in Innsbruck reported that the most popular news programmes both in the town and in the surrounding rural districts were from Switzerland and Strasbourg.[10] With time, interest in the official news media dwindled considerably, and there was a widespread feeling towards the end of the war that bad news was being held back. In June 1943, for instance, the SD in Linz reported very little interest in the official news, either in the press or on the radio, while a fortnight earlier the local public prosecutor (*Generalstaatsanwalt*) had reported a sharp increase in 'black listening' (*Schwarzhören*), that is, listening to foreign radio stations, a phenomenon which he linked directly to the fortunes of the German armies at Stalingrad and in North Africa, and to the effect on morale of aerial bombardment in the west.[11]

The eagerness of people to seek out alternatives to Nazi radio broadcasts suggests that they might also have been receptive to the propaganda of the KPÖ. The Communist Party smuggled material from abroad and distributed it in Austria. (Here again transport workers, and particularly railwaymen, played an important part.) It also produced its own illegal propaganda, above all simple flysheets with minimal contents, such as short slogans or symbols like the hammer and sickle.[12]

In 1938 the Vienna Gestapo detected 5,000 of these '*Streuzettel*' with simple slogans like 'Down with Fascism', 'Hail Moscow', 'Austria for the Austrians' and 'Don't Forget the South Tyrol'.[13] In addition 127 flysheets and 1,005 pamphlets had been found, most of the latter before distribution. The Gestapo's calculations also took into account a handful of cases where the hammer and sickle had been scratched or daubed on windows or coins.[14]

Such simpler types of propaganda became more common after the war began, when restrictions on the mails prevented the party from importing lengthier material from abroad. In Vienna in particular, there was a marked increase in the dissemination of communist propaganda activity in the winter of 1939, but this was one of the most conspicuous and dangerous activities undertaken by the KPÖ and activists were easily traced by the Gestapo. By the end of the year, 119 party members from the *Lit-Apparat* had been arrested, and their eight typewriters and three duplicating machines confiscated. Following the Gestapo crackdown, which continued into the new year, the Communist Party was compelled to resort to even simpler means of communication: the smearing of graffiti on blacked-out windows, the carving of hammer and sickle signs, and so on.[15]

Writing anti-Nazi graffiti should have been a relatively low risk activity which dispensed with the material and equipment required by the production or distribution of leaflets and fly-sheets, but because even such simple operations were generally carried out as one of a number of activities of a formally constituted 'group of five', the appearance of graffiti put the Gestapo on the alert and often led to the discovery and arrest of several activists. In Hornstein, for example, on the road between Vienna and Eisenstadt, the slogans 'Heil Moskau' and 'Red Front', and hammer and sickle signs were found daubed in red paint on two occasions in the spring of 1939. The Gestapo investigated, and a baker's apprentice was found to have a stock of fly-sheets with the same slogans. Eventually, a Communist Party cell was discovered in the village, three of whose members had painted the graffiti. The other two members of the cell were thirteen-year-old schoolboys.[16]

Not all graffiti was communist propaganda, of course. Much of it was simply the result of frustration or spontaneous defiance on the part of people not especially involved in organised oppositional politics. The motives were often clear from the culprit's case history. In 1943, for example, a Viennese worker was charged under the 'malice law' for writing on a toilet wall at work:

> 'Da wir nichts zu essen kriegen,
> Lassen wir die Arbeit liegen.'
> ('Since we get nothing to eat, let's stop working.')

He had also written 'Down with the Hitler bandits, these murderous thieves and butchers'. The man was a forty-three year old skilled worker who was doing an unskilled job. He had been out of work for the seven years before the Anschluss, and was bitter about his wages, which he claimed weren't enough to keep his family. He was not an obviously political opponent: he belonged to three Nazi subsidiary organisations himself, and his children were in the Hitler Youth and the League of German Girls (*Bund deutscher Mädel*, BDM).[17]

The boundaries between sedition, provocation and frustration were frequently unclear. Where communist activists did not write graffiti themselves, they had often already set the agenda for the occasional protester, whose vocabulary of protest was probably formed by what he had already read or seen (and, perhaps, by what he knew to be the most irritating for local Nazis). There were similarly blurred boundaries between whispering propaganda, rumour and gossip. Speculation and rumour were rife in the absence of an open media system. During the war a great deal of information was either withheld by the regime or contradicted by foreign broadcasters, and this led to speculation and rumour. By its very nature rumour disputed the official version of events; and where it was not straightforwardly political in a more conventional sense, it was *implicitly* critical. This made it difficult for the authorities to distinguish between genuine speculative rumour and deliberate rumour-mongering.

There were also persistent reports of explicit criticism of the regime. These generally reflected fluctuation in the popular mood rather than subversive intentions on the part of the speaker, and to that extent they represented a degree of popular immunity (*Resistenz*) to Nazi propaganda, at most a passive or functional opposition to the regime. The Gestapo treated such cases as sedition anyway, since criticism of the regime was prohibited. The SD on the other hand, which was more concerned with the accurate representation of the popular mood than with the prosecution of individual offenders, was inclined to be more circumspect.[18] During the first wave of disillusionment and disaffection after the Anschluss in the autumn of 1938 the Gestapo in Vienna made large numbers of arrests for seditious remarks, generally drunken outbursts, and conversations in pubs, but also criticisms voiced in shops, trams and other public places. In terms of maintaining public support and confidence this seemed to be something of a crisis for the Nazis in Austria, and security measures were undertaken against known political activists. In another sense, however, it was little more than a crisis of adjustment, a cyclical trough in the level of support for the regime which would be superseded by relief, approval and acclamation following the annexation of the Sudetenland.

Many people, in any case, were unaware that their grumbling would be taken so seriously. If they broke the law in such matters it was often accidental and happened either through ignorance, or through frustration; and to judge from Gestapo reports littered with phrases such as '*in angeheitertem Zustande*' and '*unter Alkoholwirkung*',[19] it was often simply a side-effect of maintaining political contacts at the *Stammtisch*. Little wonder that in 1940 the SD commented in a lengthy report on

the 'insufficiency' of the Austrian law on drunkenness, and suggested
replacing it with the more severe German legislation.[20]

Drunken outbursts varied in length and seriousness. Some were long,
sometimes drunken tirades taking some trivial grievance as a starting
point for a general critique of the regime, society and any other subject
that came to the speaker's attention: the army, the war, rationing and
so on. Many of the cases that came to trial in the 'special courts'
(*Sondergerichte*) during the war were for expressing scepticism or disbe-
lief about news reports, especially from the front. At other times the
offence was a simple but unambiguous slogan, such as 'Heil Moskau',
'Heil Stalin' or 'Rot Front', and a string of curses, or uncomplimentary
remarks about Nazi leaders or local party functionaries. It is clear in
some cases that the speaker knew that a Nazi or a Nazi supporter was
present and that the remarks came from a reckless drunken urge to
provoke or irritate. 'Heil Stalin' and a few choice remarks about Hitler
were enough for a charge, even before the war.[21]

Not all drunken outbursts were quite so succinct, however. An
apprentice mechanic from Donawitz in Upper Styria was thrown out of
a pub at three in the morning before he could finish his beer – he later
claimed to have drunk nine and a half litres ('17 Krügel und
2 Flaschen'). The situation itself was not an uncommon one, but outside he launched into a lengthy diatribe:

They call this the national community, I've hardly been served and paid before
they call time and I have to leave the beer standing. I've been around a lot. I've
been to Italy and Russia, and the workers are nowhere as badly off they are in
Germany and Italy. In Italy and Germany a worker with intelligence can't get
on. We'll never have it as good as the Russian workers until we have
Communism.

There is little here, in the politicisation of an everyday grievance, to
suggest a new perception of social relations on the part of this particular
customer. Warned to drop the subject by another drinker, who left him
with the greeting 'Heil Hitler', he responded 'Heil, but Moscow'.[22]

The discourse of dissent varied from one social or political milieu to
another, and critique was couched in the 'home' ideology of the speaker.
Although the German Right had been at pains to demonise Bolshevik
Russia for a generation, praise of Stalin, the Soviet Union and communism were among the most recurrent ingredients of working-class critiques of the regime. This phenomenon seems to have been largely
unaffected by the Hitler-Stalin pact. Despite the confusion the pact
caused among party members about how to proceed,[23] workers continued to use Stalin, Moscow and the Soviet Union as positive symbols

in their language of protest against Hitler, the Nazis and Germany. Criticism and protest among members of other social groups was framed in other terms, those of Christian values, for example, respect for tradition or, less frequently, admiration for the liberal democracies of western Europe.

If the language and terms of reference of popular dissent varied according to speaker and context, the content varied according to the unfolding events. But here too there were a number of predictably recurrent preoccupations which were likely to attract the attention of the police. Chief among these were Hitler, the party and its functionaries, and the war.

'Führerbeleidigung': lèse-majesté in the Third Reich

Hitler's charismatic leadership was one of the most powerful forces for political integration in the Third Reich.[24] Many people saw in the figure of the Führer a national symbol, and accepted the image which he strove to present of gifted military leader and international statesman, aloof from the politicking of lesser politicians, and exempted him from generalised criticism of the regime and its policies.[25] Whereas the government and party, other leading Nazis and official propaganda were all frequently the subject of critical and often sarcastic comment, Hitler himself was often specifically excluded from such attacks. Following a particularly gruesome description of how the Nazis should be treated one critic concluded: 'Yes, the Führer is alright, I'll fight for him; but the others. . .' In a similar case, a timber worker from Upper Austria was charged in 1941 with repeatedly insulting the leaders of both government and party, but he had always specifically excluded Hitler.[26]

However, this was not always the case. It seems that in Austria at least a significant section of the working class was not convinced. Most of the personal insults recorded by the Gestapo in Vienna in the months following the Anschluss were directed against Hitler himself, and reporters coined the convenient abbreviation 'Führerbeleidigung', denoting a sort of down-market lèse-majesté, to cover a multitude of imaginative slanders. The Führer was variously referred to as a 'brown dog' and a swindler; as a megalomaniac and an idiot; and as a 'Lausbub' and a criminal. The same terms and similar ones were also used of other leading Nazis.[27]

Insults directed against Hitler were often obscene or scatological. Perhaps the two most common were 'Ich scheiße auf den Führer' and 'Der Führer kann mich amal am Arsch lecken', the so-called 'Götz quotation'.[28] The coarsest were frequently sexual. In 1934 Hitler had been able, by presenting the SA leaders as homosexuals living a life of corruption and debauchery, to tap a rich vein of bigotry which he exploited to enhance his own image.[29] When opinion ran against him he was condemned in terms of the social values he himself articulated and manipulated so effectively. One variation of the 'Führer insult' was the accusation that Hitler himself was homosexual. Indeed, a night-watchman from the twelfth district of Vienna was arrested in October 1939 after he claimed to have slept with the Führer.[30] Similarly, the Nazis' own biological metaphors were turned against them. An apprentice furnaceman from Vienna was arrested in March 1939 for his comment that Hitler and Goering were insects and, as such, should be exterminated.[31] It was also often said that Hitler was a Jew or a freemason.

In Upper Austria, the 'Führer's *Heimatgau*', the Hitler cult was a serious business. Braunau and, to a lesser extent, Leonding became tourist centres overnight, and occasions like Hitler's fiftieth birthday were exploited to the full. As elsewhere, opinions differed on the subject of the 'greatest German of all time'; but here personal friendship or acquaintance with Hitler might be claimed. In a fawning newspaper article an ex-schoolmate wrote of the early indications of Hitler's social conscience, which prompted him to share his sandwiches with his playmates until 'very often there was nothing left for little Adolf'. A woman from Fischhalm expressed a rather different point of view: 'Don't talk to me [about Hitler] ... I went to school with the Führer. He was already a crook [*Gauner*] then, as a ten-year-old boy. And above all he loved torturing animals.'[32]

If the attempt on Hitler's life in the Munich *Bürgerbräukeller* on 8 November 1939 caused 'shock, anger, and relief at the outcome' in many quarters,[33] there was scepticism and indifference in others. An SD report from Vienna depicted widespread shock, bitterness and sympathy for Hitler, but its language was qualified with interjections such as 'among the greater part of the population' or 'the entire National Socialist population'. The reporter also added that hatred of Hitler in the most extreme opposition circles knew no limits: 'In the Steyrwerke several people were arrested who had remarked that the attempt on the Führer's life was simply a result of his repression of the Catholic population.'[34] A mechanic from Wiener Neustadt was arrested on the day following the attempt for remarking 'Those lads deserve the iron cross'. Three other arrests were made, in Vienna for similar comments, and one of the offenders had offered to go and kill Hitler himself.[35] Where sympathy or outrage *was* expressed by known opponents of the regime, reporters were in any case sceptical, and by no means convinced that the sympathy was genuine.[36]

Hitler's image was built on the recovery in Germany's economy and international position, and for many people his leadership had been successful in both fields, and that was enough. But that was not true for everybody, and the Führer cult worked both ways. It was not that Hitler was very unpopular in working-class communities, but that he provided a focus for resentment and grumbling among the disaffected, just as in good times, and among his supporters, he was a focus for acclamation and consensus. Dissent had not been fully expressed without a gratuitous swipe at the Führer. A joiner's assistant and his wife from Fünfhaus, in Vienna's working-class suburbia, were arrested on New Year's Day in 1939. The Vienna Gestapo recorded that 'according to a denunciation FB has described himself as a Marxist, criticised conditions on the motorway [construction sites], praised conditions in Russia, and insulted the Führer by use of the Götz quotation'.[37]

It was not only or always workers who were critical of Hitler. Clerks, shopkeepers and especially peasants were also looking for somebody to blame when things went wrong (although these were the people more inclined to blame other Nazis or local functionaries). Most arrests for *Führerbeleidigung*, however, were made in working-class districts, and it was here that the criticism was most emphatic, most vituperative and most personal.

The little Hitlers: people, party and protest

Hitler was, of course, not alone in attracting popular criticism.[38] Indeed other Nazi leaders, above all Goering and Goebbels generally attracted more criticism than the Führer, and local party functionaries were often disliked for their self-importance, or suspected of giving and receiving special favours, of evading military service or of operating on the black market. Typical was the accusation made by an unskilled Viennese worker shortly before Christmas 1938 that a local Nazi Party housing official was guilty of taking bribes – and that, in fact, 90 per cent of the party were swine.[39] The widespread practice of impersonating party officials cannot have helped the image of the party. In the same week a journalist with a record of impersonating lawyers and judges was arrested in Vienna for falsely claiming to be an agent of the Führer and the director of the 'Austrian secret intelligence agency'; and a few days later a physical education teacher was arrested for wearing a Nazi uniform he was not entitled to.[40]

Specific criticism was also directed against the members of organisations attached or affiliated to the party, such as the SA and the SS, and many people had particular grievances against organisations with which they frequently came into contact, such as the DAF. In 1941 an unskilled worker from Minichholz, Steyr, a worker's settlement and traditionally an unassailable 'red stronghold', was sentenced to seven months imprisonment by the local court in Linz for insulting remarks about Labour Front officials. He concluded a lengthy diatribe about wages, conditions and the curtailment of workers' rights with the remark: 'All the workers are like Chinese, all we need now are pigtails.'[41]

Party badges, greetings, uniforms and other paraphernalia were found particularly irritating by the disaffected, and were frequently mocked and insulted. One party official was told 'You can shove your party badge up your arse, it'll not be long before you're done for. The things you lot get up to these days is criminal.'[42]

Criticism of individuals did not necessarily imply general opposition to the regime or rejection of government policies (although these were also frequently criticised, too), and distinctions were often clearly being made between Reich government and local party bureaucracy, between sacrifices necessary to the war effort and officious chicanery.[43] Particularly striking are the ambivalent and often critical responses to government and party initiatives launched specifically with the intention of raising popular morale in wartime: the Nazis' good works. Campaigns such as the Winter Relief Fund (*Winterhilfswerk*), collections of winter clothes for soldiers on the eastern front, one-pot (*Eintopf*) days and so on, were intended to mobilise people, to prompt them into 'small steps of compliance' with the regime, but they were frequently resented by those who felt compromised.[44]

They were also a reminder of the unequal sacrifices being demanded and made. A labourer at the St. Pölten aerodrome remarked that: 'the Trustees [of Labour] and the Führer should try working for Rpf. 83 an hour' and later, in a local pub had declared 'they should go and fight the war themselves. I couldn't give a shit for any of them, including the Führer.' Turning his attention to some SA men nearby, he had added: 'They're the work-shy ones. They should try picking up a clap-iron and a shovel and doing some honest work.'[45]

Above all, the Nazis were ridiculed by their clandestine opponents. Many of the 'seditious' remarks that came before the courts were anti-Nazi jokes or satirical rhymes, and the 'whispered joke' (*Flüsterwitz*) was a recognised and widespread from of oral propaganda. Ernst Hanisch cites a fly-sheet from the nitrogen works in Linz as the origin of the following rhyme, although it also occurred in other places, and seems to have been quite well known. Although it was probably

Communist Party propaganda, it did articulate popular feelings and reflect the widespread practice of using traditional greetings as a defiance of the Nazis:

> Der Pifke und Profitler
> Schreit nach wie vor 'Heil Hitler'
> Der Beamte mit Verstand
> hebt nur mehr stumm die Hand.
> Der Kaufmann in seinen Sorgen
> sagt wieder Guten Morgen.
> Der Bauer in seiner Not
> sagt wie zuvor Grüß Gott.
> Der Österreicher mit Courage
> sagt leck Du mich am Arsch. . .[46]

Finally, and especially during the war, this criticism was directed less discriminatingly at Germans in general: 'The Führer is a swine, Goebbels and Goering should be hanged, they are all for the Prussians. There's an uprising in Czechoslovakia, although the swine deny it.'[47]

One of the striking elements of working-class dissent during the war was the assertive opposition of young people. If the fascism of the 1920s had been something of a generational revolt itself, it now represented an institutionalised, inflexible and disciplinarian politics which many young people from a variety of social backgrounds found unappealing.[48] Young men came to shun the Hitler Youth, coming together in informal groups (referred to by the authorities as 'cliques'). Members of such groups were drawn together by a common rejection of official youth culture in favour of tastes and behaviour which comprehensively outraged the Nazis' lower middle-class cultural values. They listened and danced to jazz and swing music, grew their hair long and cultivated English or American accents. They also got drunk and 'practised moral excesses with girls'.[49]

Such groups sprang up in most of the major urban areas of the Reich among young people from different social backgrounds, and were not simply, or even primarily, groups of anti-Nazis; nor did they always share the same tastes, outlook and behaviour.[50] A taste for American music or the affectation of English accent were more typical of middle-class than working-class youth groups, for example, although both maintained much of the insolently sloppy dress and demeanour of the 'swing' groups. In any case much of this behaviour transcended the politics of the Third Reich. It was intentionally provocative, but both recalled the youth cultures of the 1920s and anticipated those of the post-war period as much as it arose out of disaffection from the Nazis. It hardly needs to be said that long hair, unruly behaviour, and modern popular music continued to irritate the older generation, the authorities and political conservatives long after the collapse of the Third Reich.

Similarly, the distinction between youth protest and juvenile delinquency is a fine one that is dependent on perspective and context, and it was in the latter category that the authorities were inclined to place the often violently aggressive behaviour of working-class youths towards members of the Hitler Youth (HJ). In March 1941, for example, the Vienna Gestapo noted a number of disturbing incidents in the working-class districts of the city. It seemed that members of the Hitler Youth on their way home from meetings had been mocked, and sometimes 'mishandled' by adolescent boys. In one case a shot had been fired, and on another occasion a few days later a group of boys had been stopped on suspicion, and again a shot had been fired. The boys later admitted that they had set out with the intention of waylaying Hitler Youth members. Seven adolescents were eventually arrested, all from working-class districts, and all were aged between fifteen and twenty.[51] There were similar incidents all over the city. In the Prater, for example two Hitler Youth members were approached by a gang of fifteen or twenty youths and told to take off their badges. When they refused they were beaten up.[52] A similar fate befell another member, not in uniform but wearing a badge, at a roll call of seventeen-year-olds who were being called up.[53]

Sometimes there were reprisals. Two Viennese schoolboys were waylaid by a number of Hitler Youth members on the Währingerstraße and asked if they were members. When they said they were not, a pair of scissors was produced, and one of them was badly injured while the Hitler Youths tried to cut his hair. This too was investigated by the Gestapo. A few weeks later another group of Hitler Youth members was ambushed and beaten up by young workers in Brigittenau.[54]

Attacks on the Hitler Youth were probably not political in the strictest sense, but they were as much gestures against the dreary uniformity and prudish respectability the system forced on adolescents as they were a part of generational rebellion or an aspect of a new type of late twentieth-century youth culture.

Hitler, the war and the workers

For many people, including workers, the successes of Hitler's foreign policy distracted from the regime's other shortcomings. Often, however, it seems that where resentment against the regime already existed, it was reinforced rather than mitigated by the experience of the War. After all, Nazi Austria was at peace for a mere eighteen months, and even that period was characterised by an increasing 'war-psychosis' and nervous rumours.[55] As war approached there was vocal and explicit criticism of what was perceived to be an unnecessarily high-risk foreign policy, and when the war finally broke out there were reports from 'working-class circles' of condemnation of the Nazi leadership, the war, the army and the Germans in general.

In the first week of June 1939 in two separate incidents in Vienna, a driver punched a pioneer and remarked 'You lot with the uniforms, you really get on my nerves, the whole army can. . .[kiss my arse].' and a baker's assistant insisted that there would be no war, only a revolution 'worse than the one in Russia'. A couple of weeks later a manual labourer was arrested for saying 'if they were all like me, we wouldn't win a war. The workers have been betrayed before and they're being betrayed now.'[56] Nor were such attitudes restricted to Socialists and other anti-Nazis. The Gestapo in Steyr expressed concern at the scatalogical tirade directed at the regime by a local SA man, a stormtrooper from the Führer's *Heimatgau*. He had ranted for fifteen minutes about the regime's foreign policy, an outburst triggered by the issue of ration cards in August 1939:

Ration cards are the best proof that we're going to war again. I fought for four years for this state during the prohibition period [1934–38]; I'm an SA man and a policeman in Steyr. If it comes to war I'm not joining up, I'd rather go to prison, to Dachau if I have to . . . The Ostmark, the Sudetenland, Czechoslovakia, Memelland occupied, and now it's supposed to be Poland's turn. The Sudetenland conquered? [At this point he shrugged his shoulders] No, stolen, or [in a very sarcastic tone] conquered.[57]

Equally, when war finally broke out, reactions were not universally or uncritically patriotic. A railway worker from Vienna was arrested in October for remarking that 'the Danzig case' was 'robbery. It would be just the same if the French were to demand Hamburg.' A tram passenger was arrested a few days later for remarking loudly 'We can't win a war with the Führer [in charge]. The French and the English will slaughter us.' In the five days covered by the report several arrests were recorded in Vienna for *Führerbeleidigung* or criticism of the war (often a mixture of the two).[58]

The economic pressures and material deprivations of war were anticipated from the outset: 'Hitler has brought us war and hunger . . . I regret that I come from a family where one brother is a National Socialist'.[59] A tram passenger from Floridsdorf was arrested for complaining on the tram that he had run around all day for ten cheap cigarettes: 'The bigwigs', he went on 'smoke the other cigarettes. And we have to fight for them, but not me, I'd rather go to Dachau. Why should I shoot Frenchmen or Englishmen I don't even know?'[60]

An assistant painter from Vienna was arrested in October 1939 for saying, among other things 'Hitler has brought us hunger and war.' Another worker was arrested when, after complaining about his evening meal, he added: 'Austrian workers are stupid, putting up with this sort of food. Everybody was much better off under Schuschnigg'.[61] A baker's assistant was arrested for saying that Hitler was a nobody, who had only brought unhappiness, and three office workers from Wiener Neustadt were arrested in October for writing a facetious obituary for bread. People were well aware, of course, that the burdens of wartime would not be equally distributed, and the perceived extravagance was criticised. Goering, naturally, was always a prime target when the shortage and poor quality of food were at issue: 'He eats a pound of meat a day while the workers have to go hungry.'[62]

An anti-German note was to be found in much of the criticism of the war. German soldiers were 'German Nazi swine' according to a Vienna kitchen maid, who then threatened that when the Czechs (!) came to power they would 'wring the German dogs' necks'. The German police and the entire German government were all idiots, she went on, shouting a warning to her friend not to speak to 'those German Nazi swine'.[63] In November 1940 it was reported that the chief concern of Austrians was where the next meal was coming from – 'Wo und wie beschaffe ich mir Lebensmittel' – and that they were worked up most of all by the shortage of fresh fruit, especially in view of the rumour that there was fresh fruit to be had in abundance in Germany. Railwaymen confirmed that wagon-loads of fruit were being exported north from Styria and Carinthia to the *Altreich*, adding fuel to the fire: 'In Carinthia the fruit trees were laden to breaking point with fruit this year. And where did it go? To Prussia of course.' There was a general increase in anti-'Prussian' feeling among the Viennese at the beginning of the war and incidents – improbable wishful thinking, in the view of the authorities – were related by the Austrians of Berliners being beaten up or lectured at length by the Viennese.[64]

State visits of Nazi leaders and their wives from Berlin were a focus for resentment: 'If these people from Berlin bring the English air force down on our heads, they'll have us to answer to as well'. Complaints ranged from the extravagant wardrobe of Frau Goering, who was supposedly having a number of dresses made in Vienna, to the buying up of prestigious Austrian businesses by Germans. The workers of Vienna seem to have been simultaneously irritated by the patronising eulogies delivered by high-ranking German visitors and disaffected by the unfulfilled promises of wages parity with Germany: 'To hear the workers talk, you would think the factories were on the brink of mutiny'. Again, as the reporter notes, this was wishful thinking.[65] Similarly a Viennese car mechanic was arrested at the end of October for remarking that 'nobody asked the Germans to annex [*anschließen*] Austria to the Reich. We always had work and bread until today'.[66]

Pacifists and conscientious objectors were dealt with severely, and 'defeatism' was equally unacceptable. There were reports of 'defeatist' rumours even in the wake of the Polish campaign. A manual labourer from Krems, Lower Austria, told an audience in a local pub that he was a flight lieutenant just back from Warsaw, and that the capture of the city had cost the Reich 25,000 dead; thirty German aeroplanes had been shot down over the city, there were almost no houses left standing in the whole of Poland, and the dead lay unburied in the streets. More explicitly defeatist were the remarks of a Viennese washerwoman who cursed the Wehrmacht and added: 'The Führer is a mason and should stick to masonry instead of bothering himself with things he knows nothing about. The Poles should have put out more eyes and cut more of our soldiers' throats, and then we might have a bit of quiet'.[67]

These remarks were made in the wake of a successful military campaign at a time when the integrative effect of foreign policy successes and military victories is generally held to have been at a high point. There is no suggestion that such attitudes were the norm, but if the office of the *Generalstaatsanwalt* (Public Prosecutor) in Graz was able to report in February 1940 that there was no change in the 'unconditional loyalty to Reich and Führer of the overwhelming majority of the population',[68] it is clear that there was also a significant number of dissenters from this majority view. Many were Viennese workers whose political background made their observations unsurprising. Others do not fit so easily into the predictable categories. In the Tyrol, for example and in Innsbruck in particular, criticism of Hitler, the Party, the Germans and the war was provoked by the same material deprivations and frustrations as those felt by the Viennese, but was more often than not couched in terms of Austrian patriotism, and even Tyrolean particularism.[69]

Despite the success of the campaign in the west, hostility to the war and its effect on living standards persisted. In September a former Social Democrat from the Vienna municipal electricity works was arrested for saying that Hitler was 'a megalomaniac, the greatest criminal there is, because he can't justify causing a war that has cost so many lives'.[70] Criticism of the war continued to be associated with the deteriorating standard of living: 'They eat well . . . and I have to work hard and eat dry bread. Poor people have to spill their blood because the others want war.'[71] In November 1940 a worker from Wiener Neustadt was arrested for telling a joke in a pub: 'Do you know why we have no meat? Because the sheep are at the front, the swine are in the government, and the cows go round with collecting boxes.'[72]

Distinctions were made between the Nazi leadership and bureaucracy on the one hand and workers on the other: 'Don't be so stupid, working so hard. The Führer is surrounded by crooks, and the civil servants are all crooks as well. They get paid for nothing while we have to work hard and sweat'.[73] Criticism also continued to reflect hostility to the Germans, and a growing sense of Austrian identity. A master glass cutter from St. Pölten in Lower Austria remarked in the presence of twenty soldiers:

Only the *Ostmärker* are real soldiers, without them Hitler and his German cowards would never have had any victories. We shouldn't have let Hitler march in in March 1938. Any one of us could have chased off ten Germans with a wet rag. But there'll be revenge for it. We'll lose the war and the *Ostmark* will be Austria again, and a monarchy as well.[74]

Such feelings were not restricted to the urban working class, of course. Anti-German feeling was probably even more common among the rural population, where it was reinforced by Catholicism. Certainly this was an observation frequently made by the authorities, and clerical agitation was often assumed to be the cause of disaffection in the countryside. When in 1942, for example, 'a certain hostility towards guests from the *Altreich*' was noted in a small rural community in the Tyrol, religious differences were assumed to have played a part, and 'black [i.e. clerical] agitators' were thought to have been at work.[75]

On the whole, however, this was the time of the greatest popular acclamation for the regime and for the war in the provinces as well as in the capital. Reports from Styria in 1940 speak of a generally good mood among most of the population, and fewer grumbles as a result of the 'great events of the time'. Communist cells had been discovered in Upper Styria, where it was acknowledged that real food and housing shortages were being exploited, particularly in industrial areas.[76] This was really no more than the regime expected.

Interest in the war was re-awakened by the invasion of the Soviet Union, and a resurgence of confidence among communist sympathisers:

Now we just have to wait quietly. Stalin is on his way anyway. Stalin will be ruling in a few weeks at the outside. Hitler will have to do everything Stalin says, and we'll do away with all those who don't suit us. It'll be much better then. Then we can start living.[77]

There was also a feeling that this was a turning point in the war. An unskilled worker from Amstetten, Lower Austria remarked 'I always said we would lose the war, and now we will'. In July another unskilled worker from St. Pölten was arrested for telling his work mates two days after the invasion that Russia and America (!) would win the war, that the Russians would use poison gas, and that he would go over to them as soon as he was sent to the eastern front.[78] This new wave of defeatism was combined with growing anti-German feeling, assertively articulated by a fifty-year-old female factory worker:

The Russians will win the war yet... The Germans have always been bar-barians. You can tell that from our case. Before, we had everything, but since the Krauts [*Pifke*] have been here we get shit. What do we need the Nazi scoundrels for anyway? I don't want to know anything about them. I feel sick when I see them. What have we ever got from Hitler? He's only brought us poverty and misery.[79]

The effect of the Russian campaign on popular opinion was also felt even in the relatively conservative western provinces. The number of so-called cases tried for 'malice' (*Heimtückeverfahren*) increased notice-ably from the beginning of July 1941, and it was reported from Salzburg that 'a whole circle of people', 'evidently former Communists', had dared to show their convictions in public again.[80] Otherwise the general feeling of the local population was one of unease about war on the east-ern front, and about the possibility of defeating Britain. The possibility of the United States entering the war was also depressing. Nevertheless, expressions of concern about the war could generally be successfully countered by referring to the Führer's successes so far, which 'often worked wonders.' Faith in Hitler, it was reported, was clearly deeply rooted even in the most habitual grumblers.[81]

Pearl Harbour immediately concentrated popular attention on the war again and led to a further deterioration in morale throughout the Reich.[82] Security reports began increasingly to adopt a tone of reassurance, reporting nervousness and criticism, but frequently balancing them with more positive reactions to better news. It was noted, for example, that the collection of winter clothes for the eastern front was a focus for critics of the regime, but that the success of the collection itself, and more encour-aging military bulletins, served to defuse popular criticism.[83]

A year later it was considerably more difficult to be encouraging. From the Tyrol it was reported that the popular mood was serious, as one might expect from the long duration of the war, but nevertheless still positive,[84] while a report from Styria recorded the disquiet felt by many people at the course of the war, both in Russia and North Africa, and noted a certain degree of war-weariness.[85]

Popular attention was focused on events at Stalingrad during the second war winter on the eastern front. Basing their assessment on a mixture of Wehrmacht reports, letters from the front and rumours, people throughout the Reich considered the situation 'serious and worrying'.[86] Reports from Austria reflect the more general anxiety. In Upper Austria the mood of the population was 'on the whole serious, often relatively confident and only partly depressed, in those circles easily influenced by rumour'. Those who had for a long time received no news from the front were particularly anxious, and their anxiety was compounded by news from others of the difficulties German troops were experiencing, difficulties which were played down by the official media.[87]

Stalingrad was also marked by the acceleration of a tendency among Austrians to distance themselves from Germany. While it was reported by the SD that people generally considered imprisonment by the Russians a fate worse than death,[88] it was reported from Austria that many people hoped that their relatives and friends had been taken prisoner or wounded, because it was 'widely hoped that Austrian soldiers [would] be better treated by the Soviets'.[89] Similarly, many Austrians also believed that only Austrians had fought at Stalingrad, and found it unbelievable that Hitler could have allowed such a thing. There was also resentment that the special sacrifice of Austrians had not been acknowledged. This distinction between Austria and Germany continued to gain ground after the immediate shock of the defeat at Stalingrad had subsided, and rumours of better treatment for Austrian prisoners of war were extended to the other enemy powers, notably Britain, and rumours of Allied plans for an independent Austria began to circulate.[90]

The regime's credibility was considerably shaken by the defeat at Stalingrad. In particular, there was less confidence in optimistic bulletins from the front, and from the eastern front in particular. The sense that the war with Russia was of a completely different order from what had gone before seemed to have been confirmed by the reversals of 1943, and scepticism, was widespread. This changing mood coloured responses in Austria to Goebbels' 'Total War' speech. Reception of the speech was mixed, but there was scepticism in all classes, and the strongest criticism came from workers:

What Goebbels says is idiocy . . . a worker who already works 14 to 16 hours a day, is hardly in a position to go to the cinema or the theatre. So what good does it do to go on about more cinemas and other entertainments being provided. It's just the usual eyewash. After all, you have to sleep sometime, if you've been grafting all day.

It was also remarked that the situation must be desperate, 'otherwise we wouldn't have been told'.[91]

Although there was some respite from news of military reverses during the early spring, Germany suffered more defeats throughout 1943. By April of that year there was nervousness about the situation in North Africa, and it was widely feared that 'a second Stalingrad' was on the way.[92] When the Germans surrendered on 13 May, the popular reaction was one of war-weariness and resignation. There was a feeling that the enemy had the upper hand. A worker from Upper Austria commented: 'Now we have to wait for the enemy to deal us another blow. It used to be the other way round.'[93]

Although the shock of the news from Tunisia was not as great as in the case of that from Russia, the popular mood was more depressed. The defeat seemed to confirm fears that a turning point had been reached; the Allied occupation of Italy was expected next; and there was no anticipation of another German offensive that year; there was little confidence in the effectiveness of mobilisation for total war; and for some people the war was as good as lost.[94] Morale continued to deteriorate, and 'faith in final victory [was] particularly absent now among peasants and workers'. When the defeat in North Africa was indeed followed by the occupation of Sicily and the fall of Mussolini in July, it seemed that events in Italy confirmed the turn in the tide of the war.[95]

Apart from the effect of news from the front, the course of the war raised other problems, and these varied in different parts of Austria. While reports from Linz were generally relatively optimistic, the authorities in Graz were becoming more and more preoccupied with the effects of partisan activity in the south-east, and air attacks in the south. By January 1944, 181 people had been killed in air raids on Klagenfurt and 52 in Marburg.[96] From Vienna concern was expressed at the overwhelming number of foreign workers in the city and an upsurge in the activity of the communist resistance was reported.[97] It was everyday concerns and domestic matters which dominated the experience of most people in the later years of the war: the wearying disruption of their lives, and above all the shortages of food and consumer goods.

The standard of living and civilian morale

In 1939, the regime was not prepared to risk the loss of popularity which serious incursions into working-class living standards might provoke,

Table 5.1. *Food allocation per head in Vienna 1942–1944 (kg).*

	Meats	Fats	Potatoes	Flour	Fruit/Vegetables
1942	1.58	0.99	15.70	7.46	8.72
1943	1.38	0.94	16.87	8.12	8.62
1944	1.34	0.85	13.54	8.63	5.47

Source: Butschek, *Die österreichische Wirtschaft* p. 99.

and withdrew its emergency measures as soon as it could; but this did not mean that there was no fall at all in the standard of living after the outbreak of the war. Shortages were felt immediately, and they hit the working class harder than most. But despite the grumbling, and the widespread feeling that the sacrifices of war were borne unequally, there was no threat of civil disorder. During the early years of the war, Austrians, as citizens of the Reich, were spared many of the privations suffered by the citizens of occupied Europe, whose resources were exploited by Germany. In the latter part of the war, however, the situation was reversed. As the German armies retreated, sources of plunder were lost, and the increasing shortages and deteriorating quality of food came to be one of the most important factors affecting public opinion.

There is little statistical information specifically on the food situation in Austria during the latter years of the war. Austrian agricultural production was strained by the flight from the land which followed the Anschluss. Harvests declined, as did some livestock populations.[98] Of course, levels of nutrition were not directly dependent on the success of local agriculture, but in Vienna especially, the war brought a change in the types of food being consumed. Consumption of meat, fish and animal fats declined, and poultry was unheard of by the end of the war. Consumption of eggs and milk also declined. The use of carbohydrates on the other hand increased all the time (table 5.1).[99]

In January 1942 it was reported that complaints of egg shortages were a particular problem in Austria, even in the provinces. In Salzburg and Linz it had proved impossible to provide the five eggs the ration specified, and there were also complaints from Salzburg about the quality of eggs.[100] The shortages were of course most acutely felt in large cities and industrial areas; doubts were expressed about the Reich's capability for economic survival, and comparisons were drawn with 1918.[101] Rumours of forthcoming reductions in bread, meat and fat rations had a direct effect on popular opinion. There was particular concern among workers with long walks to work, and among those with no access to the work canteens, where some of the shortfall in calories and variety could be made up (such as transport workers and shift workers). Working wives also pointed out that their households in particular used more bread since lunch hours were not long enough to prepare a warm meal. The situation could only get worse after reductions in food rations in the spring.

Every effort had been made to avoid reducing the ration, but in the end it was inevitable, and although there had long been rumours of such measures the news, when it came, caused disquiet, particularly in working-class areas, throughout the Reich.[102] The cuts came into operation on 6 April 1942. Reports from Upper Austria now noted resentment of the system and severe criticism amongst both farmers and consumers, and there were accusations and recriminations against those involved in collection and distribution. Eggs, for example, already in short supply, were being hoarded by collectors, according to popular complaints. Experts blamed this situation on the shortage of transport and collectors blamed it on the inefficiency of the system,[103] and when Darré retired, ostensibly on grounds of ill health, it was generally felt that he had been sacked for failing to get to grips with the deteriorating food situation. News reports of his illness were not believed.[104]

Similarly, shortages of clothes and shoes were so acute by the end of 1941 that there were complaints from all parts of Austria of children missing school for lack of adequate footwear.[105] In fact, there were periodic shortages of a whole range of non-luxury consumer goods which were either absolutely necessary (pots and pans, soap and heating fuel), or everyday items that had taken on a new importance in wartime: torch batteries for the blackout, alarm clocks, and storage jars for preserves and pickles.

The regime's aim of avoiding the widespread hunger and deprivation of the First World War became more difficult to meet as the tide of the war turned. Finally, the scarcity of food and material goods was exacerbated and overshadowed by the consequences of aerial bombardment as first Carinthia and Styria and then Vienna came within reach of Allied air forces.

Towards demoralisation and defeat

Any remaining doubts about the course the war was taking must have been dismissed by the autumn of 1944. In September Ernst Kaltenbrunner, a leading Austrian Nazi – he had replaced Heydrich as head of the *Reichssicherheitshauptamt* – gave an unsolicited assessment of civilian morale in Austria. The mood in Vienna, among all classes, was one of dejection and confusion and the city was rife with rumour from the

eastern front, where the progress of the Red Army seemed unstoppable.
Austrian nationalism, at least in its negative manifestation of anti-
German feeling, was on the increase, creating fertile ground for the
Communist Party. In the working-class districts of the outer suburbs
the mood was particularly unpleasant, and especially so before work and
at the change of shifts.[106] Successive situation reports from the last
winter of the war confirm this impression.

Austrians were particularly anxious about the approach of the Red
Army. The greatest fear was of an imminent Russian occupation, and
this fear was intensified by rumours of Hungary's capitulation, which
started in Vienna as early as October 1943. Morale in eastern Austria,
and particularly in the Burgenland, was severely depressed as a result.
There were reports of increased absenteeism from work among the
industrial working class in Lower Austria, and increased withdrawals
from bank accounts by the rural population: many people were clearly
making preparations for flight. There was widespread scepticism about
the usefulness of new fortifications: 'What's the point of all the digging,
when even the Atlantic fortifications didn't hold, and they were built
by experts?' Again there was an element of anti-German resentment, or
at least a feeling that Austria was getting a raw deal: 'Everywhere except
in the *Ostmark* they began the fortifications in time.' The resistance tried
to exploit the mood by demanding peace at any price, and this was a
line which found some sympathy among ordinary people, particularly
women.[107]

By November 1944 Vienna in particular was feeling the strain of
almost daily air raids, which disrupted business and industry.[108] There
was a widespread impression of defencelessness: 'Twenty aeroplanes are
in a position to bring the whole of Vienna to a standstill and there's
nothing we can do about it.' Workers were not prepared to remain in
factories during air raids and left at the first sound of the siren, refusing
to take up work even after the strongest disciplinary warnings. This
added to the general defeatism: 'What are the troops going to fight with
anyway if half the factories are bombed out and the workers from the
rest spend most of their time in air raid shelters?'[109] Vienna was increasingly perceived as a front-line city, and this impression was reinforced
by the streams of refugees from the war-stricken areas of Transylvania
and southern Hungary, who arrived daily either by train or in long cara-
vans of horses and carts only to be driven further west into Upper
Austria.[110]

In the course of the winter there were transport difficulties, problems
with the provision of gas, electricity and water, and shortages of coal.[111]
In March the SD reported from Vienna that all their local offices were

unanimous in their assessment of the popular mood: it was one of sheer hopelessness; most of the population were desperate, helpless and often indifferent. The underground resistance movements were noticeably more active and air raids continued to wear the nerves of the population. While SD reports attempted to put the best light on the situation, there was no mistaking the atmosphere of defeatism by the end of the year. The people of Vienna had a shrewd idea of what awaited them, the people of eastern Lower Austria and Styria even more so: 'They should put a stop to this damned war, all the murder is senseless.' The position of the Red Army was a topic of daily speculation, and fear of the Russians alternated with war-weariness: 'Whether I lose everything through the air raids, or whether the Soviets take it away from me is all the same to me'. Workers wondered whether they would be any worse off under the Russians anyway: 'Bolshevism is for the workers, they won't be killed, and being carried off won't be all that bad. You can't work where you want now anyway.' The conscription of women to the Wehrmacht also invited unfavourable comparisons with the Russians.[112] Finally, there was a feeling that when the war was lost and the Nazis had gone, ordinary people would still be there: 'We lost the war in 1918 as well, and we're still alive today.'[113]

There were severe food shortages in the winter of 1944–1945, and in the first week of March the SD in Vienna reported unrest among the working class as a result of the cuts in the fat and bread rations.[114] A week later the reports from Vienna's working-class districts were so alarming that Berlin asked for independent confirmation. For the most part these districts were no-go areas for Nazis who were regularly cursed, threatened and even stoned. Women played a leading role in the disturbances, protecting rioters and organising protests and demonstrations. Confirmation of the reports came from Nazi district leaders in Vienna on 2 April, by which time the Soviets were already at the outskirts of the city.

A 'national community'?

Were the Nazis successful in changing workers' perceptions of themselves and society, of integrating them into a 'national community'? Certainly, working-class perceptions changed during the Third Reich, but so did the working class. During the Nazi occupation seven years of social and economic change followed a decade of stagnation, and that in itself was bound to affect workers, regardless of party propaganda. Many of the changes were a product of the war itself: industrial expansion and labour shortages; military conscription; shortages of food and consumer goods; air raids. It was these changes which determined the ups and downs of working-class life and, along with the course and eventual outcome of the war, concerned people most.

Attitudes to these matters do not reveal much sense of a 'national community'. Significant numbers of workers were outspokenly critical of the regime and sceptical about its policies and intentions, and the criticism and scepticism went beyond areas of immediate interest to workers. Certainly there was some breaking down of class boundaries and class loyalties, but the majority of workers whose position had not changed, or seemed worse under the harsher industrial regime, retained an acute sense of us and them, the latter not only bosses and bureaucrats, but Nazi party apparatchiks as well. This is reflected in the extent of satirical humour and critical comment about party leaders' lifestyles.

A variety of observers from Austria reported a diversity of working-class opinion ranging from the unenthusiastic or apathetic to the openly hostile, and Gestapo reports, which provide a rather closer focus on opposition to the regime, recorded open and often vitriolic criticism. Of course it is in the nature of such documentation that it does not record acclamation and praise, but the cumulative impression of the working class under Nazism is of a social group which was sullen and querulous. While for other sections of society at least the military successes of the Blitzkrieg years or the personality and much acclaimed achievements of the Führer, served to reconcile them, if only temporarily, with the regime, again significant numbers of workers dissented.

In order to achieve even the semblance of a 'national community' the regime had to break down the community of working-class sub-culture that already existed, such as it was. This it conspicuously failed to do. It crushed workers' political and social organisations, as it had done the trade unions, but there was no indication that in the absence of the *Arbeiterzeitung* the workers were prepared to look to the *Völkischer Beobachter* for inspiration.

On the other hand, the long absence of leadership and the coherent formation and expression of opinion by and within the labour move-ment did have some impact. New generations of industrial workers grew up without the traditions of pre-war Vienna; if they mouthed the slogans of illegal communist fly-sheets they often, too, mouthed the platitudes and clichés of Nazi radio broadcasts and newsreel film, more potent instruments of propaganda, ones which were monopolised by the regime from the outset, and to which there could be no effective challenge from the resistance within Austria (although the incidence of '*Schwarzhören*', listening in to the 'black wireless' – banned foreign broadcasts – suggests a measure of dissatisfaction with the official media). Workers were not integrated successfully into a Third Reich characterised by class harmony, but their social and political sub-culture did not emerge unscathed from the experience of Nazism either.

Conclusion

Our understanding of the history of the Third Reich has inevitably been influenced, and even distorted, by the many considerations of post-war political expedience to which it has been subjected. In Austria, not least, but in other parts of Europe, too (from Russia to the Channel Islands), the difficulties of coming to terms with the recent past have only too forcefully been made clear.[1] The relationship between the working class and fascism is one aspect of that history. The very complexity of this relationship makes it difficult to make sweeping assertions, but some points can be made with a degree of confidence.

The first of these concerns the experience and behaviour of the working class in Austria before 1934. Nowhere in Europe was as great a majority of industrial workers united as solidly and consistently behind its political and industrial leaders in a social democratic party and in social democratic trade unions than in Austria. This is not to say that labour solidarity was monolithic: the collective organisation of Styrian workers was undermined by unemployment, employer pressure and, arguably, by a neglectful party leadership at national level; and, of course, the erosion of party and union membership felt in Styria during the 1920s was experienced more widely during the depression.

The Austrian working class faced a determined political offensive from the Right. Its origins lay in a refusal to accept the political settlement of 1919 or the subsequent concessions to the Left in the fields of welfare and employment law during the period of coalition government between 1918 and 1920. The ability of workers to respond to this offensive was restricted on all sides. The hesitant labour leadership avoided open conflict for fear of losing what had been gained, while the economic position of workers deteriorated to the extent that when conflict finally came few felt certain enough of the outcome to put their livelihoods on the line.

Yet before the debacle of 1934 support for the Social Democrats in Austria held up extraordinarily well. In so far as they were successful at all during the 1920s, radical right-wing and fascist groups (*Heimwehren,*

DNSAP and NSDAP) found little response among industrial workers, and were able to make only marginal inroads into the social democratic electorate during the depression itself. Electoral support for the Christian Social Party, on the other hand, and above all for the German Nationalists, crumbled around them in a matter of months.

The government's response to its own party's electoral losses was to impose an authoritarian political settlement. Parliament was suspended on a thin procedural pretext, local elections postponed indefinitely, and eventually after a prolonged and violent conflict between workers and government security forces, a fascist constitution was promulgated. Apart from the much longer civil war in Spain, the Austrian working class mounted the most determined resistance in Europe to a fascist take-over of power. It was a significant conflict in a number of ways. Radical rhetoric in the 1920s had discussed open conflict with the Right as a measure of last resort, as if the workers in arms might reluctantly have to impose the dictatorship of the proletariat. Instead they had been quickly and completely defeated, as party leaders had expected they would be. That they had been defeated by the sheer superiority of the government's arms was a point that was not lost on workers.

It was only in the wake of this dramatic defeat and in the course of the punitive reprisals which followed it, that the social democratic *Lager* collapsed. With the leadership disabled and members disorientated, there were substantial defections to the Communists, and in a few cases to the Nazis. Despite the admonitions of socialist leaders some workers perceived the Nazi Party primarily as a radical anti-clerical party more opposed to the government than to workers' interests. There were, of course, also working-class fascists in Austria, and we should not be surprised by the phenomenon: there have been right-wing workers in all European societies since industrialisation. Many of those now supporting fascism had defected along with other Conservatives from more mainstream parties of the Right.

In so far as there was a coherent strategy common to both Revolutionary Socialists and Communists in the wake of the debacle of 1934, it was a flexible one whose aim was the maximum defence of workers' interests within the bounds of possibility. These bounds were set by the government, and if there was still some restricted possibility of winning limited and localised concessions under Dollfuss and Schuschnigg, workers' freedom of action, such as it was within the terms of the Austrofascist constitution of 1934, were further curtailed in 1938.

There was much in workers' responses to Nazi rule that was recognisable from their behaviour between 1934 and 1938, but there were also important differences in the new political context. Firstly, the Nazi regime was both more brutal and repressive than the '*Ständestaat*'. The Gestapo intervened frequently and increasingly in industrial disputes. This was recognised immediately by the Social Democrats, who abandoned any further attempts at concerted resistance (although revolutionary socialist cells continued to operate, as did the Socialist relief organisation). The difference was also recognised by the Communist Party, which was forced to dispense with the services of known activists, and to refrain from the agitation in industry which might expose its resistance networks. That these precautions were justified was demonstrated by the repeated successes of the Gestapo in the surveillance and infiltration of communist cells, and by the frequency of arrests of KPÖ activists.

The difference between 'black' and 'brown' fascists was not merely one of degree, however. The Nazis' claim to be a socialist party of any kind was, of course, specious no matter how often they repeated it in their propaganda; but the new regime nevertheless differed politically from the old in many respects. The balance of forces between radical Fascists and authoritarian Conservatives was different, as were the traditions, ideological affinities and alliances of the two governments. Above all, the Nazis had given considerable thought to the workings of plebiscitary dictatorship, and recognised the need for mobilising support and eliciting acclamation, as well as reasserting authority.

Nazi repression was more intense, but better focused than that of the clerical regime. In public the Nazis were shrewd enough not to be openly contemptuous of popular sensibilities. They were aware, indeed, of the importance of winning over important workers' leaders.[2] It helped, too, that they brought with them the German rearmament boom. In a country where the effects of the depression had been exacerbated by deflationary economic policies throughout the 1930s, and where there was much long-term unemployment, the return to work had by far the most effect on the lives of the majority of workers.

Flattery and limited improvements in their material position were not enough to effect significant changes in workers' attitudes to the Nazis, however. Austrian social democracy had had considerable success in the political schooling of its rank and file. Political conflict was neither eliminated nor dispersed into a multiplicity of minor conflicts with no common denominator.[3] Class consciousness was still very much present in the attitudes and opinions of Austrian workers, and most notably so in former social democratic strongholds (especially Vienna), and among adult male workers, whose political schooling had been most thorough. If, on the other hand, open class conflict had been suppressed during the depression by economic insecurity it was now suppressed by force or by the threat of force. The threat of dismissal, unemployment and poverty was replaced by the threat of a spell in a Gestapo prison or 'work education camp'.

This does not mean that conflict was absent. Forms of class conflict re-emerged with the advent of full employment: workers sought the best jobs and the most advantageous terms. Job-changing in itself was not, of course, economic class conflict in the accepted sense; and it was even encouraged by employers prepared to poach labour for lucrative government contracts. It was politicised by the regime itself, through attempts to introduce state regulation of labour allocation and wage levels.

On the whole workers were kept in line, but were no less aware for all that, in the context of more exploitative, rather than more harmonious class relations, of 'what was up and what was down'.[4] It mattered relatively little in everyday terms to a worker putting in longer hours for less return, whether an *arriviste* was served by an aristocrat. Work and domestic pressures dominated the lives of workers, and it mattered more, for example, to working women with families and husbands at the front, that middle-class women still had domestic servants.

Responses to Nazism varied considerably, and much of the diversity was determined by the changing structure of the workforce. Veteran Social Democrats were not only the best-schooled, but also the most disciplined in a more general sense, in accordance with labour leaders' injunctions to maintain contacts and loyalties, but avoid open conflict and foolhardy heroism. Where they expressed grievances, they were couched in the discourse of trade-unionism, and where they attempted to take industrial action they did so collectively (and almost invariably unsuccessfully). They responded to unpopular government measures in intangible ways, through widespread absenteeism or deliberate reductions in productivity. They were not inclined to become actively involved in underground resistance movements on the whole, but were willing to express solidarity in other ways, such as contributing to 'relief funds'.

Increasingly, such workers were outnumbered by new kinds of workers: younger men, labour conscripts, recruits from the agricultural sector, foreigners and women. Such workers filled the new, often de-skilled jobs created by industrial expansion as well as those vacated by men called up to the front. Their behaviour was characterised by generally much poorer industrial discipline. Absenteeism and other forms of protest were still common among such workers, but there are few discernible patterns of response to government policy or employer chicanery. Women, who worked in industry in addition to running the household single-handedly ordered their priorities as best they could, and this was especially true of working mothers. Agricultural workers drafted into the booming munitions factories also had another order of priorities, as often as not related to the demands of the agricultural calendar, and they were inclined to absent themselves at seed-time and harvest. The traditions of the countryside constituted as effective a barrier to Nazi penetration as the political sub-culture of the industrial workforce. They were often ignorant of, or indifferent to the demands of the local labour office, not to mention decrees from Berlin, and they brought their obduracy with them when they took jobs in industry, that is, if they complied with labour conscription orders in the first place. Many breaches of employment contract that came before the courts were cases of failure by peasants (or women) to take up jobs allocated to them in the expanding armaments sector.

The apparent indiscipline of many workers was not actively and consciously oppositional at all. As Wolfgang Werner has argued, poor work performance might be a result of incidental factors such as lack of skill, inadequate training, or the inability of adolescents and older workers to match the physical capacity of younger adult men for manual work. Pressures from outside the workplace increased, too, as the war took its toll, as food, clothes and other goods became scarcer, and as Vienna and larger towns became the targets of Allied air raids.

Nevertheless, the level of indiscipline that was genuinely oppositional was substantial and significant. It ranged from individual acts of sabotage that brought the offender no advantage, which were defiant but not necessarily consciously political, to aggregations of individual acts which followed specific measures sufficiently closely for the element of protest to be unmistakable. This was the case for example, with responses to the introduction of German income tax, and to the War Economy Decree.

The effect of such oppositional behaviour is a different matter. It is difficult to argue that either the ideological 'immunity' (*Resistenz*) evinced by workers, or the disruption they caused in industry constituted an effective form of 'functional' resistance, as has been argued.[5] There is little indication in the records of the authorities responsible for the smooth running of the arms industries in Austria that labour discipline was a serious problem that threatened to impede the war effort. Their reports were much more concerned with the *allocation* of sufficient numbers of workers with the right skills to the firms where they were needed, and with labour and raw materials shortages. To be sure, the caution with which workers were approached by the government may well have affected the speed and efficiency of rearmament, but this caution (and, indeed, the extreme nature of the institutionalised terrorism which accompanied it), had more long-term origins in the paranoia generated by the 'stab-in-the-back-myth', and exaggerated fears of Bolshevism, than in the reality of fragmented opposition after the Nazis came to power. The mythology of November 1918, no less potent for being mythical, inhibited the government and prompted fears of an outbreak of revolution even after relatively mild expressions of discontent.

Only in one area did the arms industries authorities face exceptional problems. In the occupied areas of Slovenia the regime faced a campaign of violent disruption unique within the self-proclaimed borders of the Greater German Reich. Here, and in neighbouring Styria and Carinthia, native Austrian opponents of the regime, for the most part Communists and Socialists, had an effective vehicle for their own resistance.

This national element in the resistance to Nazism, widespread also in the attitudes of foreign workers in Austria was not generally to be found among the native Austrian population. Attitudes towards Austrian nationality were often ambiguous, and many Austrians were in favour of the Anschluss in 1938. The actual experience of occupation did much to dissipate any illusions about the immediate benefits of union with Germany,[6] but little to reinforce a positive identification with Austria. Indeed, it has been argued that the development of a genuine sense of separate Austrian identity is to be located in the post-war period.[7] To be sure, the KPÖ adopted a pro-Austrian line, albeit in the hope of forming an anti-Nazi popular front, but mistrust of communism on the one hand, and disagreements about the nature of a future independent Austria on the other, prevented the emergence of a national Austrian resistance with genuinely shared values and common goals. The Austrian resistance is a construct imposed after 1945 on the more heterogeneous and ambivalent realities of opposition, resistance and consent during the years of occupation; it has been a rationalisation of events determined to a large extent by the conditions of the Moscow declaration and the necessity of distancing Austria from a defeated Nazi Germany. If Austrians resisted they did so primarily not as Austrians, but as Communists, Socialists, Roman Catholics, Jehovah's Witnesses and so on, and this continued to be true up to the last months of the war. Links were forged, but there was a great deal of mutual suspicion.

If a successful Austrian identity has been established since 1945 it is thanks to the successful resolution of these differences, and not least to the economic prosperity which eluded the First Republic and put its 'viability' in question. The discrediting of the Right through its association with fascism, and the rapid recovery during the 1940s of ground lost by the Social Democrats to the Communists, did much to redress the real balance of power in the Second Republic. The SPÖ has been more centrist than its predecessor, reflecting a revolutionary change in the attitude of workers, effected not by the Nazis' failed version of modernity, but by a more successful post-war modernisation of political attitudes rooted in the 'destructive dynamism' and ultimate defeat of Nazism, in economic reconstruction, and in the effective integration of Austria into the political and economic order of the west.

Notes

INTRODUCTION.

1 See F. Parkinson, 'Introduction' in F. Parkinson (ed.), *Conquering the Past. Austrian Nazism Yesterday and Today* (Detroit, 1989), pp.11–13.

2 See Gunther Mai, ' "Warum steht der deutsche Arbeiter zu Hitler?" Zur Rolle der deutschen Arbeitsfront im Herrschaftssystem des Dritten Reiches', *Geschichte und Gesellschaft*, 12 (1986), 212–34; Jürgen Falter, 'Warum die deutschen Arbeiter während des "Dritten Reiches" zu Hitler standen. Einige Anmerkungen zu Gunther Mais Beitrag über die Unterstützung des nationalsozialistischen Herrschaftssystems durch Arbeiter', *Geschichte und Gesellschaft*, 13 (1987), pp.217–31.

3 See Robert H. Keyserlingk, 'Austria Abandoned. Anglo-American Propaganda and Planning for Austria, 1938–1945', in Parkinson (ed.), *Conquering the Past*, pp.224–42. Here p. 237; Günter Bischof, 'Die Instrumentalisierung der Moskauer Erklärung nach dem 2. Weltkrieg.' *Zeitgeschichte*, 20 (1993) 345–66. Here p. 358.

4 Keyserlingk, 'Austria Abandoned', p.225.

5 Ibid., pp.245–7.

6 Bischof, 'Die Instrumentalisierung der Moskauer Erklärung nach dem 2. Weltkrieg', *Zeitgeschichte*, 20 (1993), 350.

7 Keyserlingk, 'Austria Abandoned', pp. 233–7.

8 Bischof, 'Instrumentalisierung', 357. Gruber identified Austria not only as the first victim of the Nazis, but as the first victim of appeasement.

9 Ernst Hanisch, 'Gab es einen spezifisch österreichischen Widerstand?', '*Zeitgeschichte*', 12 (1985), 339–50. Here, 340.

10 *Rot-Weiß-Rot-Buch. Darstellungen, Dokumente und Nachweise zur Geschichte und Vorgeschichte der Okkupation Österreichs (nach amtlichen Quellen)* (Vienna, 1946).

11 Fritz Molden, *Feuer in der Nacht. Opfer und Sinn des österreichischen Widerstandes 1938–1945* (Vienna, 1988), p.7.

12 There was a certain amount of *Schadenfreude* in the German press. See 'Der Fall Waldheim. Österreichs stiller Faschismus' *Der Spiegel* (14 April 1986).

13 Parallels have been drawn with the 1970 election campaign , when the ÖVP recommended its candidate, Josef Klaus, as a 'real Austrian' ('ein echter Österreicher') as the alternative to the SPÖ's popular (and Jewish) candidate, Bruno Kreisky. See Michael John and Albert Lichtblau, *Schmelztiegel*

Wien. Einst und Jetzt. Zur Geschichte und Gegenwart von Zuwanderung und Minderheiten. Aufsätze, Quellen, Kommentare, 2nd edn (Vienna, Cologne, Weimar, 1993).

14 Fritz Molden's *Feuer in der Nacht* was the most recently published history of the resistance in Austria, and did this very emphatically.

15 Robert Knight, 'The Waldheim Context', *Times Literary Supplement* (3 October 1986).

16 Andreas Unterberger, 'Die Vergangenheit als Seifenoper. Das Anhalten der Vorwürfe aus dem Ausland verunsichert die Alpenrepublik', *Die Presse* (30 December 1986) p. 3. See also Oliver Rathkolb's introduction to Robert Knight, 'Einige vergleichende Betrachtungen zur "Vergangenheitsbewälti-gung" in Österreich und Großbritannien', *Zeitgeschichte,* 15 (1987) 634–71.

17 See Gerhard Botz, 'Introduction' in Robert Schwarz, '*Sozialismus der Propa-ganda'. Das Werben des 'Völkischen Beobachters' um die österreichische Arbeiter-schaft 1938–9* (Vienna, 1975), pp. 5–46.

18 Dokumentationsarchiv des österreichischen Widerstandes, *Widerstand und Verfolgung in Wien 1934–1945,* 3 vols. (Vienna, 1975); *Widerstand und Verfol-gung im Burgenland 1934–1945* (Vienna, 1979); *Widerstand und Verfolgung in Oberösterreich 1934–1945,* 2 vols. (Vienna, 1982); *Widerstand und Verfolgung in Tirol 1934 –1945,* 2 vols. (Vienna, 1984); *Widerstand und Verfolgung in Nieder-österreich 1934–1945,* 3 vols. (Vienna, 1987); *Widerstand und Verfolgung in Salz-burg 1938–1945,* 2 vols. (Vienna, 1991); a volume on Styria is currently being prepared. The earlier volumes on Vienna and the Burgenland are dominated to a greater extent by an 'institutional' approach. Later volumes introduce new approaches, but the discussion is still dominated by opposition from the labour movement and the 'Catholic-conservative' camp. There is rela-tively little on the persecution of Austrians from outside these two political camps.

19 See Anton Pelinka, 'The Great Austrian Taboo: The Repression of the Civil War', *New German Critique,* 43 (1988), 69–82; Emmerich Tálos and Wolf-gang Neugebauer (eds.) *'Austrofaschismus', Beiträge über Politik, Ökonomie und Kultur 1934–1938* (Vienna,1984). Gerhard Melinz, 'Die Christlichsoziale Partei Wiens. Von der Majorität zur Minorität und "Kerntruppe" der Vater-ländischen Front', *Wiener Geschichtsblätter,* 49 (1994), 1–14, represents something of a new departure in approaches to the relationship between the CSP and Austrofascism.

20 Hannes Sulzenbacher, 'Homosexual Men in Vienna in 1938', in Tim Kirk and Anthony McElligott (eds.), *Community, Authority, and Popular Resistance to Fascism* (Cambridge, forthcoming); Brigitte Bailer, *Wiedergutmachung kein Thema. Österreich und die Opfer des Nationalsozialismus* (Vienna, 1993).

21 See Otto Bauer, *Zwischen Zwei Weltkriegen,* in *Otto Bauer. Werkausgabe* vol. IV (Vienna, 1976) pp. 49–329 ('Der Faschismus', pp. 136–59). See also Bauer's unfinished discussion of fascism, written shortly before his death in 1938: Otto Bauer, 'Der Faschismus. Vom Weltkrieg', *Der sozialistische Kampf,* 4 (1938), 75–83.

22 See, for example, Carl J. Friedrich and Zbigniew Brzezinski, *Totalitarian Dictatorship and Autocracy* (New York, 1956), and J.L. Talmon, *The Origins*

of Totalitarian Democracy. Political Theory and Practice during the French Revolution and Beyond (London 1952, 1986).

23 Hermann Mitteräcker, *Kampf und Opfer für Österreich. Ein Beitrag zur Geschichte des österreichischen Widerstandes 1933–1945* (Vienna, 1963); Magdalena Koch, *Der Widerstand der Kommunistischen Partei Österreichs gegen Hitler von 1938–1945* Phil. Diss. (Vienna, 1964); Hans-Josef Steinberg, *Widerstand und Verfolgung in Essen 1933–45* (Bad Godesberg, 1969); Kurt Klotzbach, *Gegen den Nationalsozialismus. Widerstand und Verfolgung in Dortmund 1933–1945* (Bad Godesberg, 1973); Kuno Bludau, *Gestapo-Geheim! Widerstand und Verfolgung in Duisburg 1933–1945* (Bad Godesberg, 1973); Helmut Konrad, *Widerstand und Verfolgung an Donau und Moldau. KPÖ und KSC zur Zeit des Hitler-Stalin-Paktes* (Vienna, 1978).

24 Tim Mason, 'Labour in the Third Reich 1933–39', *Past and Present*, 33 (1966), 112–41; Mason, *Arbeiterklasse und Volksgemeinschaft. Dokumente und Materialien zur deutschen Arbeiterpolitik 1936–1939*, (Opladen, 1975).

25 For example, Wolfgang Werner, *'Bleib 'übrig!' Deutsche Arbeiter in der nationalsozialistischen Kriegswirtschaft* (Düsseldorf, 1983); Rüdiger Hachtmann, *Industriearbeit im 'Dritten Reich': Untersuchungen zu den Lohn-und Arbeitsbedingungen in Deutschland 1933–1945* (Göttingen, 1989).

26 See Tim Mason, *Social Policy in the Third Reich. The Working Class and the 'National Community'* (Providence and Oxford, 1993).

27 See, for example, F. L. Carsten, *The German Workers and the Nazis* (Aldershot, 1995).

28 Jack R. Censer, 'Editor's Preface' in David Crew (ed.), *Nazism and German Society 1933–1945* (London, 1994), p. x.

29 Peter Baldwin, 'Social Interpretations of Nazism: Reviewing a Tradition', *Journal of Contemporary History*, 25 (1990), 5–37. Here p.6.

30 Baldwin, 'Social Interpretations', p.28. The case for a (modified) post-structuralist approach to the Russian revolution has been made more explicitly. See Ronald Grigor Suny 'Revision and Retreat in the Historiography of 1917: Social History and its Critics', *Russian Review*, 53 (1994), 165–82, an essay which discusses revisionist approaches to the Russian revolution, and covers similar ground to Baldwin, while drawing different conclusions, *recommending* a post-structuralist approach as a possible reconciliation between an older conservative generation and younger radical revisionists. See also John Eric Marot, 'A "Postmodern" Approach to the Russian Revolution? Comment on Suny', *Russian Review*, 54 (1995), 260–4.

31 Alf Lüdtke, 'The "Honor of Labor". Industrial workers and the power of symbols under National Socialism', in Crew (ed.), *Nazism*, pp.67–109. The quotation is from Crew's introductory remarks, p.67.

32 See Tim Mason, 'Whatever happened to "Fascism",' in Thomas Childers and Jane Caplan (eds.) *Reevaluating the Third Reich* (New York, 1993), pp. 253–62.

33 David Schoenbaum, *Hitler's Social Revolution*, p. xii.

34 Crew, 'General Introduction' in Crew (ed.), *Nazism*, pp. 1–37, particularly the section on 'Workers under Nazism', pp. 2–13.

35 See Tim Mason's observations on this point in Tim Mason, *Social Policy*, p.284.

36 As defined, for example, by E.P. Thompson, *The Making of the English Working Class*, (London, 1963), p.10.

37 Mason, *Social Policy*, p.285.

38 See the discussion of the 'stab-in-the-back myth', in Mason, *Social Policy*, chapter 1, pp. 19–40.

39 Detlev Peukert, *Inside Nazi Germany. Conformity, Opposition and Racism in Everyday Life* (London, 1989), pp.238–42.

40 'Kirche, Militär oder bürgerliche Jugend', in the summary of Detlev Peukert, 'Der deutsche Arbeiterwiderstand 1933–1945', *Aus Politik und Zeitgeschichte: Beilage zur Wochenzeitung 'Das Parlament'* B28–29/79 (14 July 1979), 22.

41 See Peter Steinbach, 'The Conservative Resistance' in David Clay Large (ed.), *Contending with Hitler. Varieties of German Resistance in the Third Reich* (Cambridge, 1991), pp. 89–97. Jürgen Schmädeke and Peter Steinbach (eds.), *Widerstand gegen den Nationalsozialismus. Die deutsche Gesellschaft und der Widerstand gegen Hitler* (Munich, 1985).

42 See Martin Broszat, Elke Fröhlich and Falk Wiesemann (vol. 1) and Martin Broszat, Elke Fröhlich, Falk Wiesemann and Anton Großmann (vols II–IV), *Bayern in der NS-Zeit. Soziale Lage und politisches Verhalten der Bevölkerung im Spiegel der vertraulichen Berichte* (Munich and Vienna, 1971–1981).

43 Martin Broszat, 'Resistenz und Widerstand. Eine Zwischenbilanz des Forschungsprojekts'; in Broszat *et al* (eds.), *Bayern* IV, pp. 691–709.

44 Ian Kershaw, ' "Widerstand ohne Volk?" Dissens und Widerstand im Dritten Reich', in Jürgen Schmädeke and Peter Steinbach (eds.), *Widerstand*, pp. 779–98. Here p. 780. See also the following article, Klaus Tenfelde, 'Soziale Grundlagen von Widerstand', ibid., pp. 799–812.

45 Social historians have also produced a less monolithic and polarised picture of the Soviet Union under Stalin. See Sheila Fitzpatrick, 'New Perspectives on Stalinism', *Russian Review* 45 (1986) pp.357–74. Geoff Eley, 'History with the Politics Left Out – Again?' *Russian Review*, 45, 385–94, draws parallels with German historiography. See also Robert Conquest, 'Revisionising Stalin's Russia', *Russian Review*, 46 (1987), 386–90, one of many further contributions to the debate the following year.

46 Karl Stadler, *Österreich im Spiegel der NS-Akten* (Vienna, 1966), pp. 11–12.

47 Gerhard Botz, 'Methoden und Theorienprobleme der historischen Widerstandsforschung' in Helmut Konrad and Wolfgang Neugebauer (eds.), *Arbeiterbewegung, Faschismus, Nationalbewußtsein* (Vienna, Munich and Zürich, 1983), pp. 137–51.

48 6,760,233 in 1934. *Statistisches Jahrbuch für den Bundesstaat Österreich. Die Ergebnisse der österreichischen Volkszählung vom 22. März 1934. (Tabellenheft)* (Vienna, 1935), p.2.

49 See David Good, 'Economic Union and Uneven Development in the Habsburg Monarchy' in John Komlos (ed.), *Economic Development in the Habsburg Monarchy in the Nineteenth Century. Essays* (New York, 1983).

50 See Jill Lewis, 'Red Vienna: Socialism in One City 1918–1927', *European Studies Review*, 13 (1983), 335–55.

51 Ernst Hanisch, *Nationalsozialistische Herrschaft in der Provinz. Salzburg im Dritten Reich* (Salzburg, 1983) p. 9.

52 See Evan Bukey, *Hitler's Hometown. Linz, Austria 1908–1945* (Bloomington, 1986), pp. 196–201. See also Harry Slapnicka, *Oberösterreich als es Oberdonau hieß 1938–1945* (Linz, 1978).

53 'Wien im großdeutschen Reich. Eine statistische Untersuchung über die Lage Wiens nach der Wiedervereinigung der Ostmark in das deutsche Reich', reproduced in full in Botz, *Wien vom 'Anschluß' zum Krieg, Nationalsozialistische Machtübernahme und politisch-soziale Umgestaltung am Beispiel der Stadt Wien 1938/39* (Vienna, 1978), pp.589–637. Original is in the collection of the Statistisches Amt der Stadt Wien (Magistratsabteilung 66).

54 Ferdinand Tremel, *Wirtschafts- und Sozialgeschichte Österreichs* (Vienna, 1969) pp. 353–60.

55 See Ian Kershaw, *Popular Opinion and Political Dissent in the Third Reich: Bavaria 1933–1945* (Oxford, 1984), p.6.

56 The largest published collection of such sources is Heinz Boberach (ed.), *Meldungen aus dem Reich. Die geheimen Lageberichte des Sicherheitsdienstes der SS 1938–1945*, 17 vols. (Herrsching, 1984).

57 *Deutschland-Berichte der Sozialdemokratischen Partei Deutschlands (Sopade) 1934–1940* 7 vols. (Salzhausen and Frankfurt am Main, 1980).

1 AUSTRIAN FASCISMS, 'AUSTROFASCISM' AND THE WORKING CLASS

1 The classic exposition of this interpretation is Adam Wandruszka, 'Österreichs politische Struktur' in Heinrich Benedikt (ed.) *Geschichte der Republik Österreich* (Munich, 1954), pp. 291–3. See also A. Diamant, 'The Group Basis of Austrian Politics', *Journal of Central European Affairs* (18 July 1983), pp.134–55; and Melanie Sully, *Parties and Elections in Austria* (London, 1981).

2 See F. L. Carsten, *Fascist Movements in Austria from Schönerer to Hitler* (London, 1977), pp. 9–27; Carl E. Schorske, *Fin de Siècle Vienna. Politics and Culture* (Cambridge, 1981), pp.116–20.

3 The situation was reversed after 1945. The parties heir to the liberal-national tradition have generally been excluded from coalitions, largely as a consequence of that tradition's association with Nazism.

4 See Lothar Höbelt, *Kornblume und Kaiseradler. Die deutschfreiheitlichen Parteien Altösterreichs 1882–1918* (Vienna and Munich, 1993), pp. 66–78; Andrew Whiteside, *The Socialism of Fools. Georg Ritter von Schönerer and Austrian Pan-Germanism* (Berkeley, 1975) pp. 44–8, p.131.

5 *Volk*, like the Russian *narod*, carries different connotations from those of the word 'people' as the word is used in the political discourse of the West. As used by the *völkisch* movement it invoked a racial definition of the nation which was central to the Nuremberg laws and has constituted a sub-text of German discussions about national and constitutional patriotism and German citizenship in recent years.

6 See, for example, Bruce Pauley, *Hitler and the Forgotten Nazis. A History of Austrian National Socialism* (London, 1981), pp. 19–21.

7 Andrew Whiteside, 'Austria' in Hans Rogger and Eugen Weber (eds). *The European Right. A Historical Profile* (Berkeley and Los Angeles, 1966), pp. 308–63.

8 Carsten, *Fascist Movements*, p.18.
9 For a detailed discussion of the language conflict see Mark Cornwall, 'The Struggle on the Czech-German Language Border, 1880–1940', *English Historical Review*, 109 (September 1994), pp. 914–51.
10 See Gary Cohen, *The Politics of Ethnic Survival: Germans in Prague 1861–1914* (Princeton, 1981). Fears for the future of Vienna are articulated in 'Das Tschechische Wien', the transcript of an article for *Der getreue Eckart*, monthly journal of the *Deutscher Schulverein* (1908), Austrian National Library, 461591–C. See also Karl M. Brousek, *Wien und seine Tschechen. Integration und Assimilation einer Minderheit im 20. Jahrhundert* (Vienna, 1980), pp.23–4; and Michael John and Albert Lichtblau, Česká Víden: Von der tschechischen Großstadt zum tschechischen Dorf', *Archiv. Jahrbuch des Vereins für die Geschichte der Arbeiterbewegung*, 3 (1987) 34–41.
11 Georg von Schönerer, 'Los von Rom!' in Peter Pulzer, *The Rise of Political Antisemitism in Germany and Austria*, 2nd edition (London, 1988), p. 332. See also p.122.
12 Brousek, *Wien und seine Tschechen*, p.20; Hans Mommsen 'Das Problem der böhmischen Arbeiterbewegung', in Hans Mommsen, *Arbeiterbewegung und Nationale Frage. Ausgewählte Aufsätze* (Göttingen, 1979) pp. 166–79.
13 See Höbelt, *Kornblume und Kaiseradler*, pp. 242–7; Pauley, *Hitler and the Forgotten Nazis*, pp.24–9; Carsten, *Fascist Movements*, pp.31–9.
14 See Gerhard Botz, 'Strukturwandlungen des österreichischen National-sozialismus (1904–1905)', in Isabella Ackerl, Walter Hummelberger and Hans Mommsen (eds.) *Politik und Gesellschaft im alten und neuen Österreich. Festschrift für Rudolf Neck zum 60. Geburtstag* (Vienna, 1981), pp.162–93. Here pp. 167–8; Carsten, *Fascist Movements*, p.32; Whiteside, *Socialism of Fools*, p.278.
15 Lothar Höbelt makes the point that at the time, the Agrarian movement was numerically more important, whereas the DAP has attracted the attention of historians for what it became. Höbelt, *Kornblume und Kaiseradler*, p. 242.
16 Botz, 'Strukturwandlungen', p.168.
17 Pauley, *Hitler and the Forgotten Nazis*, pp. 32–3.
18 See John W. Boyer, *Political Radicalism in Late Imperial Vienna. Origins of the Christian Social Movement* (Chicago and London, 1981) Conclusion, pp. 411–21.
19 Boyer, *Political Radicalism*, pp. 166–80; Fritz Fellner, 'The Background of Austrian Fascism' in Peter F. Sugar (ed.), *Native Fascism in the Successor States 1918–1945* (Santa Barbara, 1971), pp. 15–23; Whiteside 'Austria', pp.321–4.
20 Jill Lewis, 'Austria' in Martin Blinkhorn (ed.), *Fascists and Conservatives. The Radical Right and the Establishment in Twentieth-Century Europe* (London, 1990) pp. 98–117. Here pp. 103–6 in particular. See also Robert Stöger, 'Der christliche Führer und die "wahre Demokratie". Zu den Demokratiekonzeptionen von Ignaz Seipel', *Archiv. Jahrbuch des Vereins für die Geschichte der Arbeiterbewegung* 2 (1988) 54–67.
21 Boyer, *Political Radicalism*, p.175; Lewis, 'Austria', p.104.
22 Adolf Hitler, *Mein Kampf*, translated by Ralph Mannheim (London, 1992) pp. 90–3

23 Geoff Eley, *Reshaping the German Right. Radical Nationalism and Political Change after Bismarck* (New Haven, 1980), p. viii.

24 On the party's response to the loss of authority in its Vienna stronghold see Gerhard Melinz, 'Die Christlichsoziale Partei Wiens'.

25 Carsten, *Fascist Movements*, pp.87–9.

26 Pauley, *Hitler and the Forgotten Nazis*, p.33.

27 Gerhard Botz, 'Changing Patterns of Support for Austrian National Socialism', in Stein Larsen, J.P. Mykleburst and B. Hatvet (eds.), *Who were the Fascists?* (Oslo, 1979), pp. 202–26. Here, pp. 203–4.

28 Gerhard Botz, 'Changing Patterns', pp. 208–10; Pauley, *Hitler and the Forgotten Nazis*, pp. 40–2.

29 Gerhard Botz, 'Introduction: Varieties of Fascism in Austria', in Larsen *et al.* (eds.), *Who were the Fascists?* pp. 192–9.

30 See Edward P. Keleher, 'Austria's *Lebensunfähigkeit* and the Anschluss Question 1918–1922', *East European Quarterly*, 23/1, (March 1989), 71–83.

31 Carsten, *Fascist Movements*, pp.41–50.

32 This had prompted an Anschluss movement which had encompassed all three camps to a greater or lesser degree. See Radomir Luža, *Anglo-German Relations in the Anschluss Era* (Princeton and London, 1975), pp. 3–18.

33 There was, nevertheless, a degree of female participation before 1938. See Johanna Gehmacher, *Jugend ohne Zukunft. Hitler-Jugend und Bund Deutscher Mädel in Österreich vor 1938* (Vienna, 1934)

34 See John Haag, 'Marginal Men and the Dream of the Reich: Eight Austrian National-Catholic Intellectuals 1918–1938' in Larsen *et al.*, *Who were the Fascists?* pp.239–48

35 Botz, 'Changing Patterns', p.206; Botz, 'Austria', in Detlef Mühlberger (ed.), *The Social Basis of European Fascist Movements* (London, 1987), pp.242–80. Here pp. 254–6.

36 See the address by Rudolf Kanzler to the *Heimwehr* in Salzburg, 7 March 1920, quoted in Carsten, *Fascist Movements*, pp. 46–7; see also Tim Mason, *Social Policy in the Third Reich. The Working Class and the 'National Community'* (Providence and Oxford, 1993), chapter 1.

37 Botz, 'Austria', p.258

38 Ibid.; Botz, 'Varieties', p.196.

39 See C. Earl Edmondson, *The Heimwehr and Austrian Politics 1918–1936* (Athens, Ga, 1978) pp. 59–61, on a report by the Austrian military attaché. Franziska Schneeberger questions assumptions about the predominance of peasants in the *Heimwehr* deriving from an article in the *New York Times* in 1929, based on this report, and subsequently referred to by a number of historians, including Edmondson, Carsten, Botz and Willibald Holzer. Franziska Schneeberger, 'Die Sozialstruktur der Heimwehr' Phil. Diss. (Salzburg 1988), pp. 52–6. The composition of membership in Linz and Upper Austria seems to bear out her point. Bukey, *'Patenstadt des Führers' Eine Politik – und Sozialgeschichte von Linz 1908–1945* (Frankfurt am Main, 1993), p.118.

40 Botz, 'Austria', p.260

41 Ibid., p.258. Some caution is due with all generalisations about the social composition of fascist organisations. Much information is based on

impressionistic or anecdotal evidence. Membership records are often not complete or reliable, and turnover of membership was often very rapid.

42 Jill Lewis, *Fascism and the Working Class in Austria*, (Oxford, 1991) pp. 150–5.
43 See G.E.R. Gedye, *Fallen Bastions*, (London, 1939), chapter 2, pp.26–38 for a contemporary account of the incident by a British journalist.
44 Hans Kernbauer and Fritz Weber, 'Von der Inflation zur Depression. Österreichs Wirtschaft 1918–1934' in E. Tálos and W. Neugebauer (eds.), *'Austrofaschismus'. Beiträge über Politik, Ökonomie und Kultur 1934–1938* (Vienna 1984), pp. 1–30. Here p.5.
45 *Statistical Year Book of the League of Nations* (Geneva, 1938), p. 65. Kernbauer and Weber, citing the *Monatsberichte des österreichischen Instituts für Konjunkturforschung*, 2 (1938) p.5, put the peak unemployment rate at 38.5 per cent at the end of 1934: Kernbauer and Weber, 'Österreichs Wirtschaft', p.1.
46 School leavers were excluded from claiming benefit. Karl R. Stadler, *Austria* (London, 1971) p.124
47 Marie Jahonda, Paul F. Lazarsfeld, Hans Zeisel, *The Sociography of an Unemployed Community* (London, 1972); originally *Die Arbeitslosen von Marienthal* (Leipzig, 1933).
48 Ibid., pp. 19, 26.
49 Jill Lewis, 'The Failure of Styrian Labour in the First Austrian Republic', Ph.D dissertation (Lancaster, 1984), p.246
50 *Statistisches Handbuch für die Republik Österreich*, vol. XII (Vienna, 1931), p.170. *Year Book of the League of Nations 1937–1938* (Geneva, 1938), p.72.
51 Melanie Sully, *Continuity and Change in Austrian Socialism. The Eternal Quest for the Third Way* (Boulder, 1982), p.109.
52 *Jahrbuch der österreichischen Arbeiterbewegung 1932* (Vienna, 1933), p.88
53 Sully, *Parties and Election in Austria* (London, 1981), p.123.
54 Lewis, 'Styrian Labour', p.236.
55 Free Trade Unions were 80.27 per cent of the total in 1923, and only 72.91 per cent in 1930. Hans Hautmann and Rudolf Kropf, *Die österreichische Arbeiterbewegung vom Vormärz bis 1945. Sozialökonomische Ursprünge ihrer Ideologie und Politik* (Linz, 1974), p.149.
56 These political preferences were also reflected in elections to the Chambers of Labour. See Botz, 'Changing Patterns', p. 209, and Bukey, *Patenstadt*, p.107.
57 *Statistisches Handbuch für die Republik Österreich* (Vienna 1932), p.169.
58 Lewis, *Fascism and the Working Class in Austria*, pp.154–9.
59 Sully, *Continuity*, p.44.
60 Edmondson, *Heimwehr*, pp. 97–9.
61 In the 1927 municipal elections the SDAP and *Einheitsliste* had taken 96.8 per cent of the vote between them; before this the German Nationalists had had less support in Vienna than nationally: 5.4 per cent in the 1919 municipal elections, and 4.9 per cent in 1923.
62 Bukey, *Patenstadt*, p.67; *Statistisches Handbuch für die Republik Österreich* 1927, 1931.
63 Edmondson, *Heimwehr*, pp.138–41.

64 Bukey, *Patenstadt*, p.67.
65 *Jahrbuch der österreichischen Arbeiterbewegung, 1932* (Vienna, 1933), pp. 110–17.
66 *Arbeiterzeitung* (17 May 1933). In the event the order was prolonged by a year, during the course of which the new constitution of the Corporate State was promulgated.
67 A new, detailed analysis of NSDAP membership in the Tyrol has been provided by Thomas Albrich and Wolfgang Meixner, 'Zwischen Legalität und Illegalität. Zur Mitgliederentwicklung, Alters- und Sozialstruktur der NSDAP in Tirol und Vorarlberg vor 1938', *Zeitgeschichte*, 22 (1995), 149–87. See also Sabine Falch ' "Legaler Sturz des Systems von unten her auf dem Wege über die Länder und Gemeinden." Zu den NS-Erfolgen bei den Gemeinderatswahlen in Tirol 1932 und 1933', *Zeitgeschichte*, 22 (1995), 188–210.
68 Botz, 'Changing Patterns', p. 212. The federal provinces of Austria were not equal in size. More than ten times more people voted in Vienna and Lower Austria than in Salzburg and Vorarlberg during the four Landtag elections of 1932. (Favoriten alone had a larger resident population than Vorarlberg.)
69 Bukey, *Patenstadt*, p.67; *Jahrbuch der österreichischen Arbeiterbewegung 1932*, pp.111–12.
70 Botz, 'Changing Patterns', pp. 212–23; *Jahrbuch der österreichischen Arbeiterbewegung 1932*, pp. 111–12; Bukey, *Patenstadt*, p.149.
71 Botz, 'Changing Patterns', p.212.
72 Jürgen W. Falter and Dirk Hänisch, 'Wahlerfolge und Wählerschaft der NSDAP in Österreich von 1927 bis 1932: Soziale Basis und Parteipolitische Herkunft', *Zeitgeschichte*, 15 (1988) 223–44. Here p.227, p.231.
73 Jürgen Falter, 'Warum die deutschen Arbeiter während des "Dritten Reiches" zu Hitler standen. Einige Anmerkungen zu Gunther Mais Beitrag über die Unterstützung des nationalsozialistischen Herrschafts systems durch Arbeiter', *Geschichte und Gesellschaft*, 13 (1987), 217–31.
74 See Ernst Hanisch, *Der lange Schatten des Staates. Österreichische Gesellschaftsgeschichte im 20. Jahrhundert* (Vienna, 1994), pp. 300–4. There is no real evidence that the SDAP were ever seriously considered as coalition partners in the 1930s, although the collapse of the German Nationalists made the possibility of a new 'bourgeois block' government unlikely, and the Social Democrats the only alternative to the Nazis in the long term.
75 Clear political antecedents to the establishment of the Austrofascist regime were already present in the 1920s. See Emmerich Tálos and Walter Manoschek 'Zum Konstituierungsprozeß des Austrofaschismus', in Tálos and Neugebauer (eds.), *Austrofaschismus*, pp. 31–52. See also Gerhard Botz, 'Der "4. März 1933" als Konsequenz ständischer Strukturen, ökonomischer Krisen und autoritärer Tendenzen' in Botz, *Krisenzonen einer Demokratie* (Frankfurt am Main 1987), pp.155–80. The government was urged both by industrialists and party leaders to take such a course. 'The German presidential regime could serve as a model.' Hanisch, *Der lange Schatten des Staates*, p. 302.
76 In a debate in parliament prompted by Social Democrat demands that the order be withdrawn, members were advised by the chancellor's legal adviser Robert Hecht that its use was legitimate, even in time of peace. Wandruszka,

'Historische Einführung', in *Protokolle des Ministerrates der Ersten Republik*, VIII, vol. I p. xvi. The cabinet noted Socialist concerns: Ministerratsprotokoll Nr. 828 vom 5. Oktober 1932, ibid., p. 596.

77 A British journalist reported a few years later that Renner's decision was challenged on the grounds that a socialist deputy had handed in the voting card of a colleague who had gone to the lavatory, and commented that it was 'a melancholy reflection that six million people lost their liberty because of the weakness of one man's bladder.' Gedye, *Fallen Bastions*, p.82.

78 A British Foreign Office memorandum recorded the fact of the *coup*, and foresaw the apologetics: 'Dollfuß . . . could no doubt easily make a return to normal parliamentary procedure, and merely claim that the Austrian parliament had by its own folly fully stultified itself'. F.L. Carsten, *The First Austrian Republic. A study based on Austrian and British Sources* (Aldershot, 1986), p.180.

79 Gedye, *Fallen Bastions*, pp. 84–5. The matter was discussed in cabinet on 9 March 1933. Ministerratsprotokoll Nr. 853 vom 9. März 1933, *Protokolle*, VIII, vol. II, pp. 853.

80 For a discussion of the historiography of the *Staatstreich* see Botz, 'Die Ausschaltung des Nationalrates im Urteil von Zeitgenossen und Historikern' in Botz, *Krisenzonen*, pp.119–54.

81 Ministerratsprotokoll Nr. 851 vom 7. März 1933, Beilage A-E, *Protokolle*, VIII, vol. II, pp. 398–404. Ministerratsprotokoll Nr. 868 vom 24. April, 1933, *Protokolle*, VIII, vol. III, pp. 192–3.

82 Vienna was undermined financially by federal government interference (under the War Economy Enabling Act) with the city's revenue raising powers. See, for example, Ministerratsprotokoll Nr. 907 vom 17. November, 1933, *Protokolle*, VIII, vol. V, p. 89.

83 Proposals for constitutional reform on a corporatist basis were presented to the cabinet in December 1933. Ministerratsprotokoll Nr. 911 vom 15. Dezember, 1933, Beilage H, *Protokolle*, VIII, vol. V, pp. 242–44. At a meeting of the CSP parliamentary party leadership in March 1933 Dollfuss had spoken of combatting the Nazis by 'out-Hitlering' them (*überhitlern*), what Ernst Hanisch has called 'preventive fascism'. Hanisch, *Der lange Schatten des Staates*, p.304.

84 Gerhard Botz, 'Der Aufstandsversuch österreichischer Sozialdemokraten am 12. Februar 1934: Ursachen für seinen Ausbruch und seinen Misserfolg' in Botz, *Krisenzonen*, p.181–99. Here p. 191; Edmondson, *Heimwehr*, pp.212–18.

85 Bukey, *Patenstadt*, pp.180–97.

86 Carsten, *First Austrian Republic*, p.189; Gedye, *Fallen Bastions*, pp. 101–5.

87 The cabinet met at 6 p.m. on 12 February. Vice-Chancellor Emil Fey reported on security operations in Linz, Vienna, and Styria, and Alois Schönburg-Hartenstein, state secretary in the Army Ministry, reported on military operations. Ministerratsprotokoll Nr. 922 vom 12 Februar, 1934, *Protokolle*, VIII, vol V, pp. 580–3.

88 Kurt Peball, 'Februar 1934: Die Kämpfe' in *Das Jahr 1934: 12. Februar. Protokoll des Symposiums in Wien am 5. Februar 1974* (Vienna, 1975), pp.25–33;

Ilona Duczynska, *Workers in Arms. The Austrian Schutzbund and the Civil War of 1934* (London, 1978), pp. 167–71.

89 Peball, 'Die Kämpfe', p.30; Lewis, *Styrian Labour*, pp. 282–4. Styria was potentially problematic for the government on account of the Nazi sympathies of the *Heimatschutz*. See Ministerratsprotokoll Nr. 922 vom 12. Februar, 1934, *Protokolle*, VIII, vol. V, pp. 585–6

90 Duczynska, *Workers in Arms*, p.172.

91 Brigitte Perfahl, 'Linz und Steyr: Zentren der Kämpfe' in Josef Weidenholzer, Brigitte Perfahl und Hubert Humer, *'Es wird nicht mehr verhandelt'* . . .*Der 12 Februar in Oberösterreich* (Linz, 1984), pp. 25–56. Here pp. 49–56.

92 Duczynska, *Workers in Arms*, p. 173.

93 Peball, 'Die Kämpfe', p. 30.

94 Everhard Holtmann, *Zwischen Befriedung und Unterdrückung. Sozialistische Arbeiterbewegung und autoritäres Regime* (Munich, 1978), p.95. See also the casualty statistics received by the government from Vienna hospitals. Ministerratsprotokoll Nr. 923 vom 12. Februar, 1934, *Protokolle*, VIII, vol. V, pp. 626–8.

95 Holtmann, *Zwischen Befriedung und Unterdrückung*, p. 177

96 See, for example, Robert Stöger, 'Der christliche Führer und die "wahre Demokratie". Zu den Demokratiekonzeptionen von Ignaz Seipel', *Archiv Jahrbuch des Vereins für die Geschichte der Arbeiterbewegung*, 2 (1988) 54–67; John Haag, 'Marginal Men and the Dream of the Reich: Eight Austrian National-Catholic Intellectuals 1918–1938' in Larsen et al., *Who were the Fascists?* pp.239–48

97 *Arbeiterzeitung* (25 February 1934), p.3.

98 Holtmann, *Zwischen Befriedung und Unterdrückung*, pp. 95–143.

99 See Ministerratsprotokoll Nr. 922 vom 12. Februar, 1934, Beilage A/1, *Protokolle*, VIII, vol. V, p. 596.

100 For a survey of interpretations of the Dollfuss-Schuschnigg regime see Emmerich Tálos, 'Das Herrschaftssystem 1934–1938: Erklärungen und begriffliche Bestimmungen. Ein Resümee', in Tálos and Neugebauer, (eds.) *'Austrofaschismus'*, pp.267–84; Hanisch. *Der Lange Schatten des Staates*, pp. 310–15.

101 Holtmann, *Zwischen Befriedung und Unterdrückung*, pp. 27–8.

102 See Walter Wisshaupt, *Wir kommen wieder! Eine Geschichte der Revolutionären Sozialisten Österreichs* (Vienna, 1967).

103 Holtmann, *Zwischen Befriedung und Unterdrückung*, p.180; Radomir Luža quotes a Czech source from 1972 which puts the increase in Communist Party membership at over 500 per cent within 'a few months': Radomir Luža, *The Resistance in Austria 1938–1945* (Minneapolis, 1984), p.22.

104 'Achtung auf die Nazi!', *Arbeiterzeitung* (4 March 1934), p.3. See also the discussion of Kurt Peball's paper, 'Diskussion zum Beitrag Peball' in *Das Jahr 1934. 12. Februar*

105 Willibald I. Holzer, *Im Schatten des Faschismus. Der österreichische Widerstand gegen Hitler 1938–1945* (Vienna, 1981).

106 Botz, 'Changing Patterns', p.216; Botz 'Strukturwandlungen', p.186.

107 The Nazi Party had been banned in June 1933. On measures against those involved in the attempted *coup*, see Ministerratsprotokoll Nr. 959 vom 30. Juli, 1934, *Protokolle*, IX, vol. I, pp. 1ff.

108 *Arbeiterzeitung*, (17 February 1935), cited in *Widerstand und Verfolgung in Oberösterreich 1934–1945* (Vienna, 1982), vol I, p.165, doc. I.
109 Ibid, p. 167, doc. 6.
110 *Widerstand und Verfolgung in Oberösterreich* vol. I, p. 165, doc. I.
111 Holtmann, *Zwischen Befriedung und Unterdrückung*, pp.279–81.
112 Gedye, *Fallen Bastions*, pp. 262–8.

2 ECONOMIC INTEGRATION AND POLITICAL OPPOSITION BETWEEN THE ANSCHULSS AND THE WAR

1 For a detailed discussion of this process see Gerhard Botz, *Die Eingliederung Österreichs in das deutsche Reich. Planung und Verwirklichung des politisch-administrativen Anschlusses (1938–1940)* (Linz, 1982). See also Radomir V. Luža, 'Die Strukturen der nationalsozialistischen Herrschaft in Österreich' in Gerald Stourzh and Brigitte Zahr (eds.), *Österreich, Deutschland und die Mächte. Internationale und österreichische Aspekte des 'Anschlusses' vom März 1938* (Vienna, 1990), pp.471–92, and the responses to his points by Ernst Hanisch, 'Fragmentarische Bemerkungen zur Konzeptualisierung der NS-Herrschaft in Österreich', ibid., pp. 493–5 and Hans-Ulrich Thamer, 'Führergewalt und Polykratie in Österreich'; ibid., pp. 497–502.
2 'A large part of the working class was not in the least bitter about the removal of its persecutors, and reckoned that the change from clerical to national fascism was not the greatest misfortune if only half the promises of the thousand year Reich were fulfilled.' Quoted in Botz, *Wien* p.135.
3 For a discussion of the complexities and ambiguities of the Anschluss, and popular responses to it, see Gerhard Botz, 'Der ambivalente Anschluss 1938–1939. Von der Begeisterung zur Ernüchterung', *Zeitgeschichte*, 6 (1978), 91–109
4 *Mitteilungen des Auslandsbüros österreichischer Sozialdemokraten in Paris* (22 April 1938) reported arrests of socialist activists and leaders, many of whom had already been arrested by the previous regime. Some were held in Vienna prisons, others were taken to Dachau. See *Widerstand und Verfolgung in Wien*, vol. II, p.11. See also Karl Stadler, *Österreich im Spiegel der NS-Akten* (Vienna, 1966).
5 The so-called 'Schoberkartei', see Botz, *Wien*, p.57.
6 Botz, *Wien*, pp.130–1.
7 *Der sozialistische Kampf*, 3 (Paris, 2 July 1938), p.53f. as cited in *Widerstand und Verfolgung in Wien*, II, pp.42–3, doc.54. See also Josef Buttinger, *Am Beispiel Österreichs. Ein Beitrag zur Krise in der sozialistischen Bewegung* (Cologne, 1953), pp.541ff.; Walter Wisshaupt, *Wir kommen wieder – Eine Geschichte der revolutionären Sozialisten Österreichs* (Vienna, 1957).
8 Radomir Luža, *The Resistance in Austria 1938–1945* (Minneapolis, 1984) p.99. For a brief summary of the organisational structure and leading personnel of the KPÖ and its subsidiary organisations see Helmut Konrad, *Widerstand an Donau und Moldau. KPÖ und KSC zur Zeit des Hitler-Stalin Paktes* (Vienna, 1978), pp.19–28.
9 Konrad, *Widerstand an Donau und Moldau* pp. 52–6.
10 DÖW 5120, SD Wien, 28 June 1938.

11 *Widerstand und Verfolgung in Wien*, vol. II, p.8. and pp. 46–9, doc. 62 'Aus: Anklageschrift des Oberreichsanwaltes beim VGH gegen Friederike Nödl und andere wegen Vorbereitung zum Hochverrat.'

12 Konrad, *Widerstand an Donau und Moldau* p.174.

13 Radio ownership was relatively widespread in Austria: some 60 per cent of Viennese households had access to a receiver by 1941, and the density was greater in large provincial towns such as Graz (66 per cent) and Linz (76 per cent). *Statistisches Jahrbuch für das deutsche Reich* (Berlin, 1942), p.278. See also Wolfgang Ammanshauser, 'Fluchtversuche aus einem geschlossenen Mediensystem. Die Verordnung über außerordentliche Rundfunkmaßnahmen vom 1. September 1939. Ihre Entstehung, ihre Bedeutung, sowie ihre Auswirkung im Reichsgau Salzburg 1939–1945', Phil. Diss. (Salzburg 1984).

14 See USNA T-84 Roll 13 for Gestapo reports from Vienna during 1938 and 1939.

15 DÖW 5120. SD Wien, 28 June 1938.

16 Ibid.

17 Ibid.

18 BA R58/446 Graz, 31 August 1938.

19 Steyr, in Upper Austria is of course a notable exception.

20 BA R58/446 Klagenfurt 9 September 1938.

21 Ibid., Salzburg 6 September 1938 and Innsbruck, 1 September 1938.

22 See Evan B. Bukey 'Popular Opinion in Vienna after the Anschluss', in F. Parkinson (ed.), *Conquering the Past. Austrian Nazism Yesterday and Today* (Detroit, 1989), pp.151–64. Here p.153.

23 BA R58/446 Vienna, September 1938. The Gestapo arrested 47 Revolutionary Socialists on 22 August 1938. *Widerstand und Verfolgung in Wien*, vol. II, pp.52–4 doc. 65

24 BA R58 1081 Lagebericht über Österreich, pp.2–5.

25 DÖW 1576.

26 BA R58 1081. Lagebericht über Österreich.

27 DÖW 1578.

28 BA R58/446 Gestapo Linz 29 March 1939. Lageberichte für die Monate Jänner, Februar, März 1939 (Marxismus).

29 BA R58/446 Lageberichte für das erste Vierteljahr 1939 der Stapoleitstelle Wien (Marxismus); Lagebericht für das II. Vierteljahr 1939, Stapoleitstelle Innsbruck. The relationship between the morale of the domestic opposition in the Third Reich and the course of foreign policy developments was repeatedly stressed by the authors of the Sopade reports, who based their judgement on comprehensive nation-wide reports. The point was emphatically repeated in the wake of the Munich agreement: Sopade, 1938, pp. 939–40.

30 DÖW 1578.

31 DÖW 1571.

32 See Norbert Schausberger, 'Deutsche Wirtschaftsinteressen in Österreich vor und nach dem März 1938' in Stourzh and Zahr (eds.), *Österreich, Deutschland und die Mächte*, pp. 177–211. Here, pp. 193–4. For a lengthier

consideration of Germany's interest in the annexation of Austria see Schausberger, *Der Griff nach Österreich. Der Anschluss* (Vienna, 1978).

33 AVA, Reichskommissar für die Wiedervereinigung Österreichs mit dem deutschen Reich, (Rk) Ordner 19.

34 Ibid. See also Helmut Fiereder, *Reichswerke Hermann Göring in Österreich (1938–1945)* (Vienna and Salzburg, 1983).

35 AVA, Rk, 72. See also Felix Butschek, *Die Österreichische Wirtschaft 1938 bis 1945* (Stuttgart, 1978).

36 BA R43 1527 fol.1: Statistik der ausländischen (einschliesslich österreichischen) Arbeiter und Angestellten im Altreichsgebiet.

37 DÖW 5120 SD Aussenstelle 5, 28 June 1938.

38 Ibid., Aussenstelle 4, 28 June 1938.

39 Sopade, 1938, pp.997–9.

40 AVA, Rk, 72.

41 DÖW 5120, SD Wien, Aussenstelle 3, 28 June 1938.

42 AVA, Rk, 72/1907. Report of RTA to Bürckel, 16 September 1938.

43 DÖW 5120, SD Wien, Aussenstelle 5, 28 June 1938.

44 BA R58/446 Graz, 31 August 1938.

45 Heinz Boberach (ed.), *Meldungen aus dem Reich. Die geheimen Lageberichte des Sicherheitsdienstes der SS 1938–1944* (Herrsching, 1984), p. 204.

46 See Botz, 'Der ambivalente Anschluss', pp.103–5.

47 Fiereder, *Reichswerke*, pp.103–4.

48 BA R58/723 Stimmungsbericht von Steyr und Umgebung, August 1938.

49 Ibid., Werkschutzleiter der Steyr Daimler Puch AG an SS Oberführer Albert, 13 August 1938.

50 DÖW 1454.

51 DÖW 1578.

52 G. Morsch, 'Streik im "Dritten Reich" ' *Vierteljahreshefte für Zeitgeschichte* 36 (1988), 649–9.

53 See Tim Mason, *Arbeiterklasse und Volksgemeinschaft. Dokumente und Materialien zur deutschen Arbeitspolitik 1936–1939* (Opladen, 1975) doc. 3 on the re-emergence of industrial action in Germany in the mid 1930s and Everhard Holtmann, *Zwischen Unterdrückung und Befriedung. Sozialistische Arbeiterbewegung und autoritäres Regime in Österreich 1933–1938* (Munich, 1978), p.281, on the industrial action of the last months of the Schuschnigg regime.

54 Tim Mason, 'Workers' Opposition in Nazi Germany', *History Workshop Journal* 11 (1981), 120–37, particularly the references to the characteristics of industrial stoppages (p.124).

55 *Österreichische Informationen*, Paris, August 1938. Although the KPD equivalent, *Deutsche Informationen* has been found to be inaccurate, no evidence of inaccuracy in *Österreichische Informationen* has yet been established.

56 Ibid.

57 *Österreichische Informationen*, Paris, 9 September 1938.

58 Ibid.

59 DÖW film 99, Gestapo Wien, 17–18 November 1938.

60 *Österreichische Informationen*, Paris 15 August 1939.

61 *Der sozialistische Kampf*, No. 5, 30 July 1938. Cited in *Widerstand und Verfolgung in Wien* vol. II, p.401.

62 *Nouvelles d'Autriche*, April 1939; *Österreichische Informationen*, 14 March 1939.
63 *Österreichische Informationen*, Paris, 29 April 1939 and 6 May 1939.
64 AVA, Rk, 171, Wirtschaftlicher Wochenbericht Nr. 6, 12–24 June 1939.
65 BA R58/1081
66 *Nouvelles d'Autriche*, April 1939.
67 AVA, Rk, 171, Wirtschaftlicher Wochenbericht Nr. 6, 12–24 June 1939.
68 AVA, Rk, 171, Wirtschaftlicher Wochenbericht Nr. 3, 3 July–5 August 1939.

3 THE WAR ECONOMY AND THE CHANGING WORKFORCE 1939–1945

1 Felix Butschek, *Die österreichische Wirtschaft 1938–1945* (Stuttgart, 1978), p.122.
2 Ibid., p. 81
3 USNA T-84 Roll 14, SD Wien, 9 November 1939, Vorarlberg, 'so near to the Swiss border', was considered a particularly sensitive area. See Timothy Kirk, The Austrian Working Class under National Socialist Rule: Industrial Unrest and Political Dissent in the People's Community' Ph. D. dissertation (Manchester 1988), pp. 144–6.
4 Gerhard Botz, *Die Eingliederung Österreichs in das deutsche Reich. Planung und Verwirklichung des politisch-administrativen Anschlusses (1938–1940)* (Linz, 1972) p.125 (map).
5 On the wartime economic exploitation of Bohemia and Moravia by Germany see J. Krejci, 'The Bohemian-Moravian War Economy' in M. C. Kaser and E. A. Radice (eds.), *The Economic History of Eastern Europe 1919–1975* (Oxford, 1986), vol II, pp. 452–92.
6 There were 105,493 Czechs and 69,299 Austrians out of a total of 375,078 foreigners within Germany's 1937 boundaries.
7 Karl M. Brousek, *Wien und seine Tschechen. Integration und Assimilation einer Minderheit im 20. Jahrhundert* (Vienna, 1980), pp. 92–3.
8 Heinz Boberach (ed.), *Meldungen aus dem Reich. Die geheimen Lageberichte des Sicherheitsdienstes der SS 1938–1944* (Herrsching, 1984), p.789.
9 Ulrich Herbert, *Fremdarbeiter. Politik und Praxis des Ausländer-Einsatzes in der Kriegswirtschaft des Dritten Reiches* (Berlin, 1986), p.58.
10 Brousek, *Tschechen*, p.93.
11 See Stephen Salter, 'The Mobilisation of German Labour 1939–1945. A Contribution to the History of the German Working Class', D. Phil. (Oxford, 1983), pp. 17–37.
12 Ibid., pp. 38–48.
13 See the complaints of the Defence Economy Inspectorate (*Wehrwirtschaftsinspektion*) of Defence District XVII, covering Vienna and Upper and Lower Danube, BA/MA, RW20–17/12 report of 25 January 1940.
14 AVA, Rk, 70/1902, p.9.
15 See Florian Freund and Bertrand Perz, 'Fremdarbeiter und KZ-Häftlinge in der "Ostmark" ', in Ulrich Herbert (ed.), *Europa und der Reichseinsatz. Ausländische Zivilarbeiter, Kriegsgefangene und KZ-Häftlinge in Deutschland 1938–1945* (Essen, 1991) pp. 317–50. Here p.318.

16 BA/MA, RW 20–17/12 Report of 11 April 1940

17 See Tim Mason, *Sozialpolitik im Dritten Reich. Arbeiterklasse und Volksgemeinschaft* (Opladen, 1977), chapter 1, pp. 15–41.

18 See Gisela Bock, 'Gleichheit und Differenz in der nationalsozialistischen Rassenpolitik', *Geschichte und Gesellschaft*, 19 (1993), 277–310. Here p. 281.

19 Herbert, *Fremdarbeiter*, p. 64.

20 Ibid., pp. 53–6. Modern industrial Germany had always attracted immigrant labour, and particularly during the First World War. See Edward L. Homze, *Foreign Labour in Nazi Germany* (Princeton, 1967), p.3; Herbert, *Fremdarbeiter*, pp. 24–35.

21 See Czeslaw Łuczak, 'Polnische Arbeiter im nationalsozialistischen Deutschland während des zweiten Weltkrieges. Entwicklung und Aufgaben der polnischen Forschung' in Herbert (ed.) *Europa und der Reichseinsatz. Ausländische Zivilarbeiter, Kreigsgefangene und KZ-Häftlinge in Deutschland 1938–1945* (Essen, 1991), pp. 90–105. Here p. 94.

22 On the dismemberment and reorganisation of Poland, and the incorporation of a substantial part of Polish territory into the Reich, see M. C. Kaser and E. A. Radice (eds.), *The Economic History of Eastern Europe 1919–1975* (Oxford, 1986), vol. II, *Interwar Policy, the War and Reconstruction* p.310 and pp. 316–19.

23 Herbert, *Fremdarbeiter*, pp. 68f.

24 See Tim Mason, *Arbeiterklasse und Volksgemeinschaft*, chapters 20, 21. Oppositional responses to the measures are discussed in chapter 4 of the present book.

25 Ibid., pp. 165f.

26 Herbert, *Fremdarbeiter*, p.77.

27 BA/MA, RW 20–17/12 Report of 22 November 1939.

28 Hans Pfahlmann, *Fremdarbeiter und Kriegsgefangene in der deutschen Kriegswirtschaft* (Darmstadt, 1968), p.126.

29 Freund and Perz, 'Fremdarbeiter' p.319.

30 Ibid., p.344.

31 USNA T-84 Roll 13 SD Wien, 15 April 1940

32 Boberach (ed.), *Meldungen*, p.591 20 December 1939.

33 Herbert, *Fremdarbeiter*, pp. 92f.

34 Freund and Perz, 'Fremdarbeiter', p.318.

35 There were 58,672 prisoners of war in Defence District XVII at the end of March 1941. In the two Austrian Defence Districts (XVII and XVIII) the proportion of POWs on the land (38.5 per cent and 46.1 per cent respectively) was less than in the Reich as a whole (51.6 per cent), the proportion put to work on construction sites (44.3 per cent and 46.1 per cent respectively) twice the Reich average (23 per cent). Freund and Perz, 'Fremdarbeiter', p.318.

36 BA/MA, RW21–38/5 Anlage 1; BA/MA, RW21–38/6 Anlage 1.

37 BA/MA, RW20–18/28 III, Anlage zum Monatsbericht der Rü Jn XVIII Z. Abt. Nr. 20147 40g vom 15 November 3. Arbeitseinsatzlage. In February 1941 the same office reported that 150 from a contingent of 3,300 were deployed in the industry, while most of the rest worked on road construction.

38 BA/MA, RW20–17/15 IV, Arbeitseinsatzlage, 14 February 1942. The number of foreign workers in the Reich increased by 263 per cent, from 1,148,000 to 3,020,000 between May 1940 and May 1941. Edward L Homze, *Foreign Labour in Nazi Germany* (Princeton, 1967, p.68.

39 Homze, *Foreign Labour*, p.29

40 The most systematic studies of the exploitation of slave labour from concentration camps by Austrian industry during the war have been undertaken by Florian Freund and Bertrand Perz in the series *Industrie, Zwangsarbeit und Konzentrationslager*: Florian Freund und Bertrand Perz, *Das KZ in der "Serbenhalle". Zur Kriegsindustrie in Wiener Neustadt* (Vienna, 1987); *Arbeitslager Zement. Das Konzentrationslager Ebensee und die Raketenrüstung* (Vienna, 1989); *Projekt Quarz. Steyr Daimler-Puch und das Konzentrationslager Melk* (Vienna, 1991).

41 Homze, *Foreign Labour*, pp. 45–50.

42 Stephen Salter, 'Mobilisation', pp. 66–7.

43 Herbert, *Fremdarbeiter*, p.133. On the mass starvation of Russian prisoners of war: ibid., pp. 147–9; Homze, *Foreign Labour*, pp. 81–4.

44 Homze, *Foreign Labour*, p.74.

45 Herbert, *Fremdarbeiter*, pp. 140–3; Homze, *Foreign Labour*, pp. 70f.

46 Ibid., pp. 78f.

47 Rolf-Dieter Müller, 'Die Rekrutierung sowjetischer Zwangsarbeiter für die deutsche Kriegswirtschaft', in Ulrich Herbert (ed.), *Europa und der 'Reichseinsatz'. Ausländische Zivilarbeiter, Kriegsgefangene und KZ-Häftlinge in Deutschland 1938–1945*, pp. 234–50. Here p. 235.

48 Homze, *Foreign Labour*, p.112.

49 Herbert, *Fremdarbeiter*, p.181.

50 Slapnicka, *Oberösterreich als es Oberdonau hieß 1938–1945* (Linz, 1978), p.162.

51 52.2 per cent in July, 63.5 per cent in August, and 62 per cent in September: BA/MA, RW21–38/10, 11.

52 BA/MA, RW 21–38/10 KTB Rü-Kdo Linz, p.14.

53 See, for example, BA/MA, RW 20–18/19 Anlage 1 'Tätigkeitsbericht für Juni 1943'.

54 See Freund and Perz, 'Fremdarbeiter', pp. 336ff.

55 D. Petzina, W. Abelshauser and A. Faust (eds.), *Sozialgeschichtliches Arbeitsbuch III. Materialien zur Statistik des deutschen Reiches 1914–1945* (Munich, 1978), p.54.

56 Richard Overy, 'Mobilization for Total War in Germany' 1939–1941, *English Historical Review*, 103 (1988), 613–39. Here pp. 629ff.

57 According to Overy 37.4 per cent of the German workforce were women in 1939 (a figure which differs from Winkler's) and 25.7 per cent of the British workforce were women. In 1943 36.4 per cent of the British workforce were women and 48.8 per cent of the German workforce. These figures are used as the basis of the argument that if there was no substantial mobilisation of women after 1939 compared with Britain, that was because, unlike in Britain, there was no pool of unemployed female labour on which to draw. An increase in the proportion of women in the workforce from 37.4 per cent to 48.8 per cent seems substantial enough, however, to undermine alto-

gether the argument that there was no significant mobilisation of German women for war work after 1939.

58 John Barber and Mark Harrison, *The Soviet Home Front 1941–1945: A Social and Economic History of the USSR* (London and New York, 1991), p.216; Hachtmann, 'Industriearbeiterinnen in der deutschen Kriegswirtschaft 1936 bis 1944/45', *Geschichte und Gesellschaft*, 19 (1933), 363; Freund and Perz, 'Fremdarbeiter', p.345. Some caution is necessary with such comparisons and the statistics on which they are based. Both Hachtmann and Freund and Perz cite figures from Rolf Wagenführ, *Die deutsche Industrie im Kriege 1939–1945* (Berlin, 1954), pp. 148–157 and 139ff. respectively. The figures in Overy's comparison between Britain and Germany (immediately above, note 57) refer to the whole workforce, while those for the German-Soviet comparison refer to the industrial workforce. Methods of calculating the latter may have differed in Germany and the USSR. Some tables of female employment in both Hachtmann, 'Industriearbeiterinnen' and Winkler, *Frauenarbeit im Dritten Reich* (Hamburg, 1977), include foreign women workers and thereby give a misleading impression. The same is true of Butschek, *Die österreichische Wirtschaft 1938 bis 1945* (Vienna and Stuttgart, 1978), p.91, as Freund and Perz point out: Freund and Perz 'Fremdarbeiter', p.345.

59 For a summary of recent work and re-interpretations of the experience of women in modern Germany, see Eve Rosenhaft, 'Women in Modern Germany' in Gordon Martel (ed.), *Modern Germany Reconsidered 1870–1945* (London and New York, 1992), pp. 140–58.

60 See for example the letter of Reich Justice Minister Freisler to the Prussian authorities on the exclusion of women from senior judicial positions, BA R43/427, in Ursula von Gersdorff, *Frauen im Kriegsdienst 1914–1945* (Stuttgart, 1969), doc. 109 pp. 282f.

61 Rosenhaft, 'Women in Modern Germany' pp. 142–5.

62 See Andrea Lösch, 'Staatliche Arbeitsmarktpolitik nach dem ersten Weltkrieg als Instrument der Verdrängung von Frauen aus der Erwerbsarbeit', *Zeitgeschichte* 14, (May 1987), 313–29.

63 Jill Lewis, *Fascism and the Working Class in Austria 1918–1934* (New York and Oxford, 1991), p.85.

64 Karin Berger, *Zwischen Eintopf und Fließband. Frauenarbeit und Frauenbild im Faschismus. Österreich 1938–1945* (Vienna, 1984), p. 56.

65 Ibid., p.59; Botz, *Wien*, p. 302.

66 BA/MA, RW 21–28/1 Kriegstagebuch, Rüstungskommando Innsbruck, 6 September 1939.

67 BA/MA, RW 20–18/26 Anlage zu Rü Jn XVIII, Salzburg, 4 March 1940.

68 BA/MA, RW 21–38/5 Anlage 1.

69 Ibid., Anlage 10.

70 See Berger, *Zwischen Eintopf und Fließband*, p.65.

71 Ibid., pp. 68–72.

72 Boberach (ed.), *Meldungen*, p.1411 (22 July 1940). Such complaints were reported from a number of parts of Greater Germany, including Graz.

73 Ibid., p.1832 (2 December 1940).

74 See Berger, *Zwischen Eintopf und Fließband*, p.76.

75 Boberach (ed.), *Meldungen* p.2002. (13 February 1941)

76 Ibid., p.2453. (26 June 1941).
77 *Reichsgesetzblatt*, 1943, I, p.67, quoted in Salter, 'Mobilisation', p.75.
78 Hachtmann, 'Industriearbeiterinnen' p.357; Boberach, (ed.) *Meldungen* p. 4751, p. 4756ff (4 February 1943).
79 Ibid. p.4756. This was in Saarbrücken. The example was used to illustrate a point which had been made since at least 1941 by SD reports: that there was popular pressure for a fairer and more systematic mobilisation of women. In the particular circumstances of February 1943 it also helped to emphasise the point that there was a general willingness to make sacrifices at a time of national adversity.
80 BA/MA, RW 20–18/19 Anlage 1 'Tätigkeitsbericht für Juni 1943'.
81 See chapter 4. See also Salter, 'Mobilisation', pp. 77–80.
82 See Berger, *Zwischen Eintopf und Fließband*, p.88.
83 Boberach (ed.) *Meldungen*, p.5172.
84 BA/MA, RW 21–46/8 Vierteljahresübersicht 1.1.43–31.3.43
85 BA R43/654b. Statistik über den Einsatz von Männern und Frauen für Aufgaben der Reichsverteidigung 31 März 1943, in Gersdorff, *Frauen im Kriegsdienst*, pp. 184ff.
86 LGA Linz 394/43. The measures in question are contained in Hitler's decree of 15 January 1943 on the comprehensive deployment of both men and women for the defence of the Reich: R 43/652a, 655a. Reprinted in Gersdorff, *Frauen im Kriegsdienst*, pp. 375ff, doc. 179.
87 An 18 year old unskilled worker involved in a similar breach of contract case claimed to have left work because he was spending more on bus fares than he was earning. LGA Linz, HV 48/43B
88 BA NS6/408 fol. 1. Report of the President of the Labour Office in Upper Danube to the Gauleiter, May 1943.
89 BA R43/652a, 655a. Reprinted in Gersdorff, *Frauen im Kriegsdienst*, pp. 375ff., doc. 179.
90 BA R43/654b. Reprinted in Gersdorff, *Frauen im Kriegsdienst*, pp. 383ff., doc. 194.
91 Homze, *Foreign Labour*, p.112.

4 WORK DISCIPLINE IN THE WAR ECONOMY

1 See Rüdiger Hachtmann, *Industriearbeit im 'Dritten Reich': Untersuchungen zu den Lohn- und Arbeitsbedingungen in Deutschland 1933–1945* (Göttingen, 1989), particularly pp. 30–6; Stephen Salter 'Industrial Workers, Employers and the State in Nazi Germany', unpublished paper, pp. 9–12.
2 Salter, 'Industrial Workers', p.11; Mason, *Arbeiterklasse und Volksgemeinschaft*, pp. 667f.
3 Tim Mason, *Social Policy in the Third Reich. The Working Class and the 'National Community'* (Providence and Oxford, 1993) pp. 230–1.
4 Michael Seidmann, 'Towards a History of Workers' Resistance to Work: Paris and Barcelona during the French Popular Front and the Spanish Revolution, 1936–38' *Journal of Contemporary History* 23 (1988), pp. 191–220; and Seidmann, *Workers against Work: Labour in Paris and Barcelona during the Popular Fronts* (Berkeley, 1991) examines similar behaviour at about the

same time in a remarkably different political context. But, see the critique of his approach by Helen Graham, 'Review of Michael Seidman, *Workers against Work: Labour in Paris and Barcelona during the Popular Fronts'* *International Review of Social History*, 37 (1992), pp.276–81. See also Günter Morsch, 'Streik im Dritten Reich', *Vierteljahreshefte für Zeitgeschichte*, 36 (1988) pp. 649–89.

5 Mason, *Social Policy*, pp. 19–40
6 Kershaw, *Popular Opinion and Political Dissent in the Third Reich: Bavaria 1933–1945* (Oxford 1984), p. 315
7 Ibid., p.304.
8 The point is reinforced by the insistence of Sopade reporters up to April 1940 that people had even then still not grasped the seriousness of the war. See *Deutschland-Berichte der Sozialdemokratischen Partei Deutschlands (Sopade)* 1940, p.221. See also Ulrich Herbert, ' "Die guten und die schlechten Zeiten." Überlegungen zur diachronen Analyse lebensgeschichtlicher Interviews', in Lutz Niethammer (ed.), *'Die Jahre weiß man nicht, wo man die heute hinsetzen soll.' Faschismuserfahrungen im Ruhrgebiet* (Berlin, 1983); Herbert, 'Good Times, Bad Times: Memories of the Third Reich', in Richard Bessel (ed.), *Life in the Third Reich*, (Oxford, 1987), pp. 97–110.
9 See R. J. Overy, *War and Economy in the Third Reich* (Oxford, 1994), pp. 360–3.
10 Ibid., p. 364; Salter 'Industrial Workers', p.12. Hachtmann calculates that real net weekly wages in German industry fell from 124.3 per cent of their 1932 levels in 1942 to 119.5 per cent in 1944, according to the official statistics, which were not entirely reliable: Hachtmann, *Industriearbeit*, p. 159.
11 Overy, *War and Economy*, pp. 364–5; Salter, 'Industrial Workers', pp. 12–13.
12 See the documents on the legislation, its implementation and subsequent changes of policy in Mason, *Arbeiterklasse und Volksgemeinschaft*, pp. 1043–135.
13 USNA T-84 R14 41002 SD Wien 17 September 1939.
14 Mason, *Sozialpolitik im Dritten Reich. Arbeiterklasse und Volksgemeinschaft* (Opladen 1977), 295–9; Werner, *'Bleib übrig!' Deutsche Arbeiter in der nationalsozialistischen Kriegswirtschaft* (Düsseldorf, 1983), pp. 34–40; Herbert, 'Arbeiterschaft im "Dritten Reich". Zwischenbilanz und offene Fragen', *Geschichte und Gesellschaft*, 15 (1989), 320–60. Here pp. 345–6
15 See the SD reports from Vienna, September 1939, USNA T-84 Roll 14
16 Ibid., 25 October 1939.
17 Ibid., 6 November 1939; 30 October 1939.
18 Ibid., 18 October 1939; 20 October 1939.
19 Ibid., 21 October 1939; 3 November, 1939; 6 November 1939.
20 Ibid., 21 October 1939 – 30 October 1939.
21 Similarly, party support for a moderate wages policy, has been explained in terms of an 'NSDAP, worried because of the plebiscitary foundations of the regime'. Mason, *Social Policy*, p.252.
22 See the SD reports from Vienna, 18 October 1939.
23 AVA, Rk 73 'Antrag auf Erlassung einer Notstandsverordnung'. 29 September 1939.
24 Ibid., 73 1909/6.

25 AVA, Rk, 171 (2205/21) Wirtschaftlicher Wochenbericht, 9 October 1939,
26 USNA T-84 Roll 14 SD 25 October 1939.
27 Ibid.
28 Boberach (ed.), *Meldungen*, p.338
29 Mason, *Arbeiterklasse und Volksgemeinschaft*, doc. 223 pp. 1182–3.
30 USNA T-84 Roll 14 SD Wien, 25 October 1939. The reports 'Aus den Betrieben' in the *Deutschlandberichte* frequently contain complaints about the rate of work.
31 USNA T-84 Roll 14, SD Wien, 18 December 1939.
32 See 'Niederschrift über eine Ressortbesprechung beim Generalbevollmächtigten für die Wirtschaft am 10. November 1939' and 'Vermerk über eine Besprechung beim Generalbevollmächtigten für die Wirtschaft am 10. November 1939 (Auszug)', in Mason, *Arbeiterklasse und Volksgemeinschaft*, pp. 1183–8, docs. 224 and 225.
33 Ibid., 'Niederschrift'. See also USNA T-84 Roll 14, SD Wien 20 November 1939.
34 USNA T-84 Roll 14, SD Wien 6 December 1939.
35 USNA T-77 Roll 741, Cited by Stefan Karner, *Die Steiermark im Dritten Reich 1938–1945. Aspekte ihrer politischen, wirtschaftlich-sozialen und kulturellen Entwicklung* (Graz and Vienna), 1986.
36 BA/MA, RW 20–17/12 7–28 March 1940.
37 AVA Generalstaatsanwaltschaft (GeSta) Linz, Generalakten Az 4206.
38 BA/MA, RW 20–17/13 12 July 1940.
39 AVA Generalstaatsanwaltschaft (Gesta) Linz, Generalakten Az 4206.
40 LGA Linz, HV 102/40.
41 LGA Linz, HV 596/40.
42 See, for example, Stefan Karner, 'Arbeitsvertragsbrüche als Verletzung der Arbeitspflicht im Dritten Reich. Darstellung und EDV-Analyse am Beispiel der untersteirischen VDM-Luftfahrtwerkes Marburg/Maribor', *Archiv für Sozialgeschichte* 21 (1982), 269–328.
43 BA/MA, RW 20–17/13 12 June 1940.
44 Zweite Verordnung gegen Arbeitsvertragsbruch und Abwerbung sowie das Fordern unverhältnismässig hohe Arbeitsentgelte in der privaten Wirtschaft 3. 12. 1942, cited in Karner 'Arbeitsvertragsbrüche', pp. 280–1.
45 See Wolfgang Werner, 'Die Arbeitserziehungslager als Mittel nationalsozialistischer "Sozialpolitik" gegen deutsche Arbeiter', in Waclaw Długoborski (ed.), *Zweiter Weltkrieg und Sozialer Wandel. Achsenmächte und besetzte Länder* (Göttingen, 1981), pp. 138–47.
46 Stefan Karner, *Steiermark*, p. 355.
47 See, for example, Gerhard Botz, 'Widerstand von Einzelnen', in *Widerstand und Verfolgung in Oberösterreich*, col. II, pp. 351–63. Here p. 362.
48 LGA Linz HV 48/43B.
49 LGA Linz HV 80/44B.
50 LGA Linz HV 77/44B.
51 LGA Linz 691/43; HV 711/43.
52 DÖW film 104, Meldungen aus dem Reichsgau Oberdonau, 13,287.
53 DÖW 13,288.
54 Karner, 'Arbeitsvertragsbrüche', p.321.

55 Slapnicka, *Oberösterreich als es Oberdonau hieß 1938–1945* (Linz, 1978), p.174.
56 DÖW 5732d. Gestapo Wien, 16–17 July 1941.
57 Peukert, *Inside Nazi Germany. Conformity, Opposition and Racism in Everyday Life* (London, 1989), 135–9.
58 Herbert, *Fremdarbeiter*, p. 305.
59 DÖW 5734a. Gestapo Wien, 19–22 February 1943.
60 DÖW film 104; 5734a. Gestapo Wien, 19–22 February 1943.
61 BA/MA, RW 20–17/15 (13 September 1941).
62 Almost 1 per cent of the entire Soviet and Polish workforces in the Reich was arrested by the Gestapo every month: Herbert, *Fremdarbeiter*, p. 304.
63 DÖW 5734a, Gestapo Wien, February 1943.
64 Herbert, *Fremdarbeiter* pp. 304–5.
65 On such covert forms of resistance see James C. Scott, 'Everyday Forms of Resistance', in Forrest D. Colburn (ed.), *Everyday Forms of Peasant Resistance* (New York, 1989), pp. 3–33.
66 DÖW 5732c. Gestapo Wien, 10, 23–25 May 1941.
67 DÖW 426. 'Austrians, practise passive resistance!' (*Resistenz*).Text inciting resistance found on a film negative in Vienna.
68 DÖW 5732c, 23–24 June 1941.
69 See Luža, *Resistance in Austria 1938–1945* (Minneapolis, 1984), p.119; Gestapo report 1–2 June 1942 (DÖW 5733c), cited in *Widerstand und Verfolgung in Wien*, vol. II p. 322. Another important group was that formed by the railwaymen at Attnang Puchheim, which had contacts with the resistance in Salzburg. See *Widerstand und Verfolgung in Oberösterreich* vol I, p.84.
70 *Widerstand und Verfolgung in Wien* vol II, pp. 331–44. USNA T-84 Roll 14 40981 23 October 1939. See also the further complaints recorded about Vienna tram drivers by the SD in November 1939, ibid.
71 DÖW 5733f. Gestapo Wien, 9, 18–20 July 1940; 3, 3–5 October 1941.
72 DÖW 5733f. Gestapo Wien, 9, 9–12 October 1942.
73 DÖW 5733f. Gestapo Wien, 7, 20–2 October 1942.
74 DÖW 5734b. Gestapo Wien, 9, 27–30 April 1943.
75 DÖW 5734a. Gestapo Wien, 9, 19–22 February 1943.
76 DÖW 5734c. Gestapo Wien, 22–6 May 1943.
77 DÖW 5734d. Gestapo, 9–12 July 1943.
78 DÖW 5734d. Gestapo, 17–20 September 1943.
79 DÖW 8479.
80 DÖW 5734a. Gestapo Wien, 29 January–1 February 1943; 9, 19–22 February 1943; 5734c Gestapo Wien, 22–3 June 1943. See also Karl Flanner, *Widerstand im Gebiet von Wiener Neustadt* (Vienna, 1973).
81 See Herbert, *Fremdarbeiter*, pp. 315–16.
82 DÖW 8477. Gestapo Wien, 9–12 November 1943.
83 Ibid., 23–5 November 1943.
84 DÖW 8476. Gestapo, 2, 5–10 October 1943.
85 DÖW 8477. Gestapo Wien, 23–5 November 1943.
86 DÖW 5734a–d; 8477–9.
87 Herbert, *Fremdarbeiter*, p. 316.
88 Oberösterreichisches Landesarchiv (OÖLA) Generalakten 7, p.63.

89 See Tone Ferenc, 'The Austrians and Slovenia during the Second World War,' in F. Parkinson (ed.) *Conquering the Past. Austrian Nazism Yesterday and Today* (Detroit, 1989), pp. 207–23.

90 BA/MA, RW 20–18/28 15 August 1941.

91 These were the *Rüstungsinspektion* (Armaments Inspectorate) for *Wehrkreis* (Defence District) XVIII in Salzburg, covering Salzburg, Tyrol (including the administrative district of Vorarlberg), Carinthia and Styria (BA/MA, RW 20–18); and the *Rüstungskommandos* in Graz and Klagenfurt (BA/MA, RW 21–4 and BA/MA, RW 21–33).

92 See Timothy Kirk, 'Limits of Germandom: The Resistance to the Nazi Annexation of Slovenia', *Slavonic and East European Review*, 69 (1991), 646–67.

93 See Luža, *Resistance in Austria*, pp. 193–206; Willibald Ingo Holzer, 'Die österreichischen Bataillonen im Verband der NOV i POJ. Die Kampfgruppe Avantgarde-Steiermark. Die Partisanengruppe Leoben-Donawitz. Die Kommunistische Partei Österreichs im militanten politischen Widerstand', Phil. Diss. (Vienna 1971); Holzer 'Am Beispiel der Kampfgruppe Avantgarde/Steiermark (1944–1945)' in G. Botz, H. Hautmann, H. Konrad and J. Weidenholzer (eds.), *Bewegung und Klasse. Studien zur österreichischen Arbeitergeschichte* (Vienna 1978), pp. 377–424; Max Muchitsch, *Die Partisanengruppe Leoben-Donawitz* (Vienna, 1978). See also Karner, 'Arbeitsvertragsbrüche', and Paul Hehn, *The German Struggle against Yugoslav Guerrillas in World War II. German Counter-Insurgency in Yugoslavia 1941–1943* (New York, 1979).

94 See Luža, *Resistance in Austria*, pp. 114–17.

5 POPULAR OPINION AND POLITICAL PROTEST IN WORKING-CLASS COMMUNITIES

1 The whole problem of how far fascism was attractive, why, and to whom has been overlooked in a post-fascist eagerness to condemn it morally, with the result that the task of explaining its rise and relative stability has been rendered more difficult. See Peter Reichel, *Der schöne Schein des Dritten Reichs. Faszination und Gewalt des Faschismus.* (Munich and Vienna, 1991), pp. 7–45.

2 See Lawrence Duncan Stokes, 'The *Sicherheitsdienst* of the *Reichsführer SS* and German Public Opinion, September 1939–June 1944', Ph.D. dissertation (Johns Hopkins University, Baltimore, Maryland, 1972), pp. 3–4. See also Arlette Farge, *Subversive Words. Public Opinion in Eighteenth-Century France* (Cambridge, 1994).

3 For a discussion of the difficulty with such reports see Richard Evans, *Kneipengespräche im Kaiserreich. Die Stimmungsberichte der Hamburger Politischen Polizei 1892–1914* (Hamburg, 1989), pp. 7–33. See also Helmut Gruber, *Red Vienna. Experiment in Working-Class Culture 1919–1934* (Oxford, 1991) pp. 116–17; Lynn Abrams, *Workers' Culture in Imperial Germany. Leisure and Recreation in the Rhineland and Westphalia* (London, 1992) pp. 63–85.

4 See Michael Burleigh and Wolfgang Wippermann, *The Racial State* (Cambridge, 1991); M. Berenbaum (ed.), *A Mosaic of Victims. Non-Jews Per-*

secuted and Murdered by the Nazis, (London, 1990) explores the experience of various groups victimised by the Nazis, but whose experience has elicited relatively little attention or sympathy. Many victims, including Jews have had considerable difficulty in gaining any compensation from the authorities in post-war Austria. See Brigitte Bailer, *Wiedergutmachung kein Thema. Österreich und die Opfer des Nationalsozialismus* (Vienna, 1993). Nazi legislation recriminalising homosexuality remained on the Austrian statute book until 1971. See Hannes Sulzenbacher, 'Homosexual Men in Vienna in 1938' in Tim Kirk and Tony McElligott (eds.), *Community, Authority and Resistance to Fascism* (Cambridge, forthcoming).

5 See Tim Mason, 'Die Bändigung der Arbeiterklasse im nationalsozialistischen Deutschland', in Carol Sachse, Tilla Siegel, Hasso Spode and Wolfgang Spohn, *Angst, Belohnung, Zucht, und Ordnung. Herrschaftsmechanismen im Nationalsozialismus* (Opladen, 1982) pp. 177–98, now translated as 'The Containment of German Workers in the National Socialist System', in Tim Mason, *Nazism, Fascism and the Working Class*, ed. by Jane Caplan (Cambridge, 1995).

6 See Stokes, 'German Public Opinion', pp. 3–16; Ian Kershaw, *Popular Opinion and Political Dissent in the Third Reich. Bavaria 1933–1945* (Oxford, 1983), p.4.

7 See Martin Broszat, 'Resistenz und Widerstand. Eine Zwischenbilanz des Forschungsprojekts.' in Broszat et al. (eds.) *Bayern in der NS-Zeit*, IV, *Herrschaft und Gesellschaft im Konflikt* (Munich, 1981), pp. 691–709.

8 The term monopoly does not imply total governmental control of the media, but the existence of a complex and symbiotic system which nevertheless prevented the intrusion of critical or unwelcome ideas. See, for example Julian Petley, *Capital and Culture. German Cinema 1933–1945* (London, 1979).

9 See Konrad, *Widerstand und Verfolgung an Donau und Moldau. KPÖ und KSČ zur Zeit des Hitler-Stalin-Paktes* (Vienna, 1978) pp. 168–72, Luža *Resistance in Austria*, pp. 100–2.

10 *Widerstand und Verfolgung in Tirol*, vol. I, p. 321. See also *Widerstand und Verfolgung in Oberösterreich*, vol. I, pp. 482–512. In addition, see Wolfgang Ammanshauser, 'Fluchtversuche aus einem geschlossenen Mediensystem. Die Verordnung über ausserordentliche Rundfunkmassnahmen vom 1. September 1939. Ihre Entstehung, ihre Bedeutung, sowie ihre Auswirkungen im Reichsgau Salzburg 1939–1945' Phil. Diss. (Vienna, 1976).

11 *Widerstand und Verfolgung Oberösterreich*, vol. I, p. 367, doc. 16: Meldungen des SD-Abschnitts Linz betreffend Auswirkungen der Presse- und Rundfunklenkung im Reichsgau Oberdonau in der Zeit vom 21. bis 27.6.1943, 29.6.1943. BA NS6/409, 13.078/79 (DÖW film 54); and doc. 15, Lagebericht des Generalstaatsanwalt beim OLG Linz an den Reichsjustizminister to 1 June 1943, BA R22/3377, 74/75 (DÖW film 97).

12 See Konrad, *Widerstand an Donau und Moldau*, pp. 169–72; *Widerstand und Verfolgung in Wien*, vol. I, pp. 214–30.

13 The last of these was an unusual reference to the German-speaking South Tyrol annexed by Italy in 1919, but still claimed by Austria. It was an

unusual case, in that it was the only one of the German-speaking irredenta whose return to the Reich Hitler did not pursue.

14 DÖW 4412. *Widerstand und Verfolgung in Wien* vol. II, pp. 230–1.

15 Bericht des RSHA betreffend kommunistische Hetzschriftpropaganda, 20.2.1940. DÖW 1453, cited *Widerstand und Verfolgung in Wien* vol. II, pp. 214–15.

16 DÖW film 78, Gestapo Wien, 13, 30–1 March 1939; 7, 22–4 April 1939.

17 DÖW 13,807. Sondergericht Wien 6 SKMs 11/43. Strafsache.

18 On the rationale of the '*Meldungen aus dem Reich*' see Stokes, *German Public Opinion*, pp. 194–253.

19 Roughly translated: 'merry' and 'under the influence of alcohol'.

20 'Unzulänglichkeit des §523 des österreichischen Strafgesetzbuches gegenüber dem §330 a des Reichsstrafgesetzbuches'. T–84 Roll 14, Meldungen des SD-Leitabschnittes Wien-Niederdonau, 14 August 1940.

21 See the case of a 42-year-old Viennese Czech, a cobbler's assistant, arrested shortly before New Year's Eve in 1938. DÖW film 78, Gestapo Wien, 2 January 1939.

22 AVA Gesta, OJs 121/39

23 See Konrad, *Widerstand an Donau und Moldau*, pp. 120–35. In fact, reports of pro-Soviet remarks do not occur as frequently later in the war. This may, of course, have arisen from changes in the Gestapo's activities or record keeping.

24 See Ian Kershaw, '*The Hitler Myth*'. *Image and Reality in the Third Reich* (Oxford, 1987); Stokes, *German Public Opinion*, 471–99.

25 See Kershaw, *Hitler Myth*, pp. 83–104.

26 DÖW film 78, Gestapo, Wien, 29 September 1939; DÖW 13,539. LGA Linz 24/21.

27 *Lausbub*, literally 'louse-boy' has no real equivalent in English, but has something of the sense of scoundrel or blackguard. DÖW film 78, Gestapo Wien, 7–8 February 1939; DÖW film, Gestapo Wien, 31 July–1 August 1939.

28 18. 'I shit on the Führer'; 'the Führer can kiss my arse'. 'Gestapo Wien, 31 January–1 February 1939; Ibid, 14–16 October 1939; See Ernst Hanisch, who detects a 'concentration on the anal sphere' in the 'Austrian tradition of insults (*Schimpftradition*)', Ernst Hanisch 'Gab es einen spezifisch österreichischen Widerstand?', *Zeitgeschichte*, 12 (June/July 1985), 339–50. Here p. 345.

29 See Kershaw, *Hitler Myth*, p.92.

30 DÖW film 78, Gestapo Wien, 14–16 October 1939. His further evidence states that Hitler had indeed only got one.

31 DÖW film 78 Gestapo Wien, 9–10 March 1939.

32 Siegwald Ganglmair, ' "Ich bitte aber, daß mein Name nicht genannt wird." Die Hitler-Zeit am Beispiel Oberösterreichs', *Landstrich. Eine Kulturzeitschrift*, 3 (May 1982), 6–32. Here, p.12.

33 Kershaw, *Hitler Myth*, p.146. See also Stokes, *German Public Opinion*, pp. 477–8

34 BA R58/372 SD Wien, 10 November 1939.

35 DÖW film 78, Gestapo Wien, 11–13 November 1939, report 6, 14–15 November 1939.

36 BA R58/372, SD Wien, 11 November 1939.

37 DÖW film 78, Gestapo Wien, 3–4 January 1939.

38 Stokes distinguishes clearly between Hitler's popularity and the unpopularity of the party, particularly after the outbreak of war: Stokes, *German Public Opinion*, pp. 499–511.

39 USNA T–84 R13 Gestapo Wien, 15 and 16 December 1938.

40 Ibid., 17–18 December; 22–3 December 1938.

41 DÖW 13,539. LGA Linz 19/41.

42 Ibid., 7–8 November 1939.

43 Kershaw makes the point that 'vilification of party functionaries – the "little Hitlers" as they were frequently dubbed – did not necessarily equate with rejection of the party itself, let alone with the aims and ideology of National Socialism.' See Kershaw, *The Hitler Myth*, pp. 96–104. Here p. 96.

44 Peukert, *Inside Nazi Germany*, p. 244. One of those arrested for refusing to give to the Winter Relief Fund, was Marie Innitzer, sister of the Cardinal Archbishop of Vienna, who was asked for a donation in the *Stadtpark* shortly after a demonstration against Innitzer. USNA T–84, Roll 13 Gestapo Wien, 15–16 October 1938.

45 DÖW 12,434. GeSta Wien, 28 August 1939 to Reich Minister of Justice, Berlin.

46 Roughly: 'The Prussian and the profiteer still say Heil Hitler; the thinking civil servant only raises his hand without speaking; the businessman with all his troubles has gone back to saying Good Morning; the poor farmer has reverted to Grüß Gott; the brave Austrian says kiss my arse.' The implication is that the 'brave Austrian' is a worker. Hanisch, 'Widerstand' p.345. *Piefke* was a disparaging nickame for Prussians and by extension for all Reich Germans; *Grüß Gott* is a local Austrian (or Bavarian) greeting, and using it demonstratively instead of the 'German greeting' was an emphatic assertion of Austrian, Catholic and rural identities.

47 The words of a baker's assistant from the seventh district of Vienna. DÖW film 78, Gestapo Wien, 7–8 November 1939.

48 See Detlev Peukert, 'Protest und Widerstand von Jugendlichen im Dritten Reich' in Richard Löwenthal and Patrick von zur Mühlen (eds.), *Widerstand und Verweigerung in Deutschland* (Berlin, 1984); Peukert, *Inside Nazi Germany*, pp. 145–74.

49 Such groups sprang up across the Reich, and those of the Rhineland, Hamburg, Berlin and Bavaria are already well documented. See Peukert, *Inside Nazi Germany*, pp. 154–69, and Peukert, *Edelweisspiraten. Protestbewegungen jugendlicher Arbeiter im Dritten Reich* (Cologne, 1983); Hans Dietrich Schäfer, *Berlin im Zweiten Weltkrieg. Der Untergang der Reichshauptstadt in Augenzeugenberichten* (Munich, 1985). See pp. 192–9 on youth 'cliques' in Berlin, and especially p. 197 on the clique 'Knietief' (Reichssicherheitshauptamt, Meldung wichtiger staatspolizeilicher Ereignisse Nr.1, Juni 1944) p.8; Arno Klönne, 'Jugendprotest und Jugendopposition. Von der HJ-Erziehung zum Cliquenwesen der Kriegszeit', in Martin Broszat et al. (eds.), *Bayern in der NS-Zeit*, vol. IV, pp. 527–620. On '*Swing-Jugend*' see Horst H. Lange, 'Jazz: eine Oase der Sehnsucht', in Deutscher Werkbund e. V. and Württemberg-

ischer Kunstverein Stuttgart (eds.), *Schock und Schöpfung. Jugendästhetik im 20. Jahrhundert* (Darmstadt, 1986), pp. 320–32.

50 See Christian Gerbel, Alexander Mejstrik and Reinhard Sieder, 'Die "Schlurfs" Verweigerung und Opposition von Wiener Arbeiterjugendlichen im "Dritten Reich" ', in Emmerich Tálos, Ernst Hanisch and Wolfgang Neugebauer (eds.), *NS-Herrschaft in Österreich 1938–1845*.

51 DÖW 5732a. Gestapo Wien, 14–16 March 1941.

52 DÖW 5734a. Gestapo Wien, 29 January–2 February 1943.

53 DÖW 5734b. Gestapo Wien, 9–12 April 1943.

54 DÖW 8477. Gestapo Wien, 16–18 November 1943.

55 BA R58/1081 Lagebericht über Österreich.

56 DÖW film 78, Gestapo Wien, 3–5 June 1939 and 9, 20–1 June 1939.

57 From Ermittlungsbericht der Gestapo Linz, Sonderkommando Steyr. LGA Linz 65/40 (DÖW 13512) in *Widerstand und Verfolgung in Oberösterreich* vol. I, p.384.

58 DÖW film 78, Gestapo Wien, 14–16 October 1939.

59 DÖW film 78, Gestapo Wien, 21–3 October 1939.

60 DÖW film 78, Gestapo Wien, 17–18 October 1939.

61 Ibid., 21–3 October 1939.

62 Ibid., 31 October–1 November 1939.

63 Gestapo Wien, 28–30 October 1939.

64 R58/707 fol. 1 (Report from Novak, Vienna, 7 November 1940).

65 Ibid.

66 DÖW film 78, Gestapo Wien, 4–6 November 1939.

67 DÖW film 78, Gestapo Wien, 19–20 October 1939.

68 BA R22/3365 Situation report from *Generalstaatsanwalt*, Graz, 5 February 1940.

69 See *Widerstand und Verfolgung in Tirol* vol. I, pp. 223–321. In particular, documents 4, 13, 37, 38 and 39.

70 USNA T-84 Roll 15, Gestapo Wien, 26–7 September 1940.

71 Ibid., 9–10 April 1940.

72 Ibid., 28–30 March 1941.

73 Ibid., 9–10 April 1941.

74 Ibid.

75 BA R22/3668 Situation report from the *Generalstaatsanwalt* in Innsbruck, 27 January 1942.

76 R22/3365. Situation report from the *Generalstaatsanwalt* in Graz to the Reich Justice Minister Dr Gärtner 10 August 1940.

77 DÖW 5732d Gestapo Wien, 9–10 July 1941.

78 Ibid.

79 DÖW 13,683. Denunciation to the Gestapo, Vienna, 16 August 1941.

80 BA R 22/3668 Situation report from *Generalstaatsanwalt* Innsbruck, 22 July 1941.

81 Ibid., 1 December 1941.

82 Boberach (ed.), *Meldungen*, p.3073, 11 December 1941, and p.3089, 15 December 1941.

83 BA R 22/3668 Situation report from *Generalstaatsanwalt beim Oberlandesgericht* Innsbruck 27 January 1942.

84 BA R22/3668, p. 62: Situation report from the *Generalstaatsanwalt* in Innsbruck, 22 September 1942.

85 BA R22/3365, p.29: 'Report on the general situation' from the *Oberlandesgerichtspräsident* in Graz, 26. November 1942.

86 Boberach (ed.), *Meldungen*, p.4707, 21 January 1943.

87 BA NS6/408 Situation report from SD Linz, 11 January 1943.

88 Boberach (ed.), *Meldungen*, p.4751.

89 BA NS6/408, p.204 *Meldungen aus dem Reichsgau Oberdonau*, Linz, 8 February 1943.

90 Ibid.

91 BA NS6/408, *Meldungen aus dem Reichsgau Oberdonau*, Linz, 19 February 1943

92 Boberach (ed.), *Meldungen*, p.5125.

93 BA NS6/409, *Meldungen aus dem Reichsgau Oberdonau*, Linz, 19 May 1943.

94 Ibid., 28 May 1943. A side effect of this mood was a fall in the birth rate, which could not entirely be attributed to shortages of baby clothes and baby food. One working-class woman remarked: 'We don't want to have a second child for the present, everything is so uncertain now, we've enough trouble with just one', and a chemist reported an increase in demand for contraceptives.

95 BA R22/3365, *Generalstaatsanwaltschaft* Graz, Report on the general situation, 25 September, 1943; R22, 3377, *Generalstaatsanwalt* Linz, General Situation in the *Reichsgau* Oberdonau, 6 October 1943.

96 BA R22/3377 *Oberlandesgerichtspräsident*, Linz, 6.12.1943; BA/MA, RW 21-4 and BA/MA, RW 21-33; BA R22/3365, Report to the Reich Justice Minister from Graz, 22 January 1944.

97 BA R22/3388, *Generalstaatsanwalt*, Vienna, 1 June 1943.

98 Butschek, *Die österreichische Wirtschaft*, p. 95. The exceptions were the winter wheat and rye harvests of 1941 and 1943, which showed an improvement on the previous year, but nevertheless returned a yield of less than 80 per cent of that of 1939. The number of beef and dairy cattle remained stable and the number of sheep increased. The number of pigs and poultry, which were more difficult to feed, declined.

99 See Werner, *Bleib übrig!*, p.195.

100 Boberach (ed.), *Meldungen*, p.3189, 19 January 1942.

101 Ibid., p.3448, 12 March 1942.

102 Ibid., p.3505, 23 March 1942.

103 Ibid., p.3623, 13 April 1942.

104 Ibid., p.3754; p.3756 28 May 1942.

105 Ibid., pp. 3086–8

106 'Ein unbekannter Bericht Kaltenbrunners über die Lage in Österreich im September 1944.' in Ludwig Jedlicka, *Der 20. Juli 1944* (Vienna, 1985), pp. 92–5. Cited in Karl Stadler, *Austria* (London, 1971), p.248.

107 DÖW 5120 SD Wien, 17 October 1944. Work on the fortifications in Lower Austria had been delayed for several weeks because of the effect they might have on Hungarian morale.

108 BA R22/3388 *Oberlandesgerichtspräsident*, Vienna to Reich Minister of Justice, Berlin, 7 November 1944. Sirens were all sounded at the approach of

planes flying over Vienna to Slovakia and Silesia, disrupting the life of the city unnecessarily.

109 DÖW 5120. SD Wien, 17 October 1944.
110 BA R22/3388 *Oberlandesgerichtspräsident*, Vienna to Reich Minister of Justice, Berlin, 7 November 1944.
111 DÖW 5120. SD Wien, 22 January 1945.
112 Ibid., SD Wien, 13 December 1944
113 Ibid., 6 March 1945.
114 Karl Stadler, *Austria*, pp. 248–50.

CONCLUSION

1 See Robert Knight, 'Einige vergleichende Betrachtungen zur "Vergangenheitsbewältigung" in Österreich und Grossbritannien', *Zeitgeschichte*, 15 (1987), 63–71, and Anton Pelinka, 'The Great Austrian Taboo: The Repression of the Civil War', *New German Critique*, 43 (1988), 69–82. F. Parkinson, 'Epilogue' in F. Parkinson (ed.), *Conquering the Past. Austrian Nazism Yesterday and Today* (Detroit, 1989), pp. 313–334
2 AVA, Rk, 192, SD Donau to Bürckel, 16 February 1939: Bericht über eine Aussprache mit den nachstehend genannten ehemaligen Arbeiter-Betriebsraten, bezw. Vertrauensmännern.
3 Such a fragmentation of politics has been suggested by Schoenbaum, *Hitler's Social Revolution* (New York 1966, 1980), p. 297.
4 Ibid., p. 293.
5 Karner, 'Arbeitsvertragsbrüche', p.376.
6 See Gerhard Botz, 'Der ambivalenter Anschluss 1938–1939. Von der Begeisterung zur Ernüchterung,' *Zeitgeschichte*, 6 (1978), 91–109
7 See Robert Knight, 'Education and National Identity in Austria after the Second World War', in Ritchie Robertson and Edward Timms (eds.), *The Habsburg Legacy* (Edinburgh, 1993). pp. 178–95.

Select bibliography

ARCHIVAL SOURCES

AUSTRIAN STATE ARCHIVES, VIENNA

The Austrian State Archives were reorganised during the course of research for this book. Material deposited after the end of the First World War was transferred from the General Administration Archive (*Allgemeines Verwaltungsarchiv*, AVA) to the Archive of the Republic (*Archiv der Republik*, AdR) which was founded in 1984. Material used before that date will be cited by the original AVA reference. The State Archives have conversion lists.

Reichskommissar für die Wiedervereinigung Österreichs mit dem Deutschen Reich (Bürckel-Akten, Rk): 19, 20, 21, 33, 70, 72, 73, 74, 76, 104, 109, 124, 170, 171, 181, 182, 183.

Generalstaatsanwaltschaft (GeSta) Linz: miscellaneous cases.

DOKUMENTATIONSARCHIV DES ÖSTERREICHISCHEN WIDERSTANDS (DÖW)

Documents: 426, 1453, 1454, 1571, 1576, 1578, 4412, 5120, 5732a–d, 5733a–f, 5734a–d, 8476, 8477, 8479, 12,434, 13,288, 13,512, 13,539, 13,683, 13,807
Films: 54, 68/2, 76, 78, 97, 99, 104.

GERMAN FEDERAL ARCHIVES, KOBLENZ (*Bundesarchiv*, BA)

R22 (Justizministerium):
3365 (Generalstaatsanwalt/Oberlandesgerichtspräsident Graz)
3368 (Generalstaatsanwalt/Oberlandesgerichtspräsident Innsbruck)
3388 (Generalstaatsanwalt/Oberlandesgerichtspräsident Wien)
3377 (Generalstaatsanwalt/Oberlandesgerichtspräsident Linz)
R43 (Reichskanzlei): 427, 527, 528, 529a, 532, 542, 652a, 654b, 655a.
R58 (Reichssicherheitshauptamt): 332, 372,375, 376, 446, 603, 707, 723, 1081
NS6 (Partei-Kanzlei): 408, 409
NS19 (Persönlicher Stab Reichsführer SS)

GERMAN FEDERAL MILITARY ARCHIVE, FREIBURG IM BREISGAU (*Bundesarchiv Militärarchiv*, BA/MA)

RW 20–17 (12–15) Lageberichte der Rüstungsinspektion, Wehrwirtschaftskreis XVII (Wien)

RW 20–18 (17–28) Lageberichte der Rüstungsinspektion, Wehrwirtschaftskreis XVIII (Salzburg)
RW 21–4 (1–22) Kriegstagebücher Rüstungskommando Graz
RW 21–8 (1–18) Kriegstagebücher Rüstungskommando Innsbruck
RW 21–33 (1–14) Kriegstagebücher Rüstungskommando Klagenfurt
RW 21–38 (1–13) Kriegstagebücher Rüstungskommando Linz
RW 21–46 (1–14) Kriegstagebücher Rüstungskommando Mödling
RW 21–63 (1–6) Kriegstagebücher Rüstungskommando Wien

OBERÖSTERREICHISCHES LANDESARCHIV, LINZ (Upper Austrian State Archives, OÖLA)

Generalakten 7, 25, 34
C17 (Politische Akten): 52
C33 (Kriegswirtschaft): 4, 6, 9, 16, 19, 20, 21, 22, 25

PRIVATE COLLECTION GERHARD BOTZ/LUDWIG BOLTZMANN INSTITUT FÜR HISTORISCHE SOZIALWISSENSCHAFT, SALZBURG

Landesgerichtsarchiv (LGA) Linz: *Haftverfahren* (HV). Custodial cases dealing with breach of employment contract (copies).

UNITED STATES NATIONAL ARCHIVES, WASHINGTON (USNA, also available in published form). Captured German records, microfilmed at Alexandria

T-77: 741
T-84: 13, 14, 14

CONTEMPORARY PUBLISHED SOURCES

Arbeiterzeitung, 17 May 1933, 25 February 1934, 4 March 1934, 17 February 1935.
Otto Bauer, *Zwischen Zwei Weltkriegen* in *Otto Bauer. Werkausgabe* vol. IV (Vienna, 1976), pp. 49–329.
Otto Bauer, 'Der Faschismus. Vom Weltkrieg', *Der sozialistische Kampf*, 4 (1938), pp. 75–83.
G.E.R. Gedye, *Fallen Bastions* (London, 1939).
Jahrbuch der österreichischen Arbeiterbewegung 1932 (Vienna, 1933).
Nouvelles d'Autriche.
Österreichische Informationen.
Statistical Year Book of the League of Nations (Geneva, 1938).
Statistisches Jahrbuch für das deutsche Reich (Berlin, 1942).
Statistisches Handbuch für die Republik Österreich, (Vienna, 1927).
Statistisches Handbuch für die Republik Österreich, vol. XII (Vienna, 1931).
Statistisches Handbuch für die Republik Österreich, (Vienna, 1932).
Statistisches Jahrbuch für des Bundesstaat Österreich. Die Ergebnisse der österreichischen Volkszählung vom 22. März 1934. (Tabellenheft) (Vienna, 1935).

Statistik des deutschen Reichs, vols. 550/27, 28.
'Das tschechische Wien', *Der getreue Eckart*, monthly journal of the *Deutscher Schulverein* (1908), Austrian National Library, 461591–C.

PUBLISHED PRIMARY SOURCES

Heinz Boberach (ed.), *Meldungen aus dem Reich. Die geheimen Lageberichte des Sicherheitsdienstes der SS 1938–1945*, 17 vols. (Herrsching, 1984).
Deutschland-Berichte der Sozialdemokratischen Partei Deutschlands (Sopade) 1934–1940, 7 vols. (Salzhausen and Frankfurt am Main, 1980).
Protokolle des Ministerrates der Ersten Republik. Abteilung VIII: 20. Mai 1932 bis 25. Juli 1934:
vol. I, *Kabinett Dr. Engelbert Dollfuss 20. Mai 1932 bis 18. Oktober 1932* (Vienna, 1980).
vol. III, *Kabinett Dr. Engelbert Dollfuss, 22. März 1933 bis 14. Juni 1933* (Vienna, 1983).
vol. IV, *Kabinett Dr. Engelbert Dollfuss 16. Juni 1933 bis 27. Oktober 1933* (Vienna, 1984).
Protokolle des Ministerrates der Ersten Republik. Abteilung IX: 29. Juli 1934 bis 11. März 1938:
vol. I, *Kabinett Dr Kurt Schuschnigg 30. Juli 1934 bis 26. Oktober 1934* (Vienna, 1988).
vol. II, *Kabinett Dr Kurt Schuschnigg 30. Oktober 1934 bis 24. Mai 1935* (Vienna, 1993).
Dokumentationsarchiv des österreichischen Widerstandes:
Widerstand und Verfolgung in Wien 1934–1945, 3 vols. (Vienna, 1975).
Widerstand und Verfolgung im Burgenland 1934–1945 (Vienna, 1979).
Widerstand und Verfolgung in Oberösterreich 1934–1945, 2 vols. Vienna, 1982).
Widerstand und Verfolgung in Tirol 1934–1945, 2 vols. (Vienna, 1984).
Widerstand und Verfolgung in Niederösterreich 1934–1945, 3 vols. (Vienna, 1987).
Widerstand und Verfolgung in Salzburg 1938–1945, 2 vols. (Vienna, 1991).
Adolf Hitler, *Mein Kampf*, translated by Ralph Mannheim (London, 1992).

SECONDARY SOURCES

Lynn Abrams, *Workers' Culture in Imperial Germany. Leisure and Recreation in the Rhineland and Westphalia* (London, 1992).
Isabella Ackerl, Walter Hummelberger and Hans Mommsen (eds.), *Politik und Gesellschaft im alten und neuen Österreich. Festschrift für Rudolf Neck zum 60. Geburtstag* (Vienna, 1981).
Thomas Albrich and Wolfgang Meixner, 'Zwischen Legalität und Illegalität. Zur Mitgliederentwicklung, Alters- und Sozialstruktur der NSDAP in Tirol und Vorarlberg vor 1938', *Zeitgeschichte*, 22 (1995), 149–87.
Wolfgang Ammanshauser, 'Fluchtversuche aus einem geschlossenen Mediensystem. Die Verordnung über ausserordentliche Rundfunkmassnahmen vom 1. September 1939. Ihre Entstehung, ihre Bedeutung, sowie ihre Auswirkung im Reichsgau Salzburg 1939–1945', Phil. Diss. (Salzburg, 1984).

Brigitte Bailer, *Wiedergutmachung kein Thema. Österreich und die Opfer des Nationalsozialismus* (Vienna, 1993).

Peter Baldwin, 'Social Interpretations of Nazism: Reviewing a Tradition', in *Journal of Contemporary History*, 25 (1990), 5–37.

John Barber and Mark Harrison, *The Soviet Home Front 1941–1945: A Social and Economic History of the USSR* (London and New York, 1991)

Heinrich Benedikt (ed.), *Geschichte der Republik Österreich* (Munich, 1954).

Karin Berger, *Zwischen Eintopf und Fließband. Frauenarbeit und Frauenbild im Faschismus. Österreich 1938–1945* (Vienna, 1984).

Richard Bessel (ed.), *Life in the Third Reich* (Oxford, 1987).

Günter Bischof, 'Die Instrumentalisierung der Moskauer Erklärung nach dem 2. Weltkrieg', *Zeitgeschichte*, 20 (1993), 345–66.

Martin Blinkhorn (ed.), *Fascists and Conservatives. The Radical Right and the Establishment in Twentieth Century Europe* (London, 1990).

Kuno Bludau, *Gestapo-Geheim! Widerstand und Verfolgung in Duisburg 1933–1945* (Bad Godesberg, 1973).

Giesela Bock, 'Gleichheit und Differenz in der nationalsozialistischen Rassenpolitik', *Geschichte und Gesellschaft*, 19 (1993), 277–310.

Gerhard Botz, 'Ideologie und Wirklichkeit des "Nationalen Sozialismus" in der "Ostmark" ', introduction to Robert Schwarz, *'Sozialismus der Propaganda'. Das Werben des 'Völkischen Beobachters' um die österreichische Arbeiterschaft 1938–9* (Vienna, 1975), pp. 5–46.

Wien vom 'Anschluß' zum Krieg. Nationalsozialistsische Machtübernahme und politisch-soziale Umgestaltung am Beispiel der Stadt Wien 1938/39 (Vienna, 1978).

'Der ambivalente Anschluss 1938–1939. Von der Begeisterung zur Ernüchterung', *Zeitgeschichte*, 6 (1978), 91–109.

'Introduction: Varieties of Fascism in Austria', in Stein Larsen, J. P. Mykleburst and B. Hatvet (eds.), *Who were the Fascists?* (Oslo, 1979) pp. 192–9.

'Changing Patterns of Support for Austrian National Socialism', in Stein Larsen, J. P. Mykleburst and B. Hatvet (eds.), *Who were the Fascists?* (Oslo, 1979), pp. 202–26.

'Strukturwandlungen des österreichischen Nationalsozialismus (1904–1905)', in Isabella Ackerl, Walter Hummelberger and Hans Mommsen (eds.), *Politik und Gesellschaft im alten und neuen Österreich. Festschrift für Rudolf Neck zum 60. Geburtstag* (Vienna 1981), pp.162–93.

Die Eingliederung Österreichs in das deutsche Reich. Planung und Verwirklichung des politisch-administrativen Anschlusses (1938–1940) (Linz, 1982).

'Methoden und Theorienprobleme der historischen Widerstandsforschung', in Helmut Konrad and Wolfgang Neugebauer (eds.) *Arbeiterbewegung, Faschismus, Nationalbewußtsein* (Vienna, Munich and Zürich, 1983), pp. 137–51.

'Widerstand von Einzelnen', in *Widerstand und Verfolgung in Oberösterreich 1934–1945* (Vienna 1982), vol II, 351–63.

'Austria', in Detlef Mühlberger (ed.), *The Social Basis of European Fascist Movements* (London, 1987), pp.242–80.

Krisenzonen einer Demokratie. Gewalt, Streik und Konfliktunterdrückung in Österreich seit 1918 (Frankfurt am Main, 1987).

'Der "4. März 1933" als Konsequenz ständischer Strukturen ökonomischer Krisen und autoritärer Tendenzen', in Gerhard Botz, *Krisenzonen einer Demokratie* (Frankfurt am Main, 1987), pp.155–80.

'Die Ausschaltung des Nationalrates im Urteil von Zeitgenossen und Historikern', in Gerhard Botz, *Krisenzonen einer Demokratie* (Frankfurt am Main, 1987), pp. 119–54.

'Der Aufstandsversuch österreichischer Sozialdemokraten am 12. Februar 1934: Ursachen für seinen Ausbruch und seinen Misserfolg', in Gerhard Botz, *Krisenzonen einer Demokratie* (Frankfurt am Main, 1987), pp.181–99.

John W. Boyer, *Political Radicalism in Late Imperial Vienna. Origins of the Christian Social Movement* (Chicago and London, 1981).

Martin Broszat, Elke Fröhlich and Falk Wiesemann (vol.I) and Martin Broszat, Elke Fröhlich, Falk Wiesemann and Anton Großmann (vols. II–IV) (eds.), *Bayern in der NS-Zeit. Soziale Lage und politisches Verhalten der Bevölkerung im Spiegel der vertraulichen Berichte*, 4 vols. (Munich and Vienna, 1971–1981).

'Resistenz und Widerstand. Eine Zwischenbilanz des Forschungsprojekts', in Broszat, Fröhlich, Wiesemann and Großmann (eds.) *Bayern in der NS-Zeit* vol. IV *Herrschaft und Gesellschaft im Konflikt* (Munich, 1981), pp. 691–709.

Karl M, Brousek, *Wien und seine Tschechen. Integration und Assimilation einer Minderheit im 20. Jahrhundert* (Vienna, 1980).

Evan Bukey, *Hitler's Hometown. Linz, Austria 1908–1945* (Bloomington, 1986).

'Popular Opinion in Vienna after the Anschluss', in F. Parkinson (ed.). *Conquering the Past. Austrian Nazism Yesterday and Today* (Detroit, 1989).

'*Patenstadt des Führers*'. *Eine Politik- und Sozialgeschichte von Linz 1908–1945* (Frankfurt am Main, 1993).

Michael Burleigh and Wolfgang Wippermann, *The Racial State* (Cambridge, 1991).

Felix Butschek, *Die österreichische Wirtschaft 1938 bis 1945* (Vienna and Stuttgart, 1978).

Josef Buttinger, *Am Beispiel Österreichs. Ein Beitrag zur Krise in der sozialistischen Bewegung* (Cologne, 1953).

F. L. Carsten, *Fascist Movements in Austria from Schönerer to Hitler* (London, 1977).

The German Workers and the Nazis (Aldershot, 1995).

Jack R. Censer, 'Editor's Preface' in David Crew (ed.), *Nazism and German Society 1933–1945* (London 1994).

Thomas Childers and Jane Caplan (eds.), *Reevaluating the Third Reich* (New York, 1993).

Gary Cohen, *The Politics of Ethnic Survival: Germans in Prague 1861–1914* (Princeton, 1981).

Forrest D. Colburn (ed.), *Everyday Forms of Peasant Resistance* (New York, 1989).

Robert Conquest, 'Revisionising Stalin's Russia', *Russian Review*, 46 (1987), 386–90.

Mark Cornwall, 'The Struggle on the Czech-German Language Border, 1880–1940', *English Historical Review*, 109 (September 1994), 914–51.

David Crew, 'General Introduction' in Crew (ed.), *Nazism and German Society 1933–1945* (London, 1994), pp. 1–37.

A. Diamant, 'The Group Basis of Austrian Politics', *Journal of Central European Affairs* (18 July 1983), 134–55.

Wacław Dlugoborski (ed.), *Zweiter Weltkrieg und Sozialer Wandel. Achsenmächte und besetzte Länder* (Göttingen, 1981).

Ilona Duczynska, *Workers in Arms. The Austrian Schutzbund and the Civil War of 1934* (London, 1978).

C. Earl Edmondson, *The Heimwehr and Austrian Politics 1918–1936* (Athens, Ga, 1978).

Geoff Eley, 'History with the Politics Left Out – Again?', *Russian Review*, 45 (1986), 385–94.

Richard Evans, *Kneipengespräche im Kaiserreich. Die Stimmungsberichte der Hamburger Politischen Polizei 1892–1914* (Hamburg, 1989).

Sabine Falch, ' "Legaler Sturz des Systems von unten her auf dem Wege über die Länder und Gemeinden." Zu den NS-Erfolgen bei den Gemeinderatswahlen in Tirol 1932 und 1933', *Zeitgeschichte*, 22 (1995), 188–210.

Jürgen Falter, 'Warum die deutschen Arbeiter während des "Dritten Reiches" zu Hitler standen. Einige Anmerkungen zu Gunther Mais Beitrag über die Unterstützung des nationalsozialistischen Herrschaftssystems durch Arbeiter', *Geschichte und Gesellschaft*, 13 (1987), 217–31.

Jürgen Falter and Dirk Hänisch, 'Wahlerfolge und Wählerschaft der NSDAP in Österreich von 1927 bis 1932: Soziale Basis und Parteipolitische Herkunft', *Zeitgeschichte*, 15 (1988), 223–44.

Arlette Farge, *Subversive Words. Public Opinion in Eighteenth-Century France* (Cambridge, 1994).

Fritz Fellner, 'The Background of Austrian Fascism', in Peter F. Sugar (ed.), *Native Fascism in the Successor States 1918–1945* (Santa Barbara, 1971).

Tone Ferenc 'The Austrians and Slovenia during the Second World War', in F. Parkinson (ed.), *Conquering the Past. Austrian Nazism Yesterday and Today* (Detroit, 1989), pp. 207–23.

Helmut Fiereder, *Reichswerke Hermann Göring in Österreich (1938–1945)* (Vienna and Salzburg, 1983).

Sheila Fitzpatrick, 'New Perspectives on Stalinism', *Russian Review*, 45 (1986), 357–74.

Karl Flanner, *Widerstand im Gebiet von Wiener Neustadt* (Vienna, 1973).

Florian Freund und Bertrand Perz, *Das KZ in der "Serbenhalle". Zur Kriegsindustrie in Wiener Neustadt* (Vienna, 1987).

Arbeitslager Zement. Das Konzentrationslager Ebensee und die Raketenrüstung (Vienna, 1989).

Projekt Quarz. Steyr Daimler-Puch und das Konzentrationslager Melk (Vienna, 1991).

'Fremdarbeiter und KZ-Häftlinge in der "Ostmark" ', in Ulrich Herbert (ed.), *Europa und der Reichseinsatz. Ausländische Zivilarbeiter, Kriegsgefangene und KZ-Häftlinge in Deutschland 1938–1945* (Essen, 1991), pp.317–50.

Carl J. Friedrich and Zbigniew Brzezinski, *Totalitarian Dictatorship and Autocracy* (New York, 1956).

Siegwald Ganglmair, ' "Ich bitte aber, daß mein Name nicht genannt wird."
    Die Hitler-Zeit am Beispiel Oberösterreichs', *Landstrich. Eine Kulturzeitsch-*
    rift, 3 (May 1982), 6–32.
Christian Gerbel, Alexander Mejstrik and Reinhard Sieder, 'Die "Schlurfs"
    Verweigerung und Opposition von Wiener Arbeiterjugendlichen im
    "Dritten Reich" ', in Emmerich Tálos, Ernst Hanisch and Wolfgang
    Neugebauer (eds.), *NS-Herrschaft in Österreich 1938–1845* (Vienna, 1988).
Ursula von Gersdorff, *Frauen im Kriegsdienst 1914–1945* (Stuttgart, 1969).
David Good, 'Economic Union and Uneven Development in the Habsburg
    Monarchy', in John Komlos (ed.), *Economic Development in the Habsburg*
    Monarchy in the Nineteenth Century. Essays (New York, 1983).
Helen Graham, 'Review of Michael Seidman, *Workers against Work: Labour in*
    Paris and Barcelona during the Popular Fronts' International Review of Social
    History, 37 (1992), 276–81.
Helmut Gruber, *Red Vienna. Experiment in Working-Class Culture 1919–1934*
    (Oxford, 1991).
John Haag, 'Marginal Men and the Dream of the Reich': Eight Austrian
    National-Catholic Intellectuals 1918–1938, in Larsen, Mykleburst and
    Hatvet (eds.), *Who were the Fascists?* (Oslo, 1979).
Rüdiger Hachtmann, *Industriearbeit im 'Dritten Reich': Untersuchungen zu den*
    Lohn- und Arbeitsbedingungen in Deutschland 1933–1945 (Göttingen, 1989).
    'Industriearbeiterinnen in der deutschen Kriegswirtschaft 1936 bis 1944/45',
    Geschichte und Gesellschaft, 19 (1993), 332–66.
Ernst Hanisch, *Nationalsozialistische Herrschaft in der Provinz. Salzburg im Dritten*
    Reich (Salzburg, 1983).
    'Gab es einen spezifisch österreichischen Widerstand?', *Zeitgeschichte*, 12
    (1985), 339–50.
    'Fragmentarische Bemerkungen zur Konzeptualisierung der NS-Herrschaft in
    Österreich', in Stourzh and Zahr (eds.), *Österreich, Deutschland und die*
    Mächte (Vienna, 1990), pp. 493–5.
    Der lange Schatten des Staates. Österreichische Gesellschaftsgeschichte im
    20. Jahrhundert (Vienna, 1994).
Hans Hautmann and Rudolf Kropf, *Die österreichische Arbeiterbewegung vom Vor-*
    märz bis 1945. Sozialökonomische Ursprünge ihrer Ideologie und Politik (Linz,
    1974).
Paul Hehn, *The German Struggle against Yugoslav Guerillas in World War II.*
    German Counter-Insurgency in Yugoslavia 1941–1943 (New York, 1979).
Ulrich Herbert, ' "Die guten und die schlechten Zeiten." Überlegungen zur
    diachronen Analyse lebensgeschichtlicher Interviews', in Lutz Niethammer
    (ed.). *'Die Jahre weiß man nicht, wo man die heute hinsetzen soll.' Faschismus-*
    erfahrungen im Ruhrgebiet (Berlin, 1983).
    Fremdarbeiter. Politik und Praxis des Ausländer-Einsatzes in der Kriegswirtschaft
    des Dritten Reiches (Berlin, 1986).
    'Good Times, Bad Times: Memories of the Third Reich,' in Richard Bessel
    (ed.), *Life in the Third Reich* (Oxford, 1987), pp.97–110.
    'Arbeiterschaft im "Dritten Reich". Zwischenbilanz und offene Fragen',
    Geschichte und Gesellschaft, 15 (1989), 320–60.

Ulrich Herbert (ed.), *Europa und der 'Reichseinsatz'. Ausländische Zivilarbeiter, Kriegsgefangene und KZ-Häftlinge in Deutschland 1938–1945* (Essen, 1991).

Lothar Höbelt, *Kornblume und Kaiseradler. Die deutschfreiheitlichen Parteien Alt-österreichs 1882–1918* (Vienna and Munich, 1993).

Everhard Holtmann, *Zwischen Befriedung und Unterdrückung. Sozialistische Arbeiterbewegung und autoritäres Regime* (Munich, 1978).

Willibald Ingo Holzer, 'Die österreichischen Bataillonen im Verband der NOV i POJ. Die Kampfgruppe Avantgarde-Steiermark. Die Partisanengruppe Leoben-Donawitz. Die Kommunistische Partei Österreichs im militanten politischen Widerstand', Phil. Diss. (Vienna 1971).

'Am Beispiel der Kampfgruppe Avantgarde/Steiermark (1944–1945)', in G. Botz, H. Hautmann, H. Konrad and J. Weidenholzer (eds.), *Bewegung und Klasse. Studien zur österreichischen Arbeitergeschichte* (Vienna 1978).

Im Schatten des Faschismus. Der österreichische Widerstand gegen Hitler 1938–1945 (Vienna, 1981).

Edward L. Homze, *Foreign Labor in Nazi Germany*, (Princeton, 1967).

Marie Jahoda, Paul F Lazarsfeld, Hans Zeisel, *The Sociography of an Unemployed Community* (London, 1972); originally *Die Arbeitslosen von Marienthal* (Leipzig, 1933).

Michael John and Albert Lichtblau, 'Česká Víden: Von der tschechischen Groß-stadt zum tschechischen Dorf', *Archiv. Jahrbuch des Vereins für die Geschichte der Arbeiterbewegung*, 3 (1987), 34–41.

Schmelztiegel Wien. Einst und Jetzt. Zur Geschichte und Gegenwart von Zuwanderung und Minderheiten. Aufsätze, Quellen, Kommentare, 2nd edn (Vienna, Cologne, Weimar, 1993).

Stefan Karner, 'Arbeitsvertragsbrüche als Verletzung der Arbeitspflicht im Dritten Reich. Darstellung und EDV-Analyse am Beispiel der untersteirischen VDM-Luftfahrwerkes Marburg/Maribor', *Archiv für Sozialgeschichte*, 21 (1982), 269–328.

Die Steiermark im Dritten Reich 1938–1945. Aspekte ihrer politischen, wirtschaftlich-sozialen und kulturellen Entwicklung (Graz and Vienna, 1986).

M. C. Kaser and E. A. Radice (eds.), *The Economic History of Eastern Europe 1919–1975* (Oxford, 1986).

Edward P. Keleher, 'Austria's *Lebensunfähigkeit* and the Anschluss Question 1918–1922', *East European Quarterly*, 23/1, (March 1989), 71–83.

Hans Kernbauer and Fritz Weber, 'Von der Inflation zur Depression. Österreichs Wirtschaft 1918–1934' in E. Tálos and W. Neugebauer (eds.), *'Austrofaschismus' Beiträge über Politik, Ökonomie und Kultur 1934–1938* (Vienna, 1984).

Ian Kershaw, *Popular Opinion and Political Dissent in the Third Reich: Bavaria 1933–1945* (Oxford, 1984).

' "Widerstand ohne Volk?" Dissens und Widerstand im Dritten Reich', in Jürgen Schmädeke and Peter Steinbach (eds.), *Widerstand gegen den Nationalsozialismus. Die deutsche Gesellschaft und der Widerstand gegen Hitler* (Munich, 1985), pp. 779–98.

'The Hitler Myth'. Image and Reality in the Third Reich (Oxford, 1987).

Robert H Keyserlingk, 'Austria Abandoned. Anglo-American Propaganda and Planning for Austria, 1938–1945', in Parkinson (ed.), *Conquering the Past* (Detroit, 1989), pp.224–42.

Timothy Kirk, 'The Austrian Working Class under National Socialist Rule: Industrial Unrest and Political Dissent in the People's Community', Ph.D. dissertation (Manchester 1988).

'Limits of Germandom: The Resistance to the Nazi Annexation of Slovenia', *Slavonic and East European Review*, 69 (1991), pp. 646–67.

Arno Klönne, 'Jugendprotest und Jugendopposition. Von der HJ-Erziehung zum Cliquenwesen der Kriegszeit', in Broszat, Fröhlich, Wiesemann and Großmann (eds.) *Bayern in der NS-Zeit*, vol IV, pp. 527–620.

Kurt Klotzbach, *Gegen den Nationalsozialismus. Widerstand und Verfolgung in Dortmund 1933–1945* (Bad Godesberg, 1973).

Robert Knight, 'The Waldheim Context', *Times Literary Supplement* (3 October 1986).

'Einige vergleichende Betrachtungen zur "Vergangenheitsbewältigung" in Österreich und Grossbritannien', *Zeitgeschichte*, 15 (1987), 63–71.

'Education and National Identity in Austria after the Second World War', in Ritchie Robertson and Edward Timms (eds.), *The Habsburg Legacy* (Edinburgh, 1993), pp. 178–95.

Magdalena Koch, 'Der Widerstand der Kommunistischen Partei Österreichs gegen Hitler von 1938–1945' Phil. Diss. (Vienna, 1964).

John Komlos (ed.), *Economic Development in the Habsburg Monarchy in the Nineteenth Century. Essays* (New York, 1983).

Helmut Konrad, *Widerstand und Verfolgung an Donau und Moldau. KPÖ und KSC zur Zeit des Hitler-Stalin-Paktes* (Vienna, 1978).

J. Krejci, 'The Bohemian-Moravian War Economy' in M.C. Kaser and E.A. Radice (eds.), *The Economic History of Eastern Europe 1919–1975* (Oxford, 1986), vol II, pp.452–92.

Horst H. Lange, 'Jazz: eine Oase der Sehnsucht', in Deutscher Werkbund e.V. and Württembergischer Kunstverein Stuttgart (eds.), *Schock und Schöpfung. Jugendästhetik im 20. Jahrhundert* (Darmstadt, 1986), pp. 320–32.

David Clay Large (ed.), *Contending with Hitler. Varieties of German Resistance in the Third Reich* (Cambridge, 1991).

Stein Larsen, J.P. Mykleburst and B. Hatvet (eds.), *Who were the Fascists?*. (Oslo, 1979).

Jill Lewis, 'Red Vienna: Socialism in One City 1918–1927', *European Studies Review*, 13 (1983), 335–55.

'The Failure of Styrian Labour in the First Austrian Republic', Ph.D dissertation (Lancaster, 1984).

'Austria', in Martin Blinkhorn (ed.), *Fascists and Conservatives. The Radical Right and the Establishment in Twentieth-Century Europe* (London, 1990), pp. 98–117.

Fascism and the Working Class in Austria 1918–1934 (New York and Oxford, 1991).

Andrea Lösch, 'Staatliche Arbeitsmarktpolitik nach dem ersten Weltkrieg als Instrument der Verdrängung von Frauen aus der Erwerbsarbeit', *Zeitgeschichte*, 14 (May 1987), 313–29.

Czeslaw Łuczak, 'Polnische Arbeiter im nationalsozialistischen Deutschland während des zweiten Weltkrieges. Entwicklung und Aufgaben der polnischen Forschung' in Herbert (ed.). *Europa und der Reichseinsatz* (Essen, 1991), pp. 90–105.

Alf Lüdtke, 'The "Honor of Labor". Industrial workers and the power of symbols under National Socialism', in David Crew (ed.), *Nazism and German Society 1933–1945* (London, 1994), pp.67–109.

Radomir Luža, *Anglo-German Relations in the Anschluss Era* (Princeton and London, 1975).

The Resistance in Austria 1938–1945 (Minneapolis, 1984).

'Die Strukturen der nationalsozialistischen Herrschaft in Österreich' in Gerald Stourzh and Brigitte Zahr (eds.), *Österreich, Deutschland und die Mächte. Internationale und österreichische Aspekte des 'Anschlusses' vom März 1938* (Vienna, 1990), pp.471–92.

Gunther Mai, ' "Warum steht der deutsche Arbeiter zu Hitler?" Zur Rolle der deutschen Arbeitsfront im Herrschaftssystem des Dritten Reiches', *Geschichte und Gesellschaft*, 12 (1986), 212–34.

Gordon Martel (ed.), *Modern Germany Reconsidered 1870–1945* (London and New York, 1992).

Tim Mason, 'Labour in the Third Reich 1933–39', *Past and Present*, 33 (1966), 112–41.

Arbeiterklasse und Volksgemeinschaft. Dokumente und Materialien zur deutschen Arbeiterpolitik 1936–1939 (Opladen, 1975).

Sozialpolitik im Dritten Reich. Arbeiterklasse und Volksgemeinschaft (Opladen, 1977).

'Workers' Opposition in Nazi Germany', *History Workshop Journal*, 11 (1981), 120–37.

'Die Bändigung der Arbeiterklasse im nationalsozialistischen Deutschland', in Carol Sachse, Tilla Siegel, Hasso Spode and Wolfgang Spohn, *Angst, Belohnung, Zucht, und Ordnung. Herrschaftsmechanismen im Nationalsozialismus* (Opladen, 1982); now translated as 'The Containment of German Workers in the National Socialist System', in Tim Mason, *Nazism, Fascism and the Working Class*, ed. Jane Caplan (Cambridge, 1995).

'Whatever happened to "Fascism" ', in Thomas Childers and Jane Caplan (eds). *Reevaluating the Third Reich* (New York, 1993), pp. 253–62.

Social Policy in the Third Reich. The Working Class and the 'National Community' (Providence and Oxford, 1993).

Nazism, Fascism and the Working Class, ed. Jane Caplan (Cambridge, 1995).

Gerhard Melinz, 'Die Christlichsoziale Partei Wiens. Von der Majorität zur Minorität und "Kerntruppe" der Vaterländischen Front', *Wiener Geschichtsblätter*, 49 (1994), 1–14.

Hermann Mitteräcker, *Kampf und Opfer für Österreich. Ein Beitrag zur Geschichte des österreichischen Widerstandes 1933–1945* (Vienna, 1963).

Fritz Molden, *Feuer in der Nacht. Opfer und Sinn des österreichischen Widerstandes 1938–1945* (Vienna, 1988).

Hans Mommsen, 'Das Problem der böhmischen Arbeiterbewegung', in Hans Mommsen, *Arbeiterbewegung und Nationale Frage. Ausgewählte Aufsätze* (Göttingen, 1979), pp. 166–79.

Günter Morsch, 'Streik im "Dritten Reich" ', *Vierteljahreshefte für Zeitgeschichte*, 36 (1988), 648–89.

Max Muchitsch, *Die Partisanengruppe Leoben-Donawitz* (Vienna, 1978).

Detlef Mühlberger (ed.), *The Social Basis of European Fascist Movements* (London, 1987).

Rolf-Dieter Müller, 'Die Rekrutierung sowjetischer Zwangsarbeiter für die deutsche Kriegswirtschaft', in Ulrich Herbert (ed.), *Europa und der 'Reichseinsatz'* (Essen, 1991), pp.234–50.

Lutz Niethammer (ed.), *'Die Jahre weiß man nicht, wo man die heute hinsetzen soll.' Faschismuserfahrungen im Ruhrgebiet* (Berlin, 1983).

Richard Overy, 'Mobilization for Total War in Germany' 1939–1941, *English Historical Review*, 103 (1988), 613–39.

War and Economy in the Third Reich (Oxford, 1994).

F. Parkinson (ed.), *Conquering the Past. Austrian Nazism Yesterday and Today* (Detroit, 1989). Includes editorial introduction and epilogue (pp. 313–34).

Bruce Pauley, *Hitler and the Forgotten Nazis. A History of Austrian National Socialism* (London, 1981).

Kurt Peball, 'Februar 1934: Die Kämpfe' in *Das Jahr 1934: 12. Februar. Protokoll des Symposiums in Wien am 5. Februar 1974* (Vienna, 1975).

Anton Pelinka, 'The Great Austrian Taboo: The Repression of the Civil War', *New German Critique*, 43 (1988), 69–82.

Brigitte Perfahl, 'Linz und Steyr: Zentren der Kämpfe', in Josef Weidenholzer, Brigitte Perfahl and Hubert Humer, *'Es wird nicht mehr verhandelt' . . .Der 12. Februar in Oberösterreich* (Linz, 1984), pp. 25–56.

Julian Petley, *Capital and Culture. German Cinema 1933–1945* (London, 1979).

D. Petzina, W. Abelshauser and A. Faust (eds.), *Sozialgeschichtliches Arbeitsbuch III. Materialien zur Statistik des deutschen Reiches 1914–1945* (Munich, 1978).

Detlev Peukert, 'Der deutsche Arbeiterwiderstand 1933–1945', *Aus Politik und Zeitgeschichte: Beilage zur Wochenzeitung 'Das Parlament'* B28–29/79 (14 July 1979).

Edelweisspiraten. Protestbewegungen jugendlicher Arbeiter im Dritten Reich (Cologne, 1983).

'Protest und Widerstand von Jugendlichen im Dritten Reich' in Richard Löwenthal and Patrick von zur Mühlen (eds.), *Widerstand und Verweigerung in Deutschland* (Berlin, 1984).

Inside Nazi Germany. Conformity, Opposition and Racism in Everyday Life (London, 1989).

Hans Pfahlmann, *Fremdarbeiter und Kriegsgefangene in der deutschen Kriegswirtschaft* (Darmstadt, 1968).

Protokoll des Symposiums in Wien, 5. Februar 1974: Das Jahr 1934. 12. Februar (Munich, 1975).

Peter Pulzer, *The Rise of Political Antisemitism in Germany and Austria*, 2nd edn (London, 1988).

Peter Reichel, *Der schöne Schein des Dritten Reichs. Faszination und Gewalt des Faschismus* (Munich and Vienna, 1991).

Ritchie Robertson and Edward Timms (eds.), *The Habsburg Legacy* (Edinburgh, 1993).

Hans Rogger and Eugen Weber (eds.), *The European Right. A Historical Profile* (Berkeley and Los Angeles, 1966).

Eve Rosenhaft, 'Women in Modern Germany', in Gordon Martel (ed.), *Modern Germany Reconsidered 1870–1945* (London and New York, 1992), pp. 140–58.

Rot-Weiß-Rot-Buch. Darstellungen, Dokumente und Nachweise zur Geschichte und Vorgeschichte der Okkupation Österreichs (nach amtlichen Quellen) (Vienna, 1946).

Stephen Salter, 'The Mobilisation of German Labour 1939–1945. A Contribution to the History of the German Working Class', D. Phil. (Oxford, 1983).

Hans Dietrich Schäfer, *Berlin im Zweiten Weltkrieg. Der Untergang der Reichshauptstadt in Augenzeugenberichten* (Munich, 1985).

Norbert Schausberger, *Der Griff nach Österreich. Der Anschluss* (Vienna, 1978).
    'Deutsche Wirtschaftsinteressen in Österreich vor und nach dem März 1938', in Stourzh and Zahr (eds.), *Österreich, Deutschland und die Mächte. Internationale und österreichische Aspekte des 'Anschlusses' vom März 1938* (Vienna, 1990), pp. 177–211.

Jürgen Schmädeke and Peter Steinbach (eds.), *Widerstand gegen den Nationalsozialismus. Die deutsche Gesellschaft und der Widerstand gegen Hitler* (Munich, 1985).

Franziska Schneeberger, 'Die Sozialstruktur der Heimwehr' Phil. Diss., (Salzburg 1988).

David Schoenbaum, *Hitler's Social Revolution*, (New York, 1966, 1980).

Carl E. Schorske, *Fin de Siècle Vienna. Politics and Culture* (Cambridge, 1981).

James C. Scott, 'Everyday Forms of Resistance,' in Forrest D. Colburn (ed.), *Everyday Forms of Peasant Resistance* (New York, 1989), pp.3–33.

Michael Seidmann, 'Towards a History of Workers' Resistance to Work: Paris and Barcelona during the French Popular Front and the Spanish Revolution, 1936–38,' *Journal of Contemporary History*, 23 (1988), 191–220.
    Workers against Work: Labour in Paris and Barcelona during the Popular Fronts (Berkeley, 1991).

Maren Seliger and Karl Ucakar, *Wien. Politische Geschichte 1740–1934* (Vienna, 1985).

Harry Slapnicka, *Oberösterreich als es Oberdonau hieß 1938–1945* (Linz, 1978).

Karl Stadler, *Österreich im Spiegel der NS-Akten* (Vienna, 1966), pp. 11–12.

Peter Steinbach, 'The Conservative Resistance' in Large (ed.), *Contending with Hitler. Varieties of German Resistance in the Third Reich*, (Cambridge, 1991), pp. 89–97.

Hans-Josef Steinberg, *Widerstand und Verfolgung in Essen 1933–45* (Bad Godesberg, 1969).

Robert Stöger, 'Der christliche Führer und die "wahre Demokratie". Zu den Demokratiekonzeptionen von Ignaz Seipel,' *Archiv. Jahrbuch des Vereins für die Geschichte der Arbeiterbewegung*, 2 (1988), 54–67.

Lawrence Duncan Stokes, 'The *Sicherheitsdienst* of the *Reichsführer* SS and German Public Opinion, September 1939–June 1944', Ph.D dissertation (Johns Hopkins University, Baltimore, Maryland, 1972).

Gerald Stourzh and Brigitte Zahr (eds.), *Österreich, Deutschland und die Mächte. Internationale und österreichische Aspekte des 'Anschlusses' vom März 1938* (Vienna, 1990).

Peter F. Sugar (ed.), *Native Fascism in the Successor States 1918–1945* (Santa Barbara, 1971).

Melanie Sully, *Parties and Elections in Austria* (London, 1981).

Continuity and Change in Austrian Socialism. The Eternal Quest for the Third Way, (Boulder, 1982).

Hannes Sulzenbacher, 'Homosexual Men in Vienna in 1938', in Tim Kirk and Tony McElligott (eds.), *Community, Authority and Resistance to Fascism* (Cambridge, forthcoming).

J. L. Talmon, *The Origins of Totalitarian Democracy. Political Theory and Practice during the French Revolution and Beyond* (London 1952, 1986).

Emmerich Tálos and Wolfgang Neugebauer (eds.), *'Austrofaschismus', Beiträge über Politik, Ökonomie und Kultur 1934–1938* (Vienna,1984).

Emmerich Tálos and Walter Manoschek, 'Zum Konstituierungsprozeß des Austrofaschismus', in Tálos and Neugebauer (eds.), *'Austrofaschismus'*, pp. 31–52.

Emmerich Tálos, 'Das Herrschaftssystem 1934–1938: Erklärungen und begriffliche Bestimmungen. Ein Resümee', in Tálos and Neugebauer (eds.), *'Austrofaschismus'*, pp. 267–84.

Emmerich Tálos, Ernst Hanisch and Wolfgang Neugebauer (eds.), *NS-Herrschaft in Österreich 1938–1945* (Vienna, 1988).

Klaus Tenfelde, 'Soziale Grundlagen von Widerstand', in Jürgen Schmädeke and Peter Steinbach (eds.), *Widerstand* (Munich, 1985), pp. 799–812.

Hans-Ulrich Thamer, 'Führergewalt und Polykratie in Österreich', in Stourzh and Zahr (eds.), *Österreich, Deutschland und die Mächte* (Vienna, 1990), pp. 497–502.

E. P. Thompson, *The Making of the English Working Class*, (London, 1963).

Ferdinand Tremel, *Wirtschafts- und Sozialgeschichte Österreichs* (Vienna, 1969).

Andreas Unterberger, 'Die Vergangenheit als Seifenoper. Das Anhalten der Vorwürfe aus dem Ausland verunsichert die Alpenrepublik', *Die Presse* (30 December 1986).

Rolf Wagenführ, *Die deutsche Industrie im Kriege 1939–1945* (Berlin, 1954).

Adam Wandruszka, 'Österreichs politische Struktur', in Heinrich Benedikt (ed.), *Geschichte der Republik Österreich*, (Munich, 1954), pp. 291–3.

Josef Weidenholzer, Brigitte Perfahl und Hubert Humer, *'Es wird nicht mehr verhandelt'* . . . *Der 12. Februar in Oberösterreich* (Linz, 1984).

Wolfgang Werner, 'Die Arbeitserziehungslager als Mittel nationalsozialistischer "Sozialpolitik" gegen deutsche Arbeiter', in Waclaw Dlugoborski (ed.), *Zweiter Weltkrieg und Sozialer Wandel. Achsenmächte und besetzte Länder* (Göttingen, 1981), pp. 138–47.

'Bleib ubrig!' Deutsche Arbeiter in der nationalsozialistischen Kriegswirtschaft (Düsseldorf, 1983).

Andrew Whiteside, 'Austria' in Hans Rogger and Eugen Weber (eds.), *The European Right. A Historical Profile* (Berkeley and Los Angeles, 1966).

The Socialism of Fools. Georg Ritter von Schönerer and Austrian Pan-Germanism (Berkeley, 1975).

Dörte Winkler, *Frauenarbeit im Dritten Reich* (Hamburg, 1977).
Walter Wisshaupt, *Wir Kommen wieder! Eine Geschichte der revolutionären Sozialisten Österreichs* (Vienna, 1967).

Index

Printed in the United States
By Bookmasters